MONEY AND THE
NEW WORLD
ORDER

BY SIR PATRICK BIJOU

DESCRIPTION

The Money Pandemic, A Changing New World Order, Digitalization And The Marshall Plan. This book will illuminate your understanding as it attempts to discuss the various pros and cons of money, the current banking and financial system and The New World Order. It will try to explain how you may put this knowledge to good use and create an advantage ahead of the game plan. It aims to describe why money matters, the nature and origin of money, the importance of money, digitalization and the frighteningly disturbing New World Order. A theory of money should provide answers to three closely related questions. What is money? Where does it come from and how and why it depreciates in value? It theoretical examines the answers given by the main traditions in social sciences and describes extensively the discoveries about money and the changing global economy.

Read and discover the truth for yourself.

ACKNOWLEDGEMENTS

I cannot express enough thanks to my friend and a remarkable editor and book formatting expert, Mr Bilal Qureshi, for his continued support and encouragement: This project could not have been accomplished without his help. Thank you for the painstaking efforts and hours you have put into this project and for tolerating me.

I offer my sincere appreciation for the learning opportunities provided by my committee of specialist bankers, Fund Managers and Karen, my Editor.

Special acknowledgement to my daughter Isabella and the love, understanding and support she has shown me over the years.

My thanks go out to all the people who have supported me and helped complete this book directly or indirectly. I am overwhelmed in humbleness and gratefulness to acknowledge the depth of all those who have helped me put my ideas above the level of simplicity and into something tangible.

Finally, to my caring, loving, and supportive partner, Janice: my deepest gratitude. Your encouragement when the times got rough was much appreciated, and it was a great comfort and relief to know that you were willing to provide management of our household activities while I completed my work. My heartfelt thanks.

And, of course, my best friend and loyal companions, always by my side and inseparable, my two loving dogs, Beau and Myla; what would I do without their unconditional love towards me.

"Success in business comes from success in developing relationships with the right people".
Sir Patrick Bijou

ABOUT THE AUTHOR

S**ir Patrick Bijou** was born in Georgetown, Guyana, South America, and resides in the UK.

He is a Senior Judge for the ICJ-ICC, Ambassador for the United Nations, Investment banker, philanthropist, and best-selling author. He specialises in debt capital markets, private placements, derivatives, and futures trading. As a distinguished trader on Wall Street, he has worked with multiple leading banks such as Wells Fargo, Deutsche Bank, Credit Agricole CIB, Merrill Lynch, and others. He has established and managed Hedge Funds such as The Tiger Fund and became a notable Fund Manager at Blackstone. Sir Patrick was responsible for setting up the MTN & Private Placement Desk and dealer function at Lloyds Bank Plc. He was the first trader for Lloyd's treasury to increase self-led deals significantly from 4% to 32% in 2002.

He has excelled as an investment banker and was awarded many accolades such as the Multiple Recipient, Wells Fargo "Valley of the Stars". The Wells Fargo "Circle of Stars" award, and Member of Wells Fargo "Millionaire Club" and "Champion Circle" award throughout his illustrious career.

He has over three decades' experience in the financial markets and has worked with numerous clients, including governments, banking institutions, and corporations. Currently, he has written and published over 30 books across several genres.

His journey into content writing has allowed him to become an exceptionally motivated and enthusiastic author and professional communicator, experienced in proactive campaign-driven and responsive communications.

Website: www.bijouebook.com
www.sirpatrickbijou.com

Table of Contents

INTRODUCTION

Money has always been associated in varying degrees of closeness with religion, partly interpreted in modern times as the psychology of habits and attitudes, hopes, fears and expectations. Thus, the taboos which circumscribe spending in primitive societies are basically not unlike the stock market bears which similarly reduce expenditures through changing subjective assessments of values and incomes, so that the true interpretation of what money means to people requires the sympathetic understanding of the less obvious motivations as much as, if not more than, the narrow abstract calculations of the computer. To concentrate attention narrowly on 'the pound in your pocket' is to devalue the all-pervading significance of money.

Observers of world affairs like to point to a defining moment or pivotal event to proclaim the end of one era and the beginning of another. Not surprisingly, the novel coronavirus pandemic has already spawned much speculation that the world will undergo profound change as a consequence, even that contemporary history will forever be divided between what happened BC (before coronavirus) and AC (after coronavirus).

A theory of money should provide answers to three closely related questions. What is money? Where does it come from, or how does it gets into society? How does it get/lose

1

its value? It is theoretical and examines the answers given to them by the main traditions in the social sciences. First, the intellectual development in mainstream economics of the notion of money as a commodity and/or a neutral symbol of commodities is examined. Here I elaborate the contention that this understanding of money is deficient because it is quite unable to specify money that is to say, how money differs from other commodities. It follows that if the question of what money is cannot be answered then the other two where it comes from and how it gets and loses value are also likely to be unsatisfactory. Indeed, the question of how money gets into society has been dismissed as irrelevant.

Money is a social relation of credit and debt denominated in a money of account. In the most basic sense, the possessor of money is owed goods. But money also represents a claim or credit against the issuer monarch, state, bank and so on. Money has to be 'issued'. And something can only be issued as money, if it is capable of cancelling any debt incurred by the issuer. Money expands human society's capacity to get things done, as Keynesian economics emphasizes; but this power can be appropriated by particular interests. Moreover, the dual elements in the nature of money can also be contradictory in that particular interest's advantages may undermine the public benefits. This is a familiar theme in the ultra-liberal economic critique of the government's debt-financed spending that gives it an interest in inducing inflation to reduce the real value of the debt.

In short, money is the basis for the progressive rationalization of social life.

CHAPTER

1

History of Money And Bank Development.

Working in collaboration with lawyers in SELC in Oakland, California, an attempt to get an overview of the US financial regulation landscape and the definitions of 'money' therein began with trying to understand how the law views and categorizes the world of finance in general. Similar to the way the financial system is pictured and discussed in everyday language, the dominant approach here was to distinguish between the organizational categories in which financial service providers are grouped. In the law as in everyday language, a fundamental distinction runs between businesses that are called banks and those that are not. Despite a perceived increase in the number, diversity and importance of financial services providers that are not licensed as banks (Bank of International Settlements, 2014), this distinction is still firmly followed in financial regulations. In technical economic parlance, the latter institutions are often described as "nonbank banks" (while in the US regulatory arena they are referred to as "Alternative Financial Services" (AFS), a term that further reaffirms the primacy of banks.

Yet, in the statutes and laws of the US, the definition of what a bank is comes down to describing what its activity, or 'banking', is, or in effect, what a bank does. This follows in line with the history of banking as the practice of lending and financing, particularly since the European Renaissance. However, the technical language found in the law does not clearly reflect the current unique role and importance of companies with a banking license in our economies today. As they de facto monopolise the creation and allocation of liquidity to specific sectors without central banks having a significant influence on this process, one might expect a clear and concise definition that also relates to concepts of 'money' in the law. However, such an explicit distinction that connects the institutional definition of a bank with the definition of 'money', was not found. The history of banking in the consolidated USA (after the Civil War) is marked by two significant developmental steps, one starting with the establishment of a nationally aligned banking system from 1863, and fifty years later, the foundation of the Federal Reserve system which continues until today.

The federal statute that launched the first step was the National Bank Act from 1863/64. Before this time, all bank charters were granted by individual states. The original act (U.S. Congress, 1864) describes the new federal oversight agencies that controlled these new companies which were to operate across all states. The Office of the Comptroller of the Currency (OCC) was one of the federal institutions that was created by this act and still exists today. It also specifies the minute rules for the procurement of capital and ongoing liquidity requirements (from section and the administrative provision "to carry on the business of banking by discounting and negotiating promissory notes, drafts, bills of exchange, and other evidences of debt; by receiving deposits; by buying and selling exchange, coin, and bullion; by loaning money on personal security; by obtaining, issuing, and circulating notes".

Across the whole, of the text of the National Bank Act, there are 2,143 instances of the word "banking", which highlights the procedural characteristic of what was thus established as a new form of a bank. In contrast, the word bank itself appears only 21 times never in an explanatory sense, but always in reference to one of the individual organisations which were to be chartered by this new legislation. This illustrates how the concept of what a bank was, did not seem to require any further definition at the time. Only the change in the nature of how these new banks were to set up and operate needed to be established. In regard to 'money', the title of the act describes the purpose of these new banks as "issuing a National Currency, secured by a Pledge of United State Bonds, and to provide for the Circulation and Redemption thereof". As commonplace as this seems today, it was a novelty compared to the reality up to that moment, which saw thousands of notes from different state-chartered banks in circulation: "eight to nine thousand different-looking pieces of paper, each with the name of a bank on it and a number of dollars which the named bank promised to pay in coin if the note were presented to it. Furthermore, the US Constitution determined all of them had to be backed 1:1 by their nominal worth in gold or silver.

Article 1 of the Constitution still says:

"No state shall enter into any treaty, alliance, or confederation; grant letters of marque and reprisal; coin money; emit bills of credit; make anything but gold and silver coin a tender in payment of debts; pass any bill of attainder, ex post facto law, or law impairing the obligation of contracts, or grant any title of nobility." (U. S. Constitution, 1788, art. 1 § 10)

Therefore, at the time when the United States were consolidating their territories geographically across the whole continent, such notes, valid homogeneously across the whole nation, did in effect constitute something akin to what today is called a 'national currency'. In contrast with the way United States Code (U.S.C.) statutes are written today, no preamble explaining the used terminology was added to congressional acts at that time. Hence, it is more difficult to determine concisely what the individual terms given in the quotes above refer to. However, a full-text search of the National Bank Act reveals sufficient context to say something on the usage of "money" and "currency" and thus infer their meaning. The word "money" appears 48 times in the 64 sections of the act. Nearly half of those (22) come in the compound term "lawful money" referring to the "Greenback" notes issued by congress. To give an example, the new national banks "shall, at all times, have on hand, in lawful money of the United States an amount equal to at least twenty-five per centum of the aggregate amount of its notes in circulation and its deposits". The other 26 mentions of the word "money" appear in various generic contexts including, but not limited to, the new notes to be issued, for example in the sense that the national banks are "hereby authorised to issue and circulate the same as money".

The word "currency" appears with a very similar frequency, 50 times altogether. Although here the vast majority of mentions (44) are in the name given to one of the new regulatory agencies, the office of the comptroller of the currency. The other six examples describe the new notes to be issued by the national banks. In functional proximity to the coins, then and now only issued by governments, the term currency hence is only employed for notes that are licensed and circulate at that same national level. The many thousands other kinds of bank notes issued at the time would therefore not be recognized as currency.

To further understand the ancestry of the practice of "banking" today and its relation to the issuance and handling of money in the legacy age of the National Bank Act, it is important to look into the history of the dominant national banks in the USA today. In several prominent cases, their business derived from the shipping and safeguarding of physical forms of money. The name American Express still directly indicates this, as does the stagecoach imagery of the logo of the Wells Fargo bank. Both these companies started out in the middle of the 19th century (in 1850 and 1852 respectively) as express mail companies, with American Express serving the eastern and Wells, Fargo & Company predominantly serving the western United States (Engstrand, 2013). Their service infrastructure allowed them to not only handle conventional freight but also precious cargo like banknotes, bonds, coins, and other precious metals. In the case of Wells Fargo, it was the higher demand for safeguarding of the latter and related payment services during the California Gold Rush that led to the explicit inclusion of banking services in their early company portfolio.

Both businesses were unregulated in the young state of California and the accelerated growth in demand for banking services led to its organisational division from the freight business, first in the physical division of the respected offices in San Francisco in 1891. The two branches were finally incorporated as two separate legal entities in 1905. In the end, both American Express and Wells Fargo had to give up their domestic freight business in 1917/18 when the US government took control of the transportation infrastructure during World War I. Their banking businesses, however, continued to flourish.

Even if the cases of American Express and Wells Fargo are not entirely representative for the diverse history of banks and banking in the United States altogether, they illustrate how the business of banking and the handling and issuance of physical forms of money are closely linked in their origins, not only in America. The origin of banking is often attributed to medieval goldsmiths and their facility for the safekeeping of their customers' coins in their on-site vaults. The subsequent issuance of paper slips confirming the deposit of a certain number of coins, including the promise to return those on demand (promissory note), eventually started to circulate instead of the gold in the vaults.

Disregarding the various monetary practices in the colonies and the early United States, the issuance of Greenbacks as 'lawful money' by the US congress can then be seen as the inception of the era of unbacked 'fiat' money in the consolidated United States. Until that time the dominant form of paper money, including that issued by Wells Fargo, American Express and the like, derived its reliability and acceptance for commerce predominantly from precious metals in form of bullion and specie that the issuing banks held "in reserve" in direct continuation of the practice of goldsmiths earlier. Consequently, the establishment of different bank charters and their ability to issue notes of different kinds and validity through the National Bank Act had a direct influence on what was then considered money and currency.

In 1913, the Federal Reserve Act established the central banking system for the geographically and politically consolidated United States, including the exclusive issuance of dollar notes by the FEDs, which resembled the appearance of Dollar notes today. In that act, the term "money" appears sixteen times, nine of these in reference to "lawful money" as discussed above. The other instances refer to money held in reserve at the FEDs or the treasury and it remains unclear without further study if these were only 'lawful money' or include other notes and assets as well. Three times, in the context of reserves and assets held by the banks to be established, or the treasury respectively, the plural "moneys" is used. This could on the one hand, support the notion that reference to 'money' here meant more than just 'lawful money', or it could refer to 'lawful money' having accumulated from different sources, in the way that the term 'monies' is commonly used today: "amounts of money".

The FED act is related to an act from 1900, called the Gold Standard Act or, as its original title reads: "An Act to define and fix the standard of value, to maintain the parity of all forms of money issued or coined by the United States, to refund the public debt, and for other purposes". The wording of that act and periodic vagaries of varying relations of the US notes to gold or other precious metals until all backing was finally abolished in a presidential order by Richard Nixon in 1971 will not be analysed here. However, the wording of the title indicates that the plural of 'money' could at the time have only referred to different forms or iterations of notes issued by congress and the treasury, without including banknotes issued by private banks.

The FED Act uses the term "currency" 37 times, but 33 of those are again in the title of the Office of the Comptroller of the Currency, which after being founded in the National Bank Act discussed above continued, until today, to be the primary regulatory body concerned with the issuance of money in the US. The word "currency" is only mentioned once in regard to the notes to be issued by the FEDs, and the remaining three times in the context of the notes issued by national banks chartered by the National Bank Act. With this, the term currency is here used coherently as the notes put into circulation by banks mandated by the government.

Chronologically, this inquiry has now reached the basis of today's financial landscape's topography including the legal notion of 'money' that still serves as the basis of current legal discourses. However, contemporary with the National Bank Act, the commercial deployment of the telegraph technology had emerged and was poised to not only revolutionize the way information was transmitted across long distances, but also to go on and revolutionise banking. The widespread use of telegraph transmissions of news and personal messages from the middle of the 19th century brought about the quick demise of the now legendary Pony Express Service that hauled small volumes of messages and important papers across the American continent within ten days. Wells Fargo Company was involved in the last six months of the service's existence, but the service was made redundant simply by the installation of a continuous cable run across the breadth of the United States in 1861.

Eventually this also had fundamental implications for the way payments and banking as a whole was conducted. In 1918, the Federal Reserve System started to use morse code to realise the first long distance electronic payments. If all payments to that date relied on a physical medium of exchange of some sort, be it coins, precious metal or banknotes, the electromagnetic representations of those not only changed the practicalities of money transmission, but would also be required to be reflected in the definition of 'money' in the law. Today's modern payment and banking practices are fundamentally different then during the time before telecommonucation, and this has consequential bearings on the meaning of the term scrutinised here. Taking this into account, a final more modern legal landmark of the changing landscape of banks and 'money', the Bank Holding Company Act will now be discussed. In its current form, as part of the federal statutes called the 'U.S. Code', it defines a bank as one of two things: either a company with federally insured deposits or a company that makes commercial loans.

Deposits are defined in a preceding chapter of the U.S.C. as the "unpaid balance of money or its equivalent received or held by a bank or savings association in the usual course of business and for which it has given or is obligated to give credit" (12. U.S.C. § 1813 (i)(1), see U.S.Code, 2017a). The openness of the term "deposit" introduced by the formulation "money or its equivalent"' is further illustrated as the definitions continue. Deposits, not only occur in the process of converting a note into an account entry of 'credit' but also the consecutive receipt of such credit entries constitutes a deposit: "money received or held by a bank or savings association, or the credit given for money or its equivalent received or held by a bank or savings association" (12 U.S.C. § 1813 (i)(3), see U.S.Code, 2017a).

This appears in line with the common description of bank balances as deposits even when no centrally issued money, in form of coins, notes or central bank money, but simply a loan contract between a commercial banks and its customers has been the origin of these 'deposited' units. In this sense the extension of loans by commercial banks today is, in fact, the creation of deposits, which equal new units of money. Even if they come to exist only on the balance sheets of banks, their fungibility with notes and coins and their dominance in our everyday payments both in volume and number of transactions, consolidates their treatment as money. However, since they are not fully equivalent to the money issued by central banks or the treasury, both descriptions of what a bank is found in the Bank Holding Act ultimately relate to the convertibility of bank deposits into cash, in the worst case by the Federal Deposit Insurance Corporation (FDIC). This entity was also founded in 1913 through the Federal Reserve Act discussed above. By guaranteeing, in case of bankruptcy of a commercial bank, the convertibility of the money created by that commercial bank to the money created by the FED and the treasury, at least up to 250 thousand dollars per account holder (FDIC, 2018), this scheme provides for the practical equivalence of these different units at least where the common understanding of those instruments and their everyday use are concerned. This makes it necessary to be clear on the expansion of the term 'money' away from just referring to 'currency', but also makes the situation actually found in the law today confusing and inaccurate under the scrutiny of this thesis.

Modern Legislation Define Money And Currency

To state one of the findings upfront, it did not come as a surprise that the definitions of money in the laws and statutes of the USA were neither straightforward to determine nor coherent within or across different texts.

To give a first impression, Gillette et al. open their over 600 pages textbook on payment systems saying that "The subject comes complete with a long and intricate history; an esoteric language [...]; and a dependence on technological developments that require constant accommodations in legal doctrine". Their subsequent analysis of payment instruments is derived from the foundational process and simplisic notion of paying somebody in "cash or what is commonly called 'money' over the counter. They substantiate this equation of cash and money by citing the definition of 'money' in the US Uniform Commercial Code (UCC) which reads: "a medium of exchange authorised or adopted by a domestic or foreign government"; and they describe the different derivative forms of payment, such as cheques, debit and credit cards as "money substitutes". Despite having put the single word money into inverted commas first, the introducing of the compound term 'money substitutes' for non-cash payment forms reinforces how they see cash and money as equivalent terms, at least for the practice of law.

Their argument means that they are interpreting the term 'medium of exchange' in the UCC to mean only notes and coins, which of course contradicts both the everyday experience of using our electronic bank balances to pay for goods and services, as well as other expert readings on the matter. Yet, Gillette uphold their limited reading, and its inherent difficulties by asserting that in law 'money' is really only considered to be cash by juxtaposing it with its presumed meaning in the economics literature, where they say that 'money': "has a broader definition: it consists of whatever is accepted in exchange for goods and services.".

Applying this question to Whaley's 2006 edition of "Commercial Paper and Payment Law" one finds a reference to the same UCC definition as in Gillette, but with an addition that is not found in the current version of the UCC: "a medium of exchange authorised or adopted by a domestic or foreign government as part of its currency". An internet search for this quote revealed it being used in various legal textbooks and study guides as recently as 2012, hence it appears that this last part of the sentence seems to have been omitted from the UCC only recently. The current UCC definition however continues to state that "the term money includes a monetary unit of account established by an intergovernmental organisation or by agreement between two or more countries." This use of the term 'unit of account' does of course immediately contradict the equation of money with cash as seen in Gillette. The reference to currency in the previous version of the UCC explains however why the equation of money and currency pertains in legal treatises on the topic.

What then does the word currency mean in the law of the USA today? The Code of Federal Regulation (CFR) defines it as this: "The coin and paper money of the United States or of any other country that is designated as legal tender and that circulates and is customarily used and accepted as a medium of exchange in the country of issuance. Currency includes U.S. silver certificates, U.S. notes and Federal Reserve notes. Currency also includes official foreign bank notes that are customarily used and accepted as a medium of exchange in a foreign country." This definition of currency as the tangible forms of money (notes and coins) aligns with the explicit definitions found in the UK.

However, this very simple and clear definition of the term currency would mean that the equation of money and currency as found above would be impossible, unless one were to accept that, legally, only cash is considered money and that the electronic bank balances that we use for most of our payments, both in number of transactions and volume, are not money. For now, we will need to accept that our everyday understanding and the economists' views on the matter of money might differ from a legal understanding, even by such a large margin. Gillette confirm this as they follow on from their passage quoted above: "In the economists' definition, governmentally approved or issued currency constitutes only one subset of money, called 'fiat money' [...]", which "takes the form of pieces of paper that are worthless in themselves". Therefore, it would indeed seem that electronic bank balances are money to economists but not to the legal profession.

However, the term 'fiat money' that was introduced in that last quote seems to provide yet another synonym for the legal definition of money and currency. Indeed, no governmental definition of the term 'fiat' that would extend beyond notes and coins was found in my research. There is a second reading of that term, that is often implied in how authors writing about complementary currencies use it: a monetary unit, physical or electronic, that is not redeemable with the issuer for an underlying asset. If the agendas of several governments to abolish cash altogether were to come to pass, it would be odd to assume that the former narrow definition of 'fiat' would not be abandoned, too as if the remaining electronic units would not have always had a fiat character akin to that of the second definition, just like cash.

However, by the idiomatic 'letter of the law' it appears that 'money' in the laws of the United States is defined, along with 'currency' and 'fiat', simply as the notes and coins issued by the US treasury or the FED respectively. It is only the mention of intergovernmental "units of account" by the UCC that seems to diverge from that definition. The situation in Californian statutes mostly reflects or even copies the wording of the federal code. Only in the California Code of Civil Procedures, in the "Uniform Foreign Money Claims Act", has a slightly different definition of money defined as: a medium of exchange "for the payment of obligations". This procedural addition reflects the relevance of payment and the discharge of debt in commercial legal claims. Following this cue, the analysis will now turn to the usage of the definitions thus far described in the practice of regulating and ruling on monetary issues in the United States, with examples from the practice of complementary currencies.

As seen in the legal and compliance research of the CCIA project, the practice of complementary currency issuance presents various questions as to what laws apply, and how. In addition, when it comes to financial law the decisive question is whether CCs are deemed to be 'money' and thus need to comply or not. Many forms of CCs have existed for many years without raising the concerns of the legislator, regulator or prosecutor in the US and elsewhere. Two prominent exceptions to this statement in the US context are noteworthy.

In 2011, after several years of court proceedings, Bernard von NotHaus was convicted for the issuance of silver coins that he called "Liberty Dollars". The case had been followed by many actors in complementary currencies for fear of having wide-ranging consequences for other currencies. However, thus far no other cases have been brought on any other currency issuer. The case was distinct from the practice of other complementary currencies in that the coins he minted resembled federal currency in the use of their imagery (the Statue of Liberty) and the use of the term and symbol of "Dollars". Despite having many features distinct from federal coins and the clear statement of the silver weight on each coin, this provoked the allegation of forgery. However, seemingly independent of the potential of confusing users of Liberty Dollars as to the origin and value of the coins, the state attorney proclaimed that currencies like the one of von NotHaus amounted to attempts "to undermine the legitimate currency of this country are simply a unique form of domestic terrorism".

Another case, in the late 1970s, in which the issuance of complementary currencies caught the regulator's attention and threat of prosecution, was the Internal Revenue Service (IRS) inquiry into the possibility that the use of business-to-business (B2B) currencies constituted a tax fraud. The issue provoked the formation of the International Reciprocal Trade Association (IRTA) as an industry representative body that allowed for a concerted strategic defence and dialogue with the IRS. In the end it was deemed legitimate for businesses to trade with B2B currencies that followed the 'mutual credit' model, and a separate tax form (1099B) was developed for the reporting of such income. The IRTA has continued to argue in favour for the differentiated treatment of B2B currencies ever since. Recently the federal requirement for cryptocurrency exchanges to register as 'money transmitters' in the USA was so broadly formulated, that it prompted IRTA to state how B2B mutual credit currencies are, in effect, "not money" in order to be clearly exempt from this regulation. In their framing, operators of such currencies are not "issuers" of currency, but third party record keepers that record the trades and balances of businesses trading in their networks.

The latter example shows how the term currency is even in legal practice today not exclusively accepted in reference to material media of exchange, but also how the question of what is considered 'money' by regulators has seen novel attention since the emergence of Bitcoin. The attention to currency innovations by regulators, epitomised by the US Senate Hearing on Bitcoin in November 2013, correlated with the increase in price, and the number of media mentions and the sentiments that expressed. With the media repeating the terminology introduced by Bitcoin advocates and enthusiasts, like 'virtual currency', 'digital currency' or "a new kind of money", the baseline framing and terminological space for the ensuing discourse amongst regulators, law enforcement agencies and economists was already determined. Consequently, given the vague or even contradictory definitions of the terms money and currency that we have observed so far, it was, not surprising that the way commentators talked about it was neither conclusive nor coherent. On an expert panel with a representative of the global credit card payment processor Worldpay, a journalist from the Financial Times, a consultant to the payment system industry, the executive director of the Bank of England at the time, and myself, the only certain finding was how there was no fundamental agreement on the question of whether Bitcoin constitutes 'money', a 'currency', a new 'asset class' or something completely different or if that question was even posed sensibly.

With a further increase of its market value and newly emerging cases of criminal activities involving Bitcoin payments, not only regulatory and legislative agencies but also the courts were soon presented with the question of categorising this new phenomenon. A landmark court case was the US Securities and Exchange Commission (SEC) suing the founder of a Bitcoin related website for fraud against the people who used the website to purchase and hold Bitcoins with the expectation of a financial return (Greene, 2013).

Curiously, the defendant argued that Bitcoin has nothing to do with money and because of this the SEC and the courts had no case in this. On the face of it, his website operated in the classic form of a Ponzi scheme through which newly paid in funds provide the capital to pay previous investors. This only works as long as new people buy into it. Thus, it was not surprising that the courts affirmed their position and convicted the operator of the scheme. In the argumentation however, judge Mazzant took to likening Bitcoin to 'money' and 'currency', saying: "Bitcoin is an electronic form of currency unbacked by any real asset and without specie, such as coin or precious metal. [...] It is clear that Bitcoin can be used as money. It can be used to purchase goods or services [...]." Through the use of the comparative "as money" this still holds a certain openness as to the definition of both terms, money and currency, or their equivalence. Although in continuation he concludes more definitely: "Therefore, Bitcoin is a currency or form of money and investors wishing to invest in [the defendant's online platform] provide an investment in money."

The functional or phenomenological statement 'can be used as' is a novel approach to defining money that provides a greater openness than the definitions we have thus far found in the law. Currency is here seen as 'a form of money', which holds the two words clearly as not synonymous. Judge Mazzant is not alone in this use of language which is divergent from what the law suggests. Since 2013 several US agencies, from law enforcement to financial regulators and the IRS, have reiterated the description of Bitcoin being some sort of 'currency' which they called 'virtual'. This contradicts the above findings that the term currency is clearly defined as notes and coins in the law. If currency is defined as notes and coins, no unit existing virtually or electronically can qualify and the term "virtual currency" or "electronic currency" would amount to an oxymoron. In the case of Bitcoin, the second criterion for what a currency is, namely, being issued by state authority, makes the usage of the term additionally paradoxical.

In 2013, apparently conscious of this problem, the United States Treasury's Financial Crime Enforcement Network (FINCEN) defined "virtual currency" in their first comprehensive guidance note on bitcoin businesses in reference to the definition of currency in the CFR:

"In contrast to real currency, "virtual" currency is a medium of exchange that operates like a currency in some environments, but does not have all the attributes of real currency. In particular, virtual currency does not have legal tender status in any jurisdiction. This guidance addresses "convertible" virtual currency. This type of virtual currency either has an equivalent value in real currency, or acts as a substitute for real currency."

This position and terminology has been confirmed by an oft-quoted publication on the same matter by the Chicago FED, which not only likened Bitcoin to currency but, following the trajectory of equating money and currency, extended the issue by introducing the concept of 'digital money': the author applies this term primarily to the electronic FED reserves, used only between the FED and banks, and then likens Bitcoin to those.

This does raise up new issues for this inquiry. By contrasting 'virtual currency' with the term 'real currency', the naked term 'currency' by itself loses all definitory solidity. By pointing, to electronic reserves the term money loses all relation to and synonymity with cash. The Chicago FED could of course be seen as a commentator from the economic disciplines and not a purveyor of legal definitions. However, the ruling by judge Mazzant shows that this way of looking at the issue is not alien to the legal professions either. Through the questions posed by Bitcoin, the recognition of digital forms of money and currencies seemed inevitable. Moreover, through his practical and phenomenological approach Mazzant also showed that 'substitutes for money' are indeed treated as money by the applicants of the law, in contrast to what was discovered in the text books discussed above. In light of an ever-changing world in which new phenomena emerge and are unlikely to fit into old definitions, such a situation is perhaps to be expected, and adhering to old definitions and terminology will only grow less and less tenable over time.

One such case in which these definitions are already showing their threadbareness is the 2014 FINCEN requirement for companies that run Bitcoin exchange platforms to register as "Money Transmitter Businesses". Quoting all the definitions that have previously been outlined it was ruled that companies that facilitate the trade and exchange of bitcoins have to comply with the same rules that a conventional payment operator needs to adhere to, including a costly registration and reporting process in all states in which they offer their services (typically all 50 states of the USA for online services). In this regard, it is curious to note that the federal money transmission statutes themselves do not speak of 'money' at all, but define services that require such licensing as those involved in "the transmission of currency, funds, or other value that substitutes for currency [...] by any means" (31 CFR § 1010.100 (ff)(5)(i)(A).

However, the legal definition of currency as found above is here not adhered to either. The transport of notes and coins which constitutes the most tangible and historically predominant form of "money transmission" is explicitly excluded in a subclause of the same statute: "The term "money transmitter" shall not include a person that only [...] physically transports currency, other monetary instruments, other commercial paper, or other value that substitutes for currency" (31 CFR § 1010.100 (ff)(5)(ii)(D), see Code of Federal Regulations, 2017). What is left then of forms of money that might be covered in this transmission statute must be electronic ones, which is made explicit in their defintion of the term 'transmission': "[By] "Any means" includes, but is not limited to [...], an electronic funds transfer network" (31 CFR § 1010.100 (ff)(5)(i)(A). Electronic units also seem to be implicitly included in their vague descriptions of "other values that substitute for currency" quoted above. In line with this, the word 'funds' is explicitly defined by the Electronic Fund Transfer Act of 1978 as "a number of electronic payments" (31 CFR § 1010.100 (w). However, particularly the term "other values" seems to leave an option for including the transfer of absolutely anything valuable to fall under the 'money transmission' regulation, including, but not limited to, Bitcoin. Such interpretation also seems to be the basis for the California Financial Code's definition that "Monetary value means a medium of exchange, whether or not redeemable in money."

All the above indicates that the terms 'money' and 'currency' are, in current legislation not sufficiently defined to mark any discernible difference. Or, if one would take the statute's content literally, the name 'money transmission act' is a misnomer and would better be changed to "Something valuable other than cash transmitter legislation". The openness for this broad scope of this legislation also resonates from a subclause that states: "Whether a person is a money transmitter as described in this section is a matter of facts and circumstances."

It could be argued that any expectation of robust and non-ambivalent definitions might be lost with such mention of 'facts' and 'circumstance'. And with the 'money transmission' ruling it has, in effect, now been determined, that Bitcoin is not only described as a form of money but actually treated and regulated as such even if this is at odds with the legal definition of the term as discussed above. A final landmark for the normalization of the legal appraisal of bitcoins being treated as money or currency came in 2014 when the IRS issued their own guidance on Bitcoin. They followed to a large extent the wording of FINCEN but highlighted the caveat that Bitcoin is not considered "legal tender" by repeating, in a hyphenated addendum, that:

"Virtual currency is a digital representation of value that functions as a medium of exchange, a unit of account, and/or a store of value. In some environments, it operates like "real" currency i.e., the coin and paper money of the United States or of any other country that is designated as legal tender, circulates, and is customarily used and accepted as a medium of exchange in the country of issuance but it does not have legal tender status in any jurisdiction".

This indicates that the status and concept of 'legal tender' remains as the one definite to distinguish between new and conventional forms of 'money'. However, by now it is probably not surprising to find that this term, like the others already discussed, is more ambiguous in law as references to it in common language suggest. To many, across different countries and languages, legal tender seems to mean that a form of money or currency described as such is what a given state deems to be the official means of payment, particularly when it comes to the final discharge of tax obligations. Furthermore, by inference, any other form of money is deemed to be of lesser status or even illegal. The second peculiarity about the term is that it does not refer to all conventional forms of money, but only to specific notes and coins. Some notes like the US Dollar bills, state explicitly that they are 'legal tender for all debts, public and private'. However, when put to the test in practice, limitations exist in many countries, that bring this broad understanding into question. Businesses, for example, are allowed to refuse payments of certain amounts in coins of small denominations in many countries or implemented maximum amounts that can be paid in cash altogether.

The same limitation to the actual meaning of the term 'legal tender' can be found in the USA. The Department of the Treasury published a FAQ on this very question which first refers to the coinage act of 1965 stating that "United States coins and currency (including Federal reserve notes and circulating notes of Federal reserve banks and national banks) are legal tender for all debts, public charges, taxes, and dues." The passage goes on to explain that this "statute means that all United States money as identified above are a valid and legal offer of payment for debts when tendered to a creditor. There is, however, no federal statute mandating that a private business, a person or an organization must accept currency or coins as payment for goods and/or services." (Department of the Treasury, 2011) Hence the 'legality' of legal tender only concerns it being offered, while every person or business is free to accept that offer in principle. This renders the expression rather nondescript as the only case to which this would not apply is if a certain form of currency or payment is explicitly prohibited from being offered as for example counterfeit notes and coins "similar in size and shape to any of the lawful coins or other currency of the United States". This explicit illegality can also pertain to complementary currencies like Bitcoins which are deemed illegal to trade or use in some countries (Bajpai, no date) or even to gold e.g. in the United States from 1933 when president Roosevelt signed Executive Order 6102 that made it illegal for Americans to own and trade in gold other than what was contained in their dental fillings. This order remained in place until 1977. In absence of such explicit exclusions of what can be offered in contracts, the current legal tender definitions, at least in the countries studied here, only come into effect in a very limited range of cases.

In the USA, the idea of legal tender is closely connected with the term "lawful money" as discussed above in the discussion of the National Bank Act. This term also features prominently in the 1913 Federal Reserve Act in which the issuance of the new, national bank notes by the FEDs, and the validity of those, is discussed: "The said notes shall be obligations of the United States and shall be receivable by all national and member banks and Federal reserve banks and for all taxes, customs, and other public dues." Central banks in other countries typically issue notes with the authority and acceptance of the state but with the FED system, the situation is different. The statute continues to say that these notes "shall be redeemed in lawful money on demand at the Treasury Department of the United States, in the city of Washington, District of Columbia, or at any Federal Reserve bank." The fact that there is a difference between the notes issued by the FEDs and what is considered "lawful money" derives from the historical development of a steadily increasing centralisation of the banking system in the US as discussed above, while congress had issued "Greenback" notes directly, without a central bank, during the the civil war. Only those treasury notes were consequently considered "lawful money". Federal Reserve Notes in contrast were issued only under license of the state. In that sense, they joined a plethora of notes that were issued by private state bound and national banks. Today, even if only the FEDs can issue bank notes, the remnants of the earlier issuance regime are still in the letter of the law. While this makes contemporary references to "lawful money" obviously antiquated, the same seems to be true for the contemporary definitions of the terms money and currency.

Historian's View On Global Money

Long-Term Shifts In The Quality/Quantity Balancing Act

From early times when money first began to be used for a variety of purposes up to around the second half of the seventeenth century some form of physical commodity supplied either the only or the main form of money. In general, therefore, during that very long earlier period the limits within which money could become relatively scarce or plentiful were closer than have subsequently been the case. Even so, quite wide swings did occur from time to time in the relative quantities and velocities of circulation of money despite communities being reliant solely or mainly on commodity moneys. To some degree the alternations between inflationary and deflationary pressures are as old as money itself, although it is only after the development of modern forms of fiat money and of banking that the speed and extent of such fluctuations were able to increase without apparent limit. Modern fluctuations in the value of money are therefore simply differences of degree, not of kind, from those occurring in earlier periods, because money itself has a built-in pendulum to which extraneous forces ceaselessly add their own powerful pressures. Money is not an inert object, but a creature responsive to society's demands.

Our distant forebears yielded to temptation and returned chastized from their more modest backslidings to yield valuable lessons to modern generations, for money is among the most long-rooted of human institutions. Among the key characteristics which have given money its uniquely desirable qualities is scarcity relative to the demands made upon it for spending and saving (including conspicuous consumption and orname-ntation). Such scarcity arose either from the difficulties of growing crops or rearing animals, catching fish, dredging, quarrying, digging mines and so on to provide supplies of the preferred type of money or from the exercise of monopoly power by the main source or arbiter of the thing used as money. All these brakes on the money supply, whether natural or state-imposed, slipped from time to time. We have seen that where a state has a monopoly over money, it is extremely likely that, when pressed, it will seek salvation by such devices as printing more money, or in former times, by debasing the coinage, a process commonly carried to such an extreme that money became valueless, and a new scarce money of high quality had to be reintroduced. Such processes were invariably accompanied by and reinforced first by increases and then by decreases in the velocity of circulation.

Examples are given and in a of the five-hundred fold depreciation in the value of the cowrie shell in Uganda following the wholesale importation of such shells in the mid-nineteenth century, and of a similar though not quite so drastic fall in the value of wampum in the USA following the introduction of mechanized drilling and factory assembly of wampum in New Jersey in 1760. We also noted in our study of primitive money that many communities used a number of commodities as money at the same time, thus providing an insurance when one of these types dropped in value. A positive and long-sustained increase in both the quantity and quality of money accompanied by similarly sustained increases in trade and mercenary military activity followed the invention of coinage in Lydia and the growth of mints around the eastern Mediterranean. The Greek city-states vied to produce the finest coins, with Greek bankers becoming the civilized world's most experienced money-changers. A further enormous stimulus to trade was later provided when Alexander the Great monetized the previously stagnant, huge gold stocks of the Persian empire, much of which gold was added to the silver stocks of the Greek bankers, so bringing down the gold–silver ratio from over 13:1 to a round and convenient 10:1. The London goldsmith-bankers would readily have recognized the Greek bankers as their close relatives; both were aware of the working of Gresham's Law in practice, and of the fundamentals of the bullionist theory of value.

For the ancient world's greatest example, by far, of excessive inflation we have to remind ourselves of the great debasement of the Roman coinage in the second half of the third century AD. By AD 270 the silver content of the denarius had fallen to 4 per cent, from 50 per cent twenty years earlier. By the end of the century the prices of the main goods were over fifty times higher than during the first century AD. This runaway inflation caused Diocletian to issue his famous Edict of Prices of 301, to institute a thorough reform of the currency and to support these measures by a strong fiscal policy in the shape of the world's first annual budget. Rome produced rubbishy metallic flakes for the impecunious together with gold coins for the rich. Roman experience clearly demonstrated excessive swings from monetary scarcity to monetary oversupply, and also the possibility of carrying on simultaneously with a two-tier monetary system just as we today have relatively good currencies in most of the rich countries and bad currencies in most of the poor countries. Similarly, just as economists differ about the causes and cures of present inflationary and other ailments, so the ancient world still provides an exciting academic battleground for modernist, Marxist and primitivist historians.

After the fall of Rome Britain showed the unique spectacle of being the only former Roman province to withdraw completely from minting money, and even refrained from using coined money for nearly 200 years. The velocity of money fell quickly after AD 410, as is indicated by the increase in the number of hoards found in the following few decades. Velocity, even including 'foreign' coins, probably fell to zero within a generation. In Britain the Dark Ages were particularly sombre so far as money was concerned. The absence of money reflected and intensified the breakdown of civilized living and trading. When foreign gold coins did return to Britain from the Continent they were initially held to be too valuable for common currency and so were used mainly as ornament. Trade and velocity of monetary circulation increased together, recreating a demand for indigenous mints in Britain, so that by about the year 1000 some thirty mints were producing millions of silver pennies for trade and tribute in the form of Danegeld. The reminting of the coinage provided some of the early English kings with a rich source of income and a convenient alternative to taxes, a process which led to a more or less regular cycle of complete recoinage every few years, inevitably producing alternate shortages and surpluses of money. The value of medieval money in Europe depended crucially on securing a sufficient supply of bullion, whether from its own mines (in the case of silver) or from Africa (in the case of gold), especially when gold coins began increasingly to supplement its previously monometallic silver coinages.

The commercial revolution of the long thirteenth century (from around 1160 to 1330) was stimulated by increased supplies of both silver and gold, enabling the creation of multi-denominational currencies, comprising gold coins for very large payments with silver and copper (mostly silver) being used for the medium and small transactions which made up the vast majority of payments. A much more economically significant increase in the money supplies from this time onwards came from the development of banking and the use of bills of exchange, spreading from the leading centre of Lombardy to France, Spain, the Low Countries and then to London. The Black Death of the mid-fourteenth century illustrated the rare case where, although the absolute money stock in general remained unchanged, its relative supply was greatly increased. Even so, the inflationary effects, though patchily present, were compensated to a considerable degree by a drastic decline in the velocity of circulation.

The plentiful supplies of money in the long thirteenth century gave way to recurring bullion famines in the later Middle Ages, e.g. in the first decade of the fifteenth century, even more severely from 1440 to 1460, and again in the first half of the sixteenth century. To overcome such shortages monarchs resorted to debasement, especially on the Continent, while the Tudors also made use of other devices such as the dissolution of the monasteries, with the Church's silver plate adding to the proceeds of the sale of monastic lands. Such devices were rendered less necessary by the influx of precious metals into Europe from the

Americas, and by the simultaneous rise in the acceptance and circulation of banknotes. Printed money supplemented minted money, moderately at first when linked together through the principle and practice of 'convertibility', but later without limit when governments found it expedient to abandon convertibility despite the inflation which inevitably followed, and which in turn could be cured only by relinking paper money to gold or silver or some combination of both. Numerous examples of such alternations, under modern conditions, of monetary excesses and reforms have been detailed in the previous chapters, with the extremes of astronomical price increases followed by complete monetary breakdowns occurring more frequently and becoming more geographically widespread since the 1920s than ever before. Warnings of the repeated tendency of the quality of money to deteriorate through excess supplies exceed the span of recorded history, from the fable of the Midas touch down to the annual reports of almost every central bank in the last two decades of the twentieth century. It should be abundantly clear that the need to understand and to control money is consequently also greater today than ever before.

Developmental Money-Ratchets And The Military

Although it has been possible to achieve long periods of reasonably stable prices in times of peace, wars have almost always brought with them rising prices, for two main reasons: first, government expenditures grow during wars, while productive factors are diverted into non-productive channels and, secondly, the government's normal powers to borrow and to create money are greatly stimulated by the imperatives of war. Even when, in post-war periods, resources return to productive uses, the inflated money supplies tend to remain in existence to form a new, higher base on which the economy operates. The military ratchet was the most important single influence in raising prices and in reducing the value of money in the past 1,000 years, and for most of that time debasement was the most common, but not the only, way of strengthening the 'sinews of war'. Supplementing the periodic bouts of official debasement were the more continuous practices of counterfeiting, clipping and forgery carried out on a considerable scale to supplement the official money supply, despite being subject to the harshest punishment, including the death penalty. However morally reprehensible, such practices when widespread pointed to the demand for money exceeding the supply, leading to attempts by the more entrepreneurial elements to overcome the constraints of a money supply wherever the incentives were sufficiently profitable. Bad money did not always drive all good money out of use but usually supplemented rather than supplanted good money, the latter being kept selectively for high-priority purposes, e.g. for export or for the payment of taxes. Gresham's Law at first worked to increase both the quantity and velocity of circulation, but if carried to extremes went into reverse, as coins became of such poor quality that they were no longer readily accepted, while holders of good coin would no longer part with them. Thus, the various forms of official and unofficial debasement were accompanied by hoarding and dishoarding and so widened the swing of the monetary pendulum.

Given the ultimate disadvantages which inevitably followed the initial beneficial results of debasement, it is easy to see that in the long run increased supplies of specie obtained through trade or new mines, though of uncertain or accidental occurrence, were the best way of removing constraints on the growth of the economy. Long-run trends in depression and prosperity correlate extremely well with the specie famines and surpluses of the Middle Ages, as has been clearly demonstrated in the incomparable survey of money during this period made by Dr. Spufford. Furthermore, it was to the most prosperous areas of Europe, e.g. the towns of north Italy, that the increased supplies of gold and silver were in the main attracted, so encouraging the growth of new forms of money such as bank deposits, public debt instruments, bills of exchange and cheques. These paper additions to commodity money eventually widened the swing of the money pendulum to greater extremes than would otherwise have been the case. During this period, the pound sterling gained considerable prestige by being less frequently and less drastically debased than most continental currencies. In this connection, however, we should remind ourselves of the point emphasized earlier, that the countries which experienced the greatest economic growth were also those which had indulged in the most severe debasement. A 'sound money' such as sterling was in part purchased at the cost of crucifying the economy on the silver-cross penny or its later equivalents.

When modern paper money released prices from their metallic anchors, the military inflation ratchet began to be seen at its most powerful. The first extensive use of state paper issues (outside China) occurred in America, whose colonial governments, in a reaction to the extreme scarcity of sterling imposed by the British home government, began issuing their own notes. The 'Continentals' of the new USA fell in value by the end of the Revolutionary War to one-thousandth of their nominal value, a process repeated by the Confederate paper which similarly became worthless by the end of the Civil War. The assignats of the French Revolution and the hyper-inflation of the German mark between 1918 and 1924 are simply among the best- known of hundreds of examples of war-induced inflation.

Second only to war as an engine of inflation is the general acceptance of the need for an ever-expanding supply of money in order to facilitate economic development, a belief which in a weaker and vaguer form long preceded the Keynesian revolution, though it was the Keynesian ratchet which acted as a strong causative factor in the unusually high peacetime inflations of the second half of the twentieth century. The seventeenth-century writers on Political Arithmetic waxed lyrical on the positive powers of money to create national wealth. Sir William Petty, for instance, was convinced that, properly set up, a new public bank could 'drive the Trade of the whole Commercial World'. John Law, the Keynes of the early eighteenth century, published a Proposal for Supplying the Nation with Money virtually anticipating the 'multiplier', and which when first put into effect in France producing beneficial results before leading on to the fiasco of the Mississippi Bubble. This failure pushed French opinion back to the other extreme of opposing for more than a century the kind of banking system the country needed another example of extremes in one direction leading to equally if not more damaging extremes in the other direction. France provides one of the best examples in history of belated industrial development being to a large extent caused by delay in adopting a modern banking system.

It would therefore be difficult to quarrel with the conclusion reached by Professor Rondo Cameron in his study of Banking in the Early Stages of Industrialisation that 'both theoretical reasoning and the historical evidence suggest that the banking system can play a positive "growth-inducing" role' (1967, 291). That was the attitude of the appropriately named 'Banking School' of the mid-nineteenth century in opposition to the 'Currency School', which latter emphasized the need to maintain the quality of money by restricting banking through tying note issue strictly to variations in the amount of gold. Similar polarization of views had been put forward by the anti-bullionists and the bullionists in the previous generation. Given the pendular motion of actual money supplies over time, it is no surprise to discover that most writers on money fall into one or other of these variants of the expansionist or the restrictionist schools. It was the special circumstances of the 1930s which gave rise to Keynes's so-called General Theory. Writing in the depth of the depression in 1933, Keynes pointed out that 'the first necessity is that bank credit should be cheap and abundant', but he also advocated the urgent need for 'large-scale government loan expenditure. 'Hitherto war has been the only object of governmental loan-expenditure on a large scale which governments have considered respectable' (1933, 20–2). Thus, was the Keynesian ratchet invented. Later it was eagerly applied worldwide, especially by the newly independent nations of the post-colonial regions. However much the Keynesian revolution may be condemned for its long-run consequences of high and stubborn inflation, Keynes's enormous successes in providing cheap finance for the Second World War and in being largely responsible for the inestimable benefits of full employment for the first post-war generation, i.e. for its short-and medium-term benefits, should not be forgotten. Given its long-run drawbacks, the pendulum inevitably swung away from Keynesian expansionism back to a re-emphasis of laissez-faire, to monetarist restrictions on the money supply in particular and against government intervention and 'planning' in general. The slump of 1991–3 began to push the pendulum back away from monetarism towards new variants of Keynesianism.

CHAPTER 2

In A Global Cashless Society, Is It Possible To Trade Money For Free?

Technical improvements in media of exchange have been made for more than a millennium. Mostly they have been of a minor nature, but exceptionally there have been two major changes, the first at the end of the Middle Ages when the printing of paper money began to supplement the minting of coins, and the second in our own time when electronic money transfer was invented. ('Electronic funds transfer' is only one of a number of major improvements in communications which include the development of lasers, the use of satellites and so on, and is used here simply as a shorthand reference to the whole range of such inventions relevant to banking and finance.) Such major economies in the production of the monetary media have considerable macro- economic effects. The first stimulated the rise of banking, while the second is opening the way towards universal and instantaneous money transfer in the global village of the twenty-first century. It is hard to improve on Adam Smith's description of the revolution caused by the introduction of paper money an invention more readily adopted in his own country than in the rest of Great Britain. 'The substitution of paper in the room of gold and silver money replaces a very expensive instrument of commerce with one much less costly, and sometimes equally convenient. Circulation comes to be carried on by a new wheel, which it costs less both to erect and to maintain than the old one'.

One of the most significant but insufficiently noted results of these two major kinds of invention is the fundamental reduction they bring about in the degree of governmental monopoly power over money. When coins were the dominant form of money, monarchs were jealous of their sovereign power over their royal mints. Paper money allowed banks to become increasingly competitive sources of money, a development which led not only to significant macro-economic changes but also facilitated contemporary revolutionary constitutional changes.

It was no accident that the Whigs, who supported the limited constitutional monarchy of William and Mary, were prominent in promoting the Bank of England. Similarly in the era of electronic banking 'national' amounts of money are becoming increasingly anachronistic as millions of customers, irrespective of their country of domicile, are eagerly offered a variety of demand and savings accounts by a multitude of competing financial institutions in a variety of competing currencies. They are spoiled for choice and national money monopolies are thereby also being 'spoiled', in the sense of being reduced in effectiveness. The monetary authorities always try to reassert their monopolistic power in economic jargon, to make sure that money is exogenously created as opposed to money supplies produced elsewhere by the working of market forces or 'endogeneously' as the economists describe the process. Just as the effective working of the international gold standard at the beginning of the twentieth century was dependent on the activities of the Bank of England, so the evolving European Monetary System in the last decade of this century has been dependent on the discipline imposed by the German Bundesbank, which was readily accepted by a German population that has remained painfully aware of the hyper-inflations it suffered after each of the two world wars. Twice bitten, thrice shy.

It was not until the UK experienced a frightening annual inflation rate of 27 per cent in the mid-1970s when the trade unions rather than the Governor of the Bank of England were the real controllers of the money supply, that the Keynesian ratchet was thrown away and replaced by the monetarist policies that had long and consistently been proposed by Milton Friedman. He saw government restriction of the money supply as being by far the most important if not quite the only method of controlling inflation. However, another lifelong opponent of Keynesianism, Friedrich Hayek (1899–1992), proposed a strikingly different solution, based less on the power of government and more on the strength of the market led by consumer choice over the kinds of money to be used, with consumer sovereignty rather than government monopoly being the best guarantor of the value of money. It was in the UK's inflationary peak year of 1976 that Hayek published his two Hobart Papers of Choice in Currency and the Denationalisation of Money, updated in his book on Economic Freedom (1991). He lived to see the reversal of Keynesianism and the almost global triumph of the market over Marxism which he had prophesied. He advocated a Free Money Movement similar to the Free Trade Movement of the nineteenth century with 'the prompt removal of all the legal obstacles which have for two thousand years blocked the way for an evolution which is bound to throw up beneficial results which we cannot now foresee'. Unfortunately, the unforeseeability detracted from the acceptability of this part of his proposals. Wider credibility was given to his proposal to allow people to trade in dollars, pounds, marks etc., in the High Street but rather less to his suggestion that they should also have the right to claim their wages and so on in the currency of their preference. Echoes of this idea resurfaced in the British government's proposal of the 'hard Ecu' to compete with the other EC currencies. Retail choice of currency would replicate what had long been possible at the wholesale level in the foreign exchange markets.

This choice could include the use of gold coins, though Hayek was forced (reluctantly) to acknowledge that a return to the gold standard was impractical, since the very attempt to do so would cause huge and destabilizing fluctuations in the price of gold. Before returning to the implications of Hayek's concepts for the future of multinational currencies it is convenient here to consider briefly to what extent payments, in whatever currency, might come to be made in cashless form.

With regard to the technology of money transfer there is probably much truth in the paradox that the peaks of the longer-term future are easier to perceive than the misty low ground which comes within the compass of our more immediate vision. There is general agreement with regard to the long-term development of versatile, economic and ubiquitous money transfer systems, so that payment and credit facilities operated by the individual at home through video terminal or telephone, by the executive at the office or by the customer at the shop, all linked directly to a central computer, will at some future date be virtually on tap, enabling immediate validation and payment within agreed limits for practically everyone in western society, and probably also to the richer persons in the urban areas of the less developed countries. Disagreement arises as to exactly when this picture of a universal, direct credit-and-debit system will largely replace rather than merely supplement existing cash and paper transfer systems: it merely requires the extension of practices already in existence at the wholesale level downwards into the retail trade and greater co-ordination across regional currency systems similar to that anticipated by Hayek. A comparison with the history of development of the steamship is relevant here in that the threat of steam brought about such a remarkable improvement in the quality of sailing ships that this apparently obsolete mode of transport was extended for considerably longer than had seemed at all probable. This 'sailing-ship effect' is very much in evidence in the present paper transfer systems supplemented by electronic devices improvements which have postponed the advent of the impatiently awaited cashless society to a rather more distant future than was anticipated only a few years ago. Cash, when compared with other forms of payment, still has many virtues, including that of anonymity, obligatory for the poor and yet also much appreciated by the rich criminal (as was demonstrated in the frauds that helped to bring about the failure of the Bank of Credit and Commerce International in 1991). Thus although cash will continue its present trend in becoming relatively less and less important in the industrialized world (despite some nostalgic attempts to revive a few prestigious gold and silver coins), it will remain of considerable importance for the greater part of the world's population. Real choice in currency, as in means of payment, is an option possible only in affluent societies, where traditional boundaries between currencies, banks and other financial institutions are dissolving. Hitler was a little premature in saying that there were no longer any islands: the smart card and the satellite have made most geographical boundaries obsolete insofar as the movement of money is concerned. Even multinational action by the monetary authorities can fail to control this flood on those occasions when the global, instantly mobilized army of speculators decides to strike.

Multi-State Central Banking That Is Independent

It might at first sight seem that the reference to Hitler is irrelevant. It certainly is not. It was his legacy of war and inflation which gave rise not only to the Schuman Coal and Steel Community so as to make future European wars much less likely, but also to the historic decision to grant the German central bank an unusually high degree of independence. The Schuman Plan led on to the Common Market, and from the beginning of 1993 to the Single Market. This in turn leads on in plain and painful logic to the concept of a Single Currency. In the same line of argument, Keynes's post-war policies would not have has been adopted had he not demonstrated in How to Pay for the War his novel method of financing the most expensive war in history at rates of interest lower than ever before. His ideas were taken to extremes in the two decades following the Radcliffe Report, according to which money did not matter very much, and so economic discipline in Britain was drowned in a sea of liquidity. Thus, the new- forged Keynesian inflation ratchet took over in peacetime from the age-old military ratchet. The slow, tide-like convergence in

European inflation rates since discarding Keynesianism has been reflected in the attempts to narrow their exchange rates on the planned path towards irrevocably fixed rates of exchange, which by definition means a single currency.

A draft treaty on European Union was signed, with varying degrees of reluctance and euphoria, by EC heads of state in Maastricht in February 1992 in which the proposals for Economic and Monetary Union (EMU) were of special significance, outlining in confident detail the path towards a system of independent multi-state central banking for controlling monetary policy throughout the EC. By the end of 1993, after much political turmoil, the treaty had in general been accepted by the member states, though with opt-outs for Britain, Denmark and Sweden. In the mean time the speculative storms of September 1992 and July 1993 practically destroyed the Exchange Rate Mechanism and so greatly strengthened the hands of the opponents of the treaty that some considerable delay in implementing the original programme seemed inevitable. Nevertheless, the inner core of Germany, Benelux, France and Italy pressed ahead with a modified plan. However, when the fundamentals of the treaty were eventually put into practice, then early in the twenty-first century a European Central Bank became fully operational, which together with the central banks of the participating member countries comprise the European System of Central Banks (ESCB). In a radical departure from the traditions of a number of EC countries, ESCB was guaranteed political independence.

Despite the opposition of those who, with some justice, decry such developments as being irreversible surrenders of national sovereignty to unelected and therefore democratically unaccountable bureaucrats, there was sufficient momentum already built up to carry at least twelve member countries towards the 'convergence' required to progress eventually through the various stages on to the climax of the final stage when a single currency, at first called the Ecu (symbolically combining a medieval French currency with the reality of the modern German mark), was to become the sole legal tender of the participants.1 After all, for hundreds of years in the Middle Ages, an abstract, fictitious unit of account, the écu de marc, was used in foreign exchange to circumvent the much more numerous national and regional boundaries of that period. Thus the future, in fact though not now in name, as is especially typical of monetary history, will be repeating the half-forgotten experiences of the distant past.

Neither Britain's proposal of a thirteenth currency, the 'hard Ecu', nor Hayek's free choice in currencies stand much practical chance of widespread adoption. The maintenance of multiple currencies would deprive EMU of one of its main advantages, namely the removal of exchange costs. According to a European Commission report entitled One Market, One Money, a single currency would remove transaction and exchange costs worth up to 1 percent of GDP annually for the smaller state and around 0.5 per cent for the larger states. There would also be a saving of around Ecu 160 billion in the EC's foreign currency reserves. Such savings would not simply be of a once-for-all nature but would, dynamically, allow a higher sustainable rate of growth to be achieved (European Commission, Luxemburg, October 1990) a consideration meriting close study by those who ask 'What price, where 'Euro' not 'Ecu' became the new name for the single currency, with effect from December 1995.

Sovereignty? In any case, single sovereignty facing a financially and economically integrated Europe differs greatly from what existed previously. Either way, positively through entry or negatively through refusal, some sacrifice in traditional financial sovereignty is inevitable except, in the latter case, the sovereign right to inflate, a dubious benefit. The worldwide swing of opinion and policy in favour of removing inflation at almost any cost has exhibited common features which have been enthusiastically adopted by a range of monetary authorities of differing political colours such as New Zealand, Australia, Chile and Canada, and have been incorporated into the EC's financial programs. These includes the setting of specific targets for inflation, the strengthening of the legal independence of the central banks, and the imposition of ceilings on government deficits. Spendthrift governments are to be pilloried. The annual report of the Bank of Canada may be taken as a typical example of the new fashion of setting out a published profile for the reduction of inflation over the medium term, not simply in a wishful vague declaration but in specific figures.

In February 1991 the Bank of Canada and the Government jointly announced targets for reducing inflation. The specific targets are to reduce the year-over-year rate of increase in the consumer price index to 3 per cent by the end of 1992; 2½ per cent by the middle of 1994; 2 per cent by the end of 1995. Thereafter the objective would be further reductions until price stability was achieved.

In October 1992 the UK similarly adopted an inflation target, of 1 per cent to 4 per cent, with the Bank of England given the task of publishing each quarter its own independent assessment of progress amended to 2½ percent in 1997. Because of the inherent imperfections of almost all retail price indexes (e.g. in not being able to make allowance for the stream of new goods that feature heavily in modern consumer expenditures and in not allowing sufficiently for the increased quality of the 'same' goods) a nominal inflation of about 2 per cent is held by many authorities to be roughly equivalent to stable real prices. Attempts to go below that might well bring disproportionately greater costs. Thereafter competitive disinflation might have similar effects to the 'exporting' of unemployment by the competitive devaluations of the 1930s, or at least might depress the growth of world trade below its trend potential, causing a substantial and irrecoverable loss. On the other hand, unless the authorities are seen to make a really strong case for price 'stability' their loss of credibility might make its attainment impossible. It is in this connection that the case has arisen not only for the greater independence of central banks but also for giving to central banks the overriding priority for the achievement and maintenance of price stability. To give central banks, a number of objectives which experience has shown to be incompatible leads to impotence where it really matters the value of money.

Thus, the ESCB is explicitly committed to the primary objective of price stability, and while it has to support the general economic policy of the Community, this must be only to the extent that it does does not conflict with its primary objective. Its political independence is strengthened by a number of practical measures such as guaranteeing adequate finance for its operations, stipulating long-term appointments for its board (for eight years) and so on. The bank will not be allowed to make loans to public bodies, thus denying governments their easiest access to finance and blocking off a traditional road to inflation. The ESCB's statutory advisory duties regarding member countries' economic policies, such as the exchange rates with non-EC countries and fiscal policies particularly the size of balance of payments or budgetary deficits will reflect its primary commitment to monetary stability. ESCB has anti-inflation built into its constitution, an essential safeguard against the power of vested interests to push governments into excessive expenditure. For two generations inflation has been an almost permanent, though disguised and arbitrary, tax on the consumer. ESCB represents the consumers' response, a modern version of the revolting American colonists' cry of 'no taxation without representation', a democracy of the money box which is less inflationary than the ballot box.

Money Is Referred To As "Liberty.

The omens look promising for an era of much lower inflation in the richer countries from the mid 1990s. The Economist boldly sees zero inflation rather than merely low inflation as a distinct possibility for OECD countries which, having suffered high unemployment and low growth in the early 1990s in order to bring down the rate of inflation, would not wish this sacrifice to have been in vain. The lesson has been learned worldwide, though at great cost, that it is countries with low inflation that have achieved high growth and therefore low unemployment. Thus, the LDCs have learned the virtues of 'financial deepening', which could be obtained only through turning from Keynesian-type government planning towards allowing instead much greater freedom for market forces in general and financial liberation in particular. Even in the leading industrial countries inflation had appeared to be unstoppable for the whole of a long sixty-year period since 1933, during which the cumulative effect on the level of retail prices has been enormous, equivalent to 4,000 per cent in the UK and 950 per cent in the USA: others were far worse.

Attention has been drawn in earlier chapters to the paradox that in Britain and the USA inflation increased after the change in the mid 1970s from Keynesian to monetarist policies. This was for two reasons. First, the introduction of monetarism coincided with and complemented extensive financial deregulation. Secondly, and more importantly, inflation had become so embedded in Anglo-American society that its potential momentum, which had been suppressed by the planning controls associated with Keynesianism, was suddenly released. The frustrated inflationary horse had been given its head: it took a long time to bring its gallop to an end.

It has taken two generations for the truth finally to be fully accepted by the general public and by the political decision makers first, that the apparent short-term benefits of inflation are outweighed by its long- term costs; secondly, that inescapably one of the keys to a successful economy is control of the money supply in its changing forms; and, thirdly, that this can be achieved only by limiting national governments' sovereignty through setting up independent central banking systems. In time the patient optimism of

Lord Robbins, one of the few British economists to oppose Keynesianism when it was in full flood, has been justified: 'It really should not be beyond the with of man to maintain control over the effective supply of money; and, as I conceive matters, eventually little less than the future of free societies may very well depend on our doing so'. Thus, it would appear that in the long run Keynesianism has been killed.

However, if the concept of the long-term pendulum is correct, then the monetarists' claims regarding the death of Keynesianism are exaggerated, for, as has been repeatedly demonstrated by past experience, theories and practices favouring financial restraint tend in the course of time to give way to precisely the opposite. This comes about in part because of social amnesia, in part because constraints, if long imposed, become increasingly irksome, unfair and patchy in coverage as privileged or ingenious persons find ways around the constraints and invent acceptable money-substitutes. Perhaps the strongest force undermining monetary restrictions in the long term is the common complaint of output forgone, as shown in the various versions of countries being 'crucified on a cross of gold', or 'held to ransom by money monopolists' or being 'made bankrupt by high interest rates' and so on. Opinion begins to turn again in favor of less restrictiveand eventually, of clearly expansive monetary policies.

Furthermore when prices have remained relatively stable for some years, so that inflationary expectations have evaporated, then Keynesian-type policies really can work again, provided that they are believed to be genuinely short- to medium-term in duration and/or restricted to particular regions, or for exceptional purposes. German reunification provides a powerful example of how a country which has had an excellent long-run post-1950 record (compared with most others) in controlling inflation, has consequently been able to put Keynesian-type policies to work with good effect, deliberately seeking unbalanced budgets and running down its customarily large balance of payments surplus into a significant deficit, as a result of making huge financial transfers from West to East Germany, which in 1992 were, at DM 180 billion, equivalent to 6.5 percent of West Germany's GNP. The conversion rate for the merging of the marks, was certainly not chosen by the free market, nor, despite its blustering, by the Bundesbank, but was most definitely a political decision boldly taken by Chancellor Kohl. The balance of benefit to Germany was clear, despite some increase in inflation and in interest rates which turned out to be acceptably moderate in Germany, but unfortunately extremely awkward for the rest of the EC, forcing their rates up at a time of rising unemployment, when naturally they would have wished to reduce them. Policy synchronization in a multi-state system poses considerable difficulty for the future ESCB. In the case of countries such as Britain and the USA, which had not been able to control inflation, Keynesian policies worked perversely, making matters much worse and so contributed to a considerable degree to a debilitating process of deindustrialization. Only after the conquest of inflation can Keynesian-type weapons become again available for re-industrialization and regional stimulation, and then only for a limited, medium-term period.

In most countries the current anti-expansionist monetary pendulum probably still has until around the turn of the century before the movement back in favour of Keynesian expansion reasserts itself. Mounting, if belated, concern about the vast increase in population occurring mainly in the poorest countries, the depletion of finite resources, the problem of global pollution and other environmental concerns are at best only partially amenable to free-market solutions. The market gives no priority to posterity or the poor: silent majorities. As the costs of market failure become more obvious, so will the need for increased co-operative governmental intervention. (Perhaps concern about global warming and the ozone layer might even replicate the 'sun-spot' theories of the nineteenth century as contributory causes of economic disequilibrium.) The wide, long-term oscillations to which monetary policies are prone are brought about not only by the obviously strong destabilizing forces of wars, famines, inventions and so on, but also because money itself frequently exerts its own inherent instability. While it is readily conceded that 'real' factors can push demand and supply so much out of balance that cumulative disequilibrium may follow, it is not sufficiently emphasized that money contains within its many-sided nature dynamic features that also can be destabilizing. More notice is usually given to the other functions of money, in facilitating the myriad exchanges of daily commerce, where money is the indispensable equilibrator, a cybernetic mechanism of immense power and delicacy: but it is not infallible.

We have seen that most theories of money tend to fall into one of two contrasting groups which, however, given a long-term perspective, are complementary. Writers of the first group emphasize the importance of limiting the quantity of money in order to enhance or maintain its value or quality. The second group of writers are more concerned with allowing or encouraging an expansion in the effective quantity of money so as to stimulate economic growth or at least to remove any brake on such growth, notwithstanding the decline in the quality of money which might result from such expansion. Among this latter group, Schumpeter and Keynes were in agreement that it was the entrepreneurs with their 'animal spirits' that disturbed the 'status quo' which economists call equilibrium. In borrowing to fulfil their ambitions, the entrepreneurs alter the previous flows of saving, investment and income in ways which not uncommonly become cumulatively destabilizing. Briefly, then, the money pendulum is likely to be set in motion even when there are no external shocks, but its amplitude tends to be increased by the frequent though random appearance of such shocks.

In the normal course of events money is rarely 'passive' or 'neutral', while the safe haven of equilibrium on which so much economists' ink has been spilled and which still appears to inspire the dangerous, earth-flattening zeal of the Brussels bureaucracy, is equally rarely attained. An assumption, possibly unconscious, of some ideal equilibrium may lie behind Euro-planners' enthusiasm for 'level playing fields' for all the Community's financial and other economic units, and so carries the danger of imposing a far too restrictive network of rules and regulations with regard to fiscal, financial and industrial policies. In this connection Lord Robbins's view is even more relevant now than when he first produced his masterly analysis over fifty years ago: 'There is no penumbra of approbation round the theory of equilibrium. Equilibrium is just equilibrium'. Sir

Gordon Richardson, when Governor of the Bank of England, wrote of his experience as follows:

I regret to say that I have little direct experience with economic equilibrium indeed, so far as I am aware, none at all. I sometimes see suggestions that we shall be moving towards equilibrium next year or perhaps the year after: but somehow this equilibrium remains firmly in the offing. In the mean time, governments and central banks are likely to be faced with a series of difficulties which have to be addressed.

While the swings of the pendulum cannot thus be held fixed at mid-point, the art of monetary policy consists of moderating their amplitude rather than seeking to achieve some unobtainable, unreal, theoretic goal of equilibrium. There is ample evidence to show that monetary policies, whether expansive or restrictive, can when appropriately applied and supported, work remarkably well but only for a limited short to medium-term period, without having to be radically readjusted. If pushed too far or carried out for too long, as happens when policy-makers become convinced of the eternal verities of the scribblings of some transient economist, then both kinds of policy suffer from a pernicious form of macro-economic diminishing returns. Sound money, in the sense of an optimally adjusted supply, is the foundation both of capitalism and of freedom. It is therefore fitting and timely that the last two comments on the fundamental importance of money should be ascribed to two famous Russian writers. 'Lenin is said to have declared that the best way to destroy the Capitalist System was to debauch the currency' (Keynes 1920, 220). Dostoevsky's comment is more concise and positive:

"The Only Constant Is Change"

Why Does Money Matter?

As a UK passport holder, I am regularly confronted with stereotypes of 'the diligent and industrious Germans'. It is impossible to prove or challenge these stereotypes from a first person perspective. However, when looking at economics with a disciplinary distance, other more tangible factors come to light to explain concrete phenomena like the highly specialised and widely distributed German SME sector. Yet such heterodox views are seldom mentioned in any discussion about macro-phenomena like the post-WWII economic success of Germany. To give but one example related to the topic of this research, the banking system in Germany is fundamentally different from many countries, particularly when compared to the UK. There are more than just the handful of big household names in international banking institutions operating on the high streets in Germany. Of course, there are big corporate Banks in the German banking sector, one iconically named 'Deutsche Bank', however they are complemented by a profuse sector of fully licensed local, cooperative and public banking institutions, that cover the bigger share of consumer services and SME lending in the country. These local banks cannot move services or profits out of their localities, but are tied, for better or worse, to the local economy in their immediate surroundings. Therefore, they have been vital for the financing of start-ups and SMEs throughout the country during the recent decades of economic uplift. Even after the credit crunch following the financial crisis in 2008, they continued to provide productive loans to the 'real economy' whereas in other countries lending to small businesses came all but to a halt.

This example from the world of banking is just one illustration of how institutional elements of our financial system can have a more profound influence on the fabric of our economies and societies than is often recognised or acknowledged. That the arena of finance as a whole has a strong grip on our societies and democracies became apparent in the aftermath of the global financial crisis and it continues to make headlines with the continuing sovereign debt crises and quantitative easing programs in the UK, the USA and Europe. In fact, even before this recent crisis, the World Bank had identified 96 banking and 176 financial crises between the years 1971, the beginning of our current monetary regime, and 1996 alone. This number indicates that it could not simply be bad management, greedy individuals or inappropriate regulation that ails our financial systems, but that the issue is "systemic".

However, that systemic issue and the topic of this thesis is not primarily to do with banking, finance, or what is commonly called the 'financial system' as a whole. Instead it is the most fundamental element common to all these: money. And, in contrast to how money is often discussed, it is not about how much or how little of it is available or what any individual or government ought to do with it. Instead it is the nature of money that is posed as the central issue here. As much as it might seem that financial or banking crises have nothing to do with the kind of money that is used to measure their effects, but rather depend on political or behavioural decisions made by the individuals and institutions that use it, it will be argued here that the two are intrinsically linked. Money is not a neutral given, but exists because of the way people think about, talk about, and use it.

With this perspective, the nature of money does not only influence the instability of our financial system, but limits our capacity to achieve sustainability in all major societal spheres. Money, and our relationship to it, is implicated in inequalities locally and globally, as well as the environmental arena, where the need for climate mitigation runs against so called economic constraints.

The potential for an exponential increase in wealth is not only measured, but also facilitated by a monetary system that has emerged in step with the capitalist, shareholder oriented paradigm, for which inequalities and ecosystem destruction appear more as symptoms then independent issues. It is the "pathological growth imperative" built into our current globalised monetary and financial systems that cannot be changed by calls for government intervention towards redistribution and a turn to conventional 'green finance'. A more fundamental change of our monetary and financial systems is needed to achieve social stability and environmental sustainability. From natural ecosystems to technological and social complex flow systems, diversity is a necessary ingredient for systemic resilience. In the economic domain, this is relevant for the organisational set-up of national banking systems as much as for the number of different exchange systems that facilitate economic activity in service to the provision of needs, rather than an increase in shareholder value.

Monetary Diversification

It was not only the financial crisis which started in 2007/08 that brought up questions about the nature of today's monetary system and calls for it to change. A second factor that sparked discussion of change and showed how money can, in principle, be very different was the rise of Bitcoin since 2009, or actually the exponential increase of the market price of individual units that are transacted on the Bitcoin network. The media coverage about windfall gains for early bitcoin investors led to a widespread awareness that there are potential alternatives to the money we commonly use. In addition, with the price of a bitcoin peaking at nearly 20,000 USD a the end of 2017 and a plethora of new cryptocurrencies contributing to, and benefiting from the hype, the topic even made headline news on main stream media and started an active field of research and practice. However, Bitcoin or the blockchain technology underlying it were not the first innovations in the field of 'new money'. A much broader practice of non-governmental monetary systems has existed in parallel to mainstream money throughout large part of history although for most parts, these have been thinly spread, fragmented and consequently marginal and continue to be hardly visible to the contemporary public. Advances in information technology in the 1980s have led to a faster spread of ideas and implementation tools, which ultimately coalesced under a unifying term 'complementary currencies' (hereafter abbreviated to CCs) used as a common identifier amongst practitioners and researchers around the world. Cryptocurrencies fall within this field, along with so-called 'local currencies', 'time banks', tradeable loyalty systems and business-to-business currencies. Not counting Bitcoin and other blockchain based currencies, three waves of innovations have already been identified in this field over the last 3 decades, which have moved from sectoral or grassroots initiatives to systems that also involve or are even driven by the public sector. Even established academics like David Graeber have recognized CCs as an "essential element in any solution" to the financial and economic issues described above.

However, despite the general awareness of potential alternatives searches about Bitcoin made it into the most queried search terms of 2017 (#2 in the news category and #3 amongst 'how to' questions) - what is missing for a widespread democratic debate about reforming money, is the broad knowledge about money as it is, amongst both the public and politicians. The Positive Money campaign group that is advocating for the change in the issuance arrangements of the Pound Sterling has recently commissioned survey amongst members of parliament and found that 70% of all Members of Parliament still believe that money in the UK is only issued by the government via the Bank of England and the Royal Mint, and that over 62% stated that it was false to believe that commercial banks create money when they issue a loan. This ignorance amongst politician can be assumed to be similar amongst the general public.

On the other hand, many people who are enthusiastic about Bitcoin espouse misguided beliefs about what it is or what it is good for. If the hope for an easy windfall can be counted amongst the most obvious motivations to invest in cryptocurrencies, big and small, the potential for actual deep-rooted change in the monetary domain seems even further off. Under scrutiny Bitcoin appears not any more egalitarian or sustainable than conventional currencies. Even though it is ultimately impossible to know which person or organisation owns which or how many Bitcoin wallets and the bitcoins therein, it is assumed that on some indicators, such as wealth inequality, Bitcoin fares even worse than the global economy.

While many complementary currencies are deliberately designed for the benefit of the disenfranchised, they are not only hampered by public ignorance about the concept and practice of money, but actually threatened by the ambiguity of what money is even in legal terms. For example, Will Ruddick, currency innovator in Kenya, and his collaborators found themselves imprisoned just ahead of the launch of the Bangla Pesa, a currency designed to provide the small traders in an informal settlement near Mombasa with self-issued media of exchange to bridge the lack of liquidity in the local micro-economy. The charges of forgery, which were based on the impression of local law enforcement that the private issuance of something akin to money must be illegal, were later dropped. The group was released, and their model has since spread with endorsements of local governments to other localities in Kenya and South Africa. Other examples, none so dramatic but all hampering the implementation and adoption of currency innovations, will be discussed.

Common to all these cases is that the dominant discourse of money, as established by the media, financial regulators, and the law, has direct effects on the implementation of CCs in terms of their compliance with law or illegality. This conceptual under-determination of money also appears in the different and sometimes conflicting framings of money and currency employed by different practitioners and approaches. Yet with no coherent theoretic frameworks to understand all kinds of complementary currencies along with conventional currencies such as the Pound Sterling, the US Dollar or the Euro, the contribution that novel monetary practices make to theory and as tools for systemic financial change and sustainable development remains underappreciated.

With the broader conceptual framework for money and currencies here proposed, there are other emergent social and economic phenomena which can be understood as part of this inquiry even if they seem to fall far outside the conventional definitions of money. Rachel Botsman, looking at new business models and collaboration platforms of what she called the 'Sharing Economy', had started to use the term 'reputation capital', in concurrence with financial capital, and also described, along with other commentators, trust and reputation metrics as 'currency'. As far removed from conventional currencies as those might seem, the latest developments of a state-mandated citizen reputation system currently being tested in China, links those two terms directly. This form of reputation is not only said to determine access to public services but also bank credit.

In fact, credit ratings are already a well established practice for commercial financial institutions, and reputation already plays an important role on internet based businesses like AirBnB (accreditation and user reviews) or eBay (star rating for vendors and buyers). However, considering those systems as 'money', in a broader sense, allows for a fundamental reappraisal of the kind of metrics we want to base our societal relations and collaborations on, which includes national currencies as much as private systems. In this sense, money will here be framed as "a social design that then designs the social" and the phenomena of novel technologies and currencies of various forms serves as a starting point to better understand and conceptualise fundamental theories of money today. In the words of Jérôme Blanc as one of the preeminent scholars on the topic: "The empirics of contemporary, so-called community and complementary currencies display various links that help to understand this complexity: it constitutes a field of observation that contributes to the critical examination of both orthodox and heterodox economist approaches to money."

Before giving an overview of how this thesis will contribute to the understanding of complementary currencies and monetary theory a few points will be raised to position not only the topic and the findings of this thesis, but the research itself. For the duration of my Ph.D. program I was based at the Institute for Leadership and Sustainability (IFLAS) which is part of the University of Cumbria's business school. Combined with an academic background in natural sciences (master-level degree (Diplombiologe) in Neuroscience, University of Freiburg, Germany 2007) and philosophy and business administration (Magister Artium at the same university in 2009) the methodological approach to the topic of money had been informed by various disciplines from the start of the learning journey that finds its conclusion with this thesis. In the years prior to the inception of this current study, I had been working on complementary currency, and for initiatives in that field, in several countries. This non-academic 'on the ground' engagement with the topic necessarily added a distinct practitioner's perspective to the conceptual and methodological approach to this thesis.

Most relevant for the development of the final research question and the progression of the analysis, however, was a position as the principal researcher and project manager for the EU Inter-programme 'Community Currencies in Action (CCIA, 2012) at the New Economics Foundation in London. The aim of that project was to showcase complementary currencies of different kinds as policy delivery tools for local governments. With project partners including the City of Amsterdam, the public bank of the City of Nantes, the Borough of Lambeth in London and the public waste disposal company of the region of Limburg in Belgium, six different currencies in England, Wales, France, Belgium and the Netherlands were implemented or scaled up during the three-year project, all of which continue today and one of which will be analyzed. The research and advocacy of the project included the impact assessment of complementary currencies, a robust implementation framework (CCIA, 2015h), the development of an online trading platform and the survey of legal and compliance issues for currency initiatives. The latter was also a precursor to the legal aspects of the research in this thesis, and the establishment of collaborations that were drawn upon for. During the lifetime of the project and beyond I was also called upon for expertise and commentary on novel currency phenomena, particularly Bitcoin, on national and international media.

Predicated in parts by this previous engagement with the topic, the research question that guided this inquiry was whether and to what extent the framings and presentations of money in financial regulatory discourses are consistent with modern monetary practices, particularly when broadening the scope of what is considered as money to include complementary currencies. This broad scope required the research to be not solely defined by existing theories and research programmes about money, neither from disciplines of economics nor sociology. They will be, however, integrated as a backdrop to this inquiry and will be supplemented and discussed in regard to a clear distinction between the two meanings of the word, the concept of money and the actual money we use. This in turn led to the development of an inclusive theory of money, in both its meanings, as a 'discursive institution' or a system that regulates our ideas and behaviour, but is itself constituted and changed by these same ideas and behaviors. It also required the application of a transdisciplinary suite of methods to three varied sets of data. This approach consistently encompasses the conceptual as well as the concrete phenomena from Pound Sterling in the form of paper notes, coins and electronic bank balances to Bitcoin and all other forms of complementary currencies.

In this way, the analysis presented here amounts to an ontological account of money that aspires to be applicable to everything that is presented as such, across such diverse texts as the publications of the Bank of England, the law of the United States or the literature on complementary currencies. Apart from this conceptual work, the original contribution of this thesis is: to present complementary currencies as activity systems and to highlight the inconsistencies of what counts as money and currency in publications of the Bank of England and in the law of the USA. The findings from this thesis are relevant for monetary theory in general and in particular for its relations to the emergent field of multidisciplinary research on complementary currencies. It also bears implications for policy and advocacy in regards to monetary reform and the implementation of and engagement with monetary innovations.

With this relatively broad scope, any answer to the question of 'What is money?' cannot only rely upon economic or sociological perspectives, as it needs to consider how individual actors use, define and, particularly in the case of complementary currencies, issue money. This necessarily also encompasses organisational and political dimensions and it would seem impossible to arrive at conclusions that are entirely free from the influence of individual preferences, or socio-cultural ideologies, both in terms of the constituencies that use money in its different forms and the authors that write about it.

More so than with other narrower research topics, any broad treatise on money is informed by and prone to reflect, if only implicitly, my own interest and impetus as a researcher. The results of this can be schematically positioned on a scale from the purely descriptive ('what is') to the normative ('what ought to be'), and the researcher's disposition can be either theoretic or practice orientated in nature. To exemplify this different approaches to the topic of money as polar positions, the following matrix has been adapted from one of my previous research papers. Pointing out these different ways of engaging with the topic of money comes without any claim that the positions marked in this matrix are exclusive to a particular methodological or disciplinary practice and without pretence that such strict separation is found in the existing literature on money, or this thesis. However, in light of the above epistemological question, this schema is helpful in discerning the underlying predispositions found in the studied literature and to help reflect on the thesis at hand.

Two Inquiries: Where Does Money Originate?

As was alluded to in the introduction, a critical engagement with money can take many forms and perspectives. Firstly, an overview of theories of money, and secondly the introduction of a novel way to describe money that will form the underlying understanding or 'hypothesis' for that analysis. This way of looking at money as a 'discursive institution' will implicitly be tried out and tested in the following chapters. However, before setting out with either of these, two more fundamental conceptual points will be made in regard to the way this thesis will discuss money.

The first of those two points concerns an ambiguity of the term 'money' that appears in most contexts but is particularly relevant when discussing novel and heterodox theories. The title of a seminal book written and published in 2011 by researchers at the New Economics Foundation, the Positive Money campaign and the University of Southampton helps to illustrate that point: The question that the authors had chosen as the title of their book and which they set out to answer, namely "Where does money come from?", can be read in two interconnected but distinct ways. To start with the more practical one, the question can simply refer to the notes and coins we have in our pockets and the numbers shown in our bank accounts. "For many people 'money' means 'coin' and what [...] is really being asked is 'How did coinage begin? '" In this more naive interpretation of the question, the contemporary answer would simply point towards the Royal Mint in Wales for coins and the Bank of England in London for banknotes. Also, much more relevant today than in the days when Grierson wrote the above quote, it is the computer terminals at any local bank branch which the electronic units in our bank accounts, that are commonly identified and used as money, originate from. However, that would only refer to the origin of those concrete units with which we count our personal wealth and use to pay for the necessities and niceties of life.

An extension of that same reading of the question would ask for the authorities and their rules or laws that govern the issuance, or the 'putting-into-circulation' of those same units. The answer in this case is likely to be more abstract as it includes power structures, legislative procedures, licenses by the Financial Conduct Authority (FCA), the setting of capital and liquidity requirements, and the influence of rating agencies, central bank, and monetary policies. It would also include concepts such as 'quantitative easing' and ultimately the question of democratic or public involvement in setting those rules versus the delegation of all those elements to expert committees. This extended reading of the question "Where does money come from?" looks at money not only as a material or digital 'object', but as a political, and by the natural extension of that term, a social phenomenon. It considers not only the object of money but also the subjects and entities that spend, receive, create, allow, commission and ultimately 'do' money. A paraphrasing of this reading would be "How come we have, today, this kind of money and monetary system and no other? And how does it work in detail?".

There is, however, a second completely different reading of the same question that leads to the point of ambiguity of 'money' that needs to be made explicit at the outset of this inquiry. This second reading refers to the concept or idea of money in general, independent from the current monetary regime with its concrete units, material or virtual which we use as money and with which economists count and recount the world. A paraphrasing of this second reading would ask how it came to be that such a thing as 'money' exists in the world, and what the nature of it is and if we could not do without it. These are, ultimately, questions of ontology or the nature of money and it is this kind of inquiry that this thesis is concerned with. This reading does not look primarily at the practicalities of money, how it is put into circulation and subsequently used, but invokes the heuristics of philosophy, sociology, and the sub-disciplines of historic anthropology and economic history.

However, as distinct and deep as this reading of the question, "Where does money (as a concept) come from?" is, it also has bearings on the first reading of the question. This is because no actually existing money or monetary regime can do without an underlying, conceptual theory of money at least implicitly. On the other hand, as will be illustrated further on, the interdependence between those two readings of the question and the two meanings of the term 'money', the concrete and the conceptual, is also relevant in reverse: the money we find in our pockets right now, influences the personal and collective ideas we have about money on a conceptual level. The concrete money we were first sent to the shop with when we were small children, to buy milk or sweets, gives form and, if never challenged, a limitation to our imagination as to what money could be in general. We develop a bias towards what Keynes called "money as we know it". Even if most people will readily be able to name a few historic forms of money like shells, gold coins, cigarettes etc. that are so very different from today's Pound Sterling, it is not only our concept of money that determines its possible implementations, but it is the commonly used implementations that in turn affect our collective conceptualisation.

One correlate of this limitation can be seen in the way economists and even anthropologists appraise the monetary phenomena they historically found in far away places, like wampum belts, or that can be observed today in the various forms of 'complementary currencies'. Where those are seen as 'not like money', because they do not resemble the forms and use cases of the money that the observers knew from their own cultural context, the concrete forms of 'money as we know it' have set the limits of conceivability for the concept of money. Given this interaction between the concrete and the conceptual any straightforward answer to the question "What is money?" can hardly be expected to both empirically and theoretically robust. Depending on the motivation and intended audience most answers will fall somewhere between the trivial and the vague. If the way of viewing money that this chapter is building up to can offer any epistemological advantages and provide both universality on the conceptual level as well as operability in practice will be reviewed in the concluding chapters of this thesis.

The book that lent its title to this section is primarily lauded for the first comprehensive and systematic answers to the first readings of the question "Where does money come from?". It describes in detail how the three predominant forms of money in the UK - bank deposits, cash (notes and coins) and electronic central bank money enter circulation in what was later dubbed "the modern economy". However, as technical and revelatory as that process might be in and to itself, at least for most lay readers, neither that book nor the later publications by the Bank of England, that confirmed the contemporary process of money creation by commercial banks, do without excursions into the historical and philosophical territory that pertains to the second reading of the question as discussed above.

This inclusion of easy to picture 'stories' like that of medieval goldsmiths seems to provide some conceptual respite to these otherwise technical texts. However, they can also be seen as a deliberate stylistic choice to support a certain conceptual theory of money instead of being an explicatory necessity for the clarification of the creation of concrete money. In the same way the iconography and graphics presented in or along with these texts and their recourse to everyday and personal experiences in regard to money seem conducive to the acceptance of the argument with wider-than-expert audiences. They also shroud the presentation of the concrete in a cloud of what Dodd calls the semi-normative "origin myths" of money.

For now, two meanings of the word 'money' will be submitted as the first foundational distinction of this thesis. On the one hand the word refers to 'money as we know it', the units we use every day and with which most of us will have been familiar since childhood. In the UK, that is Pound Sterling in its different forms, in other constituencies the same is known by different names like Euro, Dollar or Yen. On the other hand there is 'money as a concept', the wider and more elusive idea that seems as familiar and taken-for-granted and yet, if asked about, becomes strange and hard to describe.

To mark this distinction, the capitalisation of the word 'Money' will be used to refer to the 'concept of Money'. This is in direct analogy to the use of capital letters in Platonic idealistic philosophy16 where a word written with a capital letter refers to the idealistic concept of something, an archetype. The word Chair, for example, with a capital C means the general concept for all the everyday material objects that fall into this category. Written with a small c, the same word refers to any one of the particular instances or representations of that category, for example the chair one might be sitting on while writing or reading this paragraph. In this latter sense the word money with a small m will be used in this thesis to refer to the particular form or implementation of the general concept of Money that we carry around with us and which probably comes up in our minds when we are asked to picture 'money'. This categorisation of Money and money is an original suggestion and should not be harder, in theory, to observe as with other analogous distinctions. It seems obvious, for example, not to speak of identity in general when we discuss national passports, or not to use the word transport as synonymous with cars. In practice however, steering clear of the ambiguous use of the two meanings of 'money' is difficult to achieve.

The confusion of the two, money and Money, is one of the heuristic difficulties and epistemological shortcomings in the way 'money' is discussed both in everyday language and, as this thesis will highlight, also in expert and academic texts. Hence, 'money' with single inverted commas will be deployed when referring to the ambiguous use of the word found in the specific texts that are analysed in the following chapters. The degree to which the two, the concept Money and the 'concrete' money we use today, are distinct will become more pronounced when novel and unusual forms of money. Maintaining this separation of the two, at least when considering questions of what money 'is', may help resolve the state that some authors describe as "schizophrenic for the most, as we indeed perceive it at once as a universal and a particular" which this thesis argues is an unnecessary state of confusion. We are used to the difference between ideal concepts and real instantiations of many things of everyday life. Extending this awareness in regard to 'money' is a precondition to enable critical engagement and enable change both in theory and practice.

The relation of the two terms, money and Money, is here visually depicted as two concentric circles. The way they have been presented so far clearly assigns the smaller circle to money, the particular and specific implementations that can never fully exhaust all the different forms that could theoretically be imagined in the scope of the big circle which represents the concept of Money. However, the graphical representation of this distinction raises the question why the different forms of money that people use in different countries are not depicted as individual subsets of Money. This is because of the contrast of all forms of 'money as we know it' with what will later be introduced as 'complementary currencies'. Compared to these very different forms of money, all 'national currencies', the Euro, Pound Sterling, Dollar, Peso, etc., seem very much like the same kind of money. Thus they are here treated as the same implementation of the concept of Money, which in the following will also be called 'conventional money'. This conceptual point is also consistent with the homogeneous way most of those 'national currencies' are issued today. Particularly since the Bretton Woods Conference at the end of the Second World War, the monetary and banking systems all around the world have converged on very similar modi operandi, with the US Dollar as their common 'reference currency' and various international institutions, like the World Bank, the International Monetary Fund (IMF) and the Bank for international Settlements (BIS) contributing to the recognition and consolidation of this dominant monetary regime.

Social Constructivism

The theory of knowledge called social constructivism can be traced back to the 1970s when it emerged at the confluence of certain research questions in philosophy, psychology, cognitive theory, and sociology. It posits that knowledge is only ever a property of, and constituted by, our perceiving and processing minds. According to this proposition, to 'know' something becomes a process, rather than a certainty, because the predisposition of the observer physical, psychological, emotional and mental and his or her expression of what is being observed are of equal importance with the 'nature' of the object that is observed or talked about. There is no 'objectivity' that requires us to talk about a certain phenomenon in a certain way. "Everything said is said by an observer to another observer that could be him or herself."

What follows from this is a sceptical alertness about the subjective nature of all descriptions of the world, even when personal descriptions are joined into collective ideas. Notions of truth, reality and objectivity become less robust or self-evident and need to be equally reconsidered as socially constructed as the objects, statement or 'facts' that would commonly be described as true, real or objective. "Truth cannot be out there cannot exist independently of the human mind because sentences cannot so exist, or be out there. The world is out there, but descriptions of the world are not.".

Furthermore, for the radical social constructivist, this is even valid when talking about material objects of which our senses give us a very convincing impression of their 'reality'. Even while we knock our hand on the table in front of us, nothing about that table can ever be expressed other than in words and those very words and the concepts they express are always socially constructed. This creates fundamental divide between what we can know about the world and what the world out there might 'actually' be like, including that table that we might even have bruised our insistently banging knuckles on.

This turn away from the realism of the phenomena observed in the world towards an acute awareness of the limitation of what we can know about them and the way we can talk about them is known as the 'linguistic turn' in social sciences. The foundational work that enabled and demanded this turn, a long time before the idea of social constructivism emerged, were the later works of Ludwig Wittgenstein. In his concept of 'language games' (Wittgenstein, 1986) he unravelled how the words we use cannot so much be seen as representations of the world around us but rather as entities to themselves that are in principle independent from that which we employ them to describe. In this way he warned that the correspondence of our words with the phenomena outside of us purely depends on the way we use those words in our communication, be it written or verbal. No other relation can safely be assumed.

This does not only lead to many equally valid but potentially conflicting descriptions of the world, but also allows for a certain resolution or dissolution of those conflicts, at least on a meta-linguistic level. Because as long as we are aware of the social construction of everything we express, the encountered contradictions do not appear as insurmountable conflicts but simply as a rich diversity of expressions that can help us to explore the social world.

These ideas have not only informed a careful reconsideration of many aspects of the subjects and methods of philosophy and social sciences but have also been applied to the otherwise methodologically self confident natural sciences and their positivist assumptions. However, when applied to the material world, constructivism alone often seems inadequate in giving a satisfactory description of the effect that the world out there has on us as part of that world. Even if we admit that the sentence "I hurt my hand on this table" is only useful within an interpersonal language game and might not express anything 'real' about the world, we are still certain that something has occurred and it will happen again unless we change our behavior and stop hitting the table. "Counter to some extreme constructivist positions, [the recognition of] the constitutive role of language should not lead to the idealist conclusion that the world emanates from people's heads and/or mouth."

This idea is expressed in a theory called 'critical realism', pioneered by Roy Bhaskar, which establishes a methodological middle-ground between radical idealism and crude positivist materialism. In his Ph.D. thesis, University of Lancaster student Hidenori Suzuki has deemed this middle ground of critical realism to be the necessary starting point for any study of money in order to make sense of the material means of transactions found in everyday use: notes, coins, cheques, credit cards. However, for this present study, those material transaction media of 'money as we know it' are not the reason to call upon a critical realist standpoint as their materiality is not likely to pose particular epistemological difficulties for the analytical framework here proposed. Rather is it important that the critical realist stance reminds us as observers about the lifeworld relevance of the object we study. Therefore, even if the following portrays both Money and money as socially constructed, their effects will not play out in the world of ideas alone. Monetary theory sits at the heart of economics and finance and thus exercises a very real and visceral influence on the world including the material bodies therein. To view monetary phenomena "and their protocols as performative or as fictional is thus not to deny their force". Or poignantly expressed in the words of a remorseful ex-investment banker in the 2015 movie "The Big Short" (McKay and Lewis, 2015): "You know what I hate about fucking banking? It reduces people to numbers. Here's a number every 1% unemployment goes up, 40,000 people die, did you know that?"

Some theories and concepts of 'money', discussed in the following, explicitly address its socially constructed nature. The implications of social constructivism and critical realism for other conceptualizations of the nature of 'money' will be discussed in the next chapter. In order to understand the scope of this philosophical framework for theories of 'money', one illustrative example is given here. It is chosen because it reappears explicitly or implicitly in the concepts of 'money' discussed and analysed throughout this thesis. It is also often used to represent the essence of material objectivity when it comes to money: the so called 'intrinsic' value of gold. Not only are gold coins probably the most iconic representation of money, maybe rivaled only by the US dollar symbol, but for many, they are also the quintessence of 'good money': stable in value, safe from manipulation or inflation of the monetary supply, independent from legitimizing authorities. The argument heard is that it carries its value within, what is called intrinsic value, by merit of its scarcity and its ultimate stainless nature.

If value was deemed to be a social construct, that would make it the opposite of 'intrinsic' as it would depend on the observers, who construct it, and not the object itself. But how far could a claim of social construction be made regarding the value of gold? Under the premises of critical realism, it remains straightforward to acknowledge that there exists such a thing which is elsewhere called a chemical element, a metal identified by the word 'gold'. Its mere existence does not depend on us as observers. This is what is referred to as a 'brute fact', a term that will be explored further in the next chapter which considers the constructivist theory of philosopher John Searle (1996). Along with the material existence of gold come, in relation to other brute material realities, certain properties: it is, for example, non-corrosive even in presence of strong oxidizing agents and it is easily malleable even within the range of forces that can be exerted by the unaided human body. Those two properties mean it can be easily polished and will maintain its shine for a long time. But that shine also depends on such material realities of the literal eye of the beholder as the arrangements of light receptors therein.

These two properties can be said to be intrinsic to gold, if not in the sense of a radical constructivist epistemology as nothing can be shiny or golden without an observer so at least in a critical realist appraisal. However, do they constitute value? Certain optical qualities can be said to have aesthetic value, at least to the human observer. In addition, gold's malleability and durability are valuable in a practical sense, being advantageous in the production of coinage and storage of media of exchange made from gold. However, that usefulness is analogous to the way that modern contactless payment technologies are of value to the retail and payment industries because they are easier for consumers to handle when compared to 'chip and pin' or even 'cashier's cheque' technologies. In this sense it seems more elucidating to talk about gold's use value rather than its intrinsic value. The unique qualities of gold here mentioned also mean that it has a certain use value in the electronics and medical industries. Furthermore, another brute fact about gold is that it is a relatively scarce chemical element.

However, are those qualities taken together enough to uphold the idea that the value of gold is intrinsic and not a social construct? Does scarcity necessarily predicate value? At the time of writing, a fine ounce of gold was valued at about 1300 USD. The same quantity of the element silver trades at roughly one percent of that price (16 USD on December 27th 2017). To give another point of comparison, an ounce of aluminium can be purchased for about 5 cents. Is this difference justified by the use value of those metals, their scarcity or other factors? When looking at what the available amounts of those metals are used for, it turns out that silver seems to outstrip gold by far in its usefulness. For example, half of the total available silver in 2016 (1027 tons) went into industrial use whilst a fifth went into coins and silver bars. Gold, on the other hand, was much more abundant that year, 4372 tons altogether. However, only 7% (320 tons) of that went into industrial use, a quarter of it (1029 tons) became bullion and coins and further purchases by central banks and other financial institutions accounted for another 25%. The rest, over 2000 tons, went into the single largest use of gold, fin 2017 and probably any other year: jewelry (Statista, 2017a).

However, only a fraction of jewellery is ever worn at any given time and it can be safely assumed that many purchases in that segment is of a similar nature as the purchases of gold bullion and coins. However, even if it is hard to tell genuinely aesthetic value from primarily speculative value apart, these numbers add to an argument against the concept of using 'intrinsic' value to account for the two orders of magnitude between the prices of gold and silver. The largest part of the value of gold seems to be socially constructed in the end: we value it because it is pretty and because many others before us have deemed it valuable on those ground, and many more will probably continue to do so. This realization might not be as much a striking dismantling of the appeal of gold as that of mystical King Midas who gained the power to turn all that was put before him to gold, and ultimately died from starvation due to this power, and that which the North American first peoples had warned the western settlers about 'one can't eat it!' but at least for the following discussions of different theories of 'money' it will be useful to bear it in mind.

CHAPTER

The Nature And Origins Of Money And Barter

Money's Importance

Perhaps the most common claim with regard to the importance of money in our everyday life is the morally neutral if comically exaggerated claim that 'money makes the world go round'. Equally exaggerated but showing a deeper insight is the biblical warning that 'the love of money is the root of all evil', neatly transformed by George Bernard Shaw into the fear that it is rather the lack of money which is the root of all evil. However, whether it is the love or conversely the lack of money which is potentially sinful, the purpose of the statement in either case is to underline the overwhelming personal and moral significance of money to society in a way that gives a broader and deeper insight into its importance than simply stressing its basically economic aspects, as when we say that 'money makes the world go round'. Consequently, whether we are speaking of money in simple, so- called primitive communities or in much more advanced, complex and sophisticated societies, it is not enough merely to examine the narrow economic aspects of money in order to grasp its true meaning. To analyse the significance of money it must be broadly studied in the context of the particular society concerned. It is a matter for the heart as well as for the head: feelings are reasons, too.

Money has always been associated in varying degrees of closeness with religion, partly interpreted in modern times as the psychology of habits and attitudes, hopes, fears and expectations. Thus the taboos which circumscribe spending in primitive societies is basically not, unlike the stock market bears which similarly reduce expenditures through changing subjective assessments of values and incomes, so that the true interpretation of what money means to people requires the sympathetic understanding of the less obvious motivations as much as, if not more than, the narrow abstract calculations of the computer. To concentrate attention narrowly on 'the pound in your pocket' is to devalue the all-pervading significance of money.

Personal attitudes to money vary from the disdain of a small minority to the total preoccupation of a similarly small minority at the other extreme. The first group paradoxically includes a few of the very rich and the very poor. Sectors of both are unconsciously united in belittling its significance: the rich man either because he delegates such mundane matters to his servants or because the fruits of compound interest exceed his appetite, however large; the poor man because he makes a virtue out of his dire necessity and learns to live as best he can with the very little money that comes his way, so that his practical realism makes his enforced self-denial appear almost saintly. He limits his ambition to his purse, present and future, so that his accepted way of life limits his demand for money rather than, as with most of us, the other way round. At the other extreme, preoccupation with money becomes an end in itself rather than the means of achieving other goals in life.

Virtue and poverty, however, are not necessarily any more closely related than are riches and immorality. Thus, Boswell quotes Samuel Johnson: When I was a very poor fellow I was a great arguer for the advantages of poverty . . . but in a civilized society personal merit will not serve you so much as money will. Sir, you may make the experiment. Go into the street, and give one man a lecture on morality, and another a shilling, and see which will respect you most . . . Ceteris paribus, he who is rich in a civilised society, must be happier than he who is poor.

Johnson's commonsense approach to the human significance of money not only rings as true today as it did two centuries ago but may be mirrored in the statements and actions of much earlier civilizations. The minority who find it possible to exhibit a Spartan disdain for money has always been exceptionally small and in modern times has declined to negligible proportions, since the very few people concerned are surrounded by the vast majority for whom money plays a role of growing importance. Even those who as individuals might choose to belittle money find themselves constrained at the very least to take into account the habits, views and attitudes of everyone else. In short, no free man can afford the luxury of ignoring money, a universal fact which explains why Spartan arrogance was achieved at the cost of an iron discipline that contrasted with the freedom of citizens of other states more liberal with money. This underlying principle of freedom of choice which is conferred on those with money became explicitly part of the strong foundations of classical economic theory in the nineteenth century, expounded most clearly in the works of Alfred Marshall, as 'the sovereignty of the consumer', a concept which despite all the qualifications which modify it today, nevertheless still exerts its considerable force through the mechanism of money.

Financial Policy Sovereignty

This essential linkage between money, free consumer choice, and political liberty is the central and powerful theme of Milton Friedman's brand of monetarism consistently proclaimed for at least two decades, from his Capitalism and Freedom (1962) to what he has called his 'personal statement', Free to Choose, published in 1980. An even longer crusade championing the essential liberalism of money-based allocative systems was waged by Friedrich Hayek, from his Road to Serfdom in 1944 to his Economic Freedom of 1991. Yet for a generation before Friedman, the eminent Cambridge economist Joan Robinson called into question the conventional basis of consumer sovereignty in her pioneering work on Imperfect Competition (1933). Indeed, she doubted 'the validity of the whole supply-and-demand-curve analyses. Many years later, with perhaps too humble and pessimistic an assessment of the tremendous influence of her writing, she felt forced to lament: 'All this had no effect. Perfect competition, supply and demand, consumer's sovereignty and marginal products still reign supreme in orthodox teaching. Let us hope that a new generation of students, after forty years, will find in this book what I intended to mean by it'.

By the mid-1970s it became obvious that, as in the inter-war period, the fundamental beliefs of economic theory were again being challenged, and nowhere was this probing deeper or more urgent than with regard to monetary economics. Mass unemployment had pushed Keynes towards a general theory which, when widely accepted, helped to bring full employment, surely the richest reward that can ever be laid to the credit (if admittedly only in part) of the economist's theorizing. But persistent inflation posed questions which Keynesians failed to answer satisfactorily, while the return of mass unemployment combined with still higher inflation finally destroyed the Keynesian consensus, and allowed the monetarists to capture the minds of our political masters.

Nevertheless, Joan Robinson's view is quite true in that the modifications of classical value theory (now being painfully and patchily refurbished by the New Classical School) were as nothing compared with the surging revolutions in monetary theories which have occurred since the 1930s, mainly taking the form of a forty years' war between Keynesians and monetarists, until the latter ultimately achieved control over practical policies in much of the western world by the end of the 1970s, despite the continuing strong dissent of the now conventional Keynesian economists. Whereas the man in the street knows nothing of the economics of imperfect competition or the theory of contestable markets, he feels himself equipped and more than willing to take sides in the great monetarist debates of the day. Without being dogmatic about this, it is unlikely that in any previous age monetary affairs and monetary theories have ever captured so vast an army of debaters, professional and amateur, as exists in today's perplexing world of uncertainty, inflation, unemployment, stagnation and recession. Can the control of money, one wonders, be the sovereign remedy for all these ills?

Never before has monetary policy openly and avowedly occupied so central a role in government policy as from the 1980s with the 'Thatcherite experiment' in Britain and the 'Reaganomics' of the United States. Needless to say, if monetary policy finally reigns supreme in the two countries of the world which have together dominated economic theory and international trade and finance over the last two centuries this fact is bound to have an enormous influence on current financial thought and practice throughout the world. If money is now of such preponderant importance in the North it cannot fail also to exert its powerful sway over the dependent economies and 'independent' central banks of the developing countries of the South. This tendency is of course strongly reinforced by the growing burden of sovereign debt, i.e., debts mainly owed or guaranteed by governments and government agencies in countries like Mexico, Brazil, Argentina, Poland, Romania, Nigeria, India and South Korea, and to private and public banks and agencies in the West. The unprecedented scale of this long-term debt, coupled with the vast short-term flows of petro-dollars and Euro-currencies, is in part reflection and in part cause of the worldwide inflationary pressures, again of unprecedented degree, which have raised public concern about the subject of money to its present pinnacle. There are far more people using much more money, interdependently involved in a greater complex of debts and credits than ever before in human history. However, despite man's growing mastery of science and technology, he has so far been unable to master money, at any rate, with any acceptable degree of success, and to the extent that he has succeeded, the irrecoverable costs in terms of mass unemployment and lost output would seem to outweigh the benefits.

If money were merely a tangible technical device so that its supply could be closely defined and clearly delimited, then the problem of how to master and control it, would easily be amenable to man's highly developed technical ingenuity. In the same way, if inflation had simply a single cause government and money supply came simply from the same single source, then mechanistic controls might well work. However, although government is powerful on both sides of the equation it is only one among many complex factors. Among these neglected factors, according to H. C. Lindgren, in a rare book on the psychology of money, 'the psychological factor that continually eludes the analysts and planners is the mood of the public'.

Furthermore, technology in solving technical problems often create yet more intractable social and psychological problems, which is why, according to Dr. Bronowski, 'there has been a deep change in the temper of science in the last twenty years: the focus of attention has shifted from the physical to the life sciences' and 'as a result science is drawn more and more to the study of individuality'. It is ironic that just when physical scientists are seeing the value of a more humanistic approach, economics, and particularly monetary economics, has become less so by attempting to become more 'scientific', mechanistic and measurable.

Unprecedented Inflation Of Population

There is an additional factor, 'real' as opposed to 'financial', which helps to explain the sustained strength of worldwide inflationary forces and yet remains unmentioned in most modern works on money and inflation, viz. the pressure of a rapidly expanding world population on finite resources virtually a silent explosion so far as monetarist literature is concerned. Thus nowhere in Friedman's powerful, popular and influential book Free to Choose is there even any mention of the population problem, nor the slightest hint that the inflation on which he is acknowledged to be the world's greatest expert might in any way be caused by the rapidly rising potential and real demands of the thousands of millions born into the world since he began his researches. Further treatment of these matters must await their appropriate place in later chapters, but since the size and distribution of this tremendous growth of population is crucial to an understanding of why the study of money is currently of unprecedented importance, a few introductory comments appear to be essential. One neglected reason why monetary policy may appear to be so attractively powerful in the richer North and West is precisely because there population pressures are least. In contrast, whereas monetary policy is of special importance in the poor developing countries of the South and East, its scope and powers are considerably reduced because this is where population pressures are greatest. Too many people are chasing too few goods.

The currently fashionable monetarist explanations of inflation fail, then, to take into account the rapid rise in real pressure on resources stemming from the population explosion. This forces communities to react by creating, by means of various devices easily learned from the West, the moneys required to help to accommodate such pressures. The enormous size of these increases since 1945 is such that millions of relatively rich have added their effective demand to the frustrated potential demands of the thousands of millions more who have remained abysmally poor. The trend of demand increases year by year causing relatively greater scarcities of primary resources and also of manufactured goods and services such as consumer durables, health care and education. The vastly increased competition for such goods and services helps to give an upward twist to the inflationary spiral despite the periodic changes in the terms of trade for certain primary products. World population has ultimately increased, in some ways as Malthus predicted over two hundred years ago, at a pace exceeding productivity, since productivity is at or near its lowest in those areas where population growth is at or near its greatest.

It took man a million years or so, until about 1825, to reach a total population of 1,000 million, but only about one hundred years to add another 1,000 million and only some fifty years, from 1925 to 1975 to double that total to 4,000 million, by which time the population was already increasing by 75 million annually. In the generation from 1975 to the year 2000, according to a consensus of opinion among experts in Britain, USA and the United Nations Organization, world population will increase by 55 per cent or 2,261 million to a total of 6,351 million and will then be increasing by around 100 million annually, so that, if currently projected growth rates continue, world population may reach 10,000 million by around the year 2030, well within the life expectancy of persons now reaching adult years in the western world.

The whole world has now broken the link with commodity money which once acted as a brake on inflation. The less developed countries are even less able than the industrialized countries to avoid the mismanagement of money, so that in their attempts to create monetary claims, including borrowing, to compete for resources which are tending to grow ever scarcer relatively to demand, runaway inflation with rates of up to 100 per cent or more per annum are not uncommon. Added to these unprecedented monetary problems over 90 per cent of the projected increase in population to the end of the century will take place in these poor and less developed countries, which by their very nature find it more difficult than their richer, industrialized neighbours to stem the full tide of inflation. Intensifying this trend is the increasing urbanization of previously predominantly rural communities, with the greater emphasis on money incomes that is the inevitable concomitant of such migration. A few telling examples must suffice, taking the population in 1960 and the projections for the year 2000 in parenthesis based on UN estimates and medium projections: Calcutta 5.5 m (19.7 m); Mexico City 4.9 m (31.6 m); Bombay 4.1 m (19.1 m); Cairo 3.7 m (16.4 m); Jakarta 2.7 m (16.9 m); Seoul 2.4 m (18.7 m); Delhi 2.3 m (13.2 m); Manila 2.2 m (12.7 m); Tehran 1.9 m (13.8 m), and Karachi 1.8 m (15.9 m). These ten towns alone will increase from a total of 31.5 m to 178 m. (Global 2000 1982, 242). This gives a new twist to William Cowper's claim: 'God made the country and man-made the town.'

The young age composition of such vastly expanding populations increases mobility, the acceptance of change and the political pressures for change, including the desire to have at least some share in the rising standards of living of the richer countries, of which, through rapidly improved communications, they are becoming increasingly conscious. This international extension of the 'Duesenberry effect' (Duesenberry 1967), viz. that the patterns of consumption of the next highest social class are deemed most desirable, again helps to create increased expenditure pressures throughout the developing world and particularly in those populous pockets of relatively rich areas which exist almost cheek by jowl among the urban poor. Duesenberry also makes the important point that 'the larger the rate of growth of population the larger the average propensity to consume'. Confronted with the magnitude of the problem of world poverty, western man may feel uncomfortable, individually helpless and perplexed by the merits of 'aid versus trade'. There is an imbalance in awareness as between North and South, and whereas it would be a caricature to say 'They ask for bread, and we give them . . . Dallas', nevertheless the three-quarters of the world's people in the hungry south are increasingly aware of how the other quarter lives. This caricature is not unlike Picasso's definition of art as a 'lie which helps us to see the truth'. Be that as it may, the expenditure patterns of society throughout the world are becoming westernized, breaking down indigenous social patterns and so leading to modern habits which, unfortunately, tend to encourage inflationary monetary systems. Thus, the worldwide expansion of money has been partly caused by, but has far exceeded, the vast expansion of population.

Although the question of whether the world is approaching the limits of growth may cause a growing number of fortunate men in modern affluent societies to cast doubt on the need for greater economic growth, nevertheless there is no question that economic growth affords the only means whereby approximately half the world's population its women can escape from the daily drudgery that has brutalized life for millions throughout time. The appalling persistence of poverty and what it means for families and especially mothers is brought out (insofar as these matters can ever meaningly be described in words) by the Brandt Report in 1980 which gives the estimate of the United Nations Children's Fund that in 1978 more than twelve million children under five years of age died of hunger. UNICEF's estimate for 1979, the 'Year of the Child', rose to seventeen million. It may be an eminently debatable point as to whether man without money is like Hobbes's famous picture of man without government: 'No arts; no letters; no society; and which is worst of all, continual fear and danger of violent death; and the life of man, solitary, poor, nasty, brutish, and short'. However, there can be no such doubt as to the direct ameliorative influence of economic growth on the standard of living of the female half of the human race, growing numbers of whom, at long last, are beginning to enjoy a diffusion of welfare that helps to raise, patchily and hesitatingly, the quality of family life over a large part of the world, and a welcome fall in the average family size.

Increasingly wealth, i.e. additions to capital stock, mostly takes place through a rise in incomes and expenditures, which necessarily leads to an increased use of money. Therefore, an increasing proportion as well as an increasing amount of trading in the rapidly growing less developed countries of the world is now based on abstract developments of money, and far less than formerly on barter and more primitive forms of money. Thus the individual finds release from irksome restraint and is able to exercise greater freedom of choice as a necessary corollary of the monetization of the economies of the less developed countries. In the aggregate, however, hundreds of millions of people, though still poor, have moved out of what were still largely subsistence economies into market economies where money naturally plays a bigger role. The speed of political, social, economic and financial change (partly but by no means entirely because of technological development) is telescoping what were previously secular trends in the West into mere decades. This is particularly so with regard to the dramatic change from primitive to modern money. Before turning to look at barter and what is still for us today the important but generally neglected subject of primitive moneys we may therefore conclude our preliminary assessment of the importance of modern money by stating that there are good reasons for believing that money means much more today to many more people throughout the world than it has ever meant before in human history.

Barter: As Old As The Hills

The history of barter is as old, indeed in some respects very much older, than the recorded history of man himself. The direct exchange of services and resources for mutual advantage is intrinsic to the symbiotic relationships between plants, insects and animals, so that it should not be surprising that barter in some form or other is as old as man himself. What at first sight is perhaps more surprising is that such a primeval form of direct exchange should persist right up to the present day and still show itself vigorously, if exceptionally, in so many guises, particularly in large-scale international deals between the eastern bloc and the West. However, barter is crudely robust and adaptable, characteristics which help to explain both its longevity and its ubiquity. Thus, when the inherent advantages of barter in certain circumstances are carefully considered, then its coexistence with more advanced and convenient forms of exchange is more easily appreciated and should occasion no surprise. Foremost among these advantages is the concrete reality of such exchanges: no one parts with value in return for mere paper or token promises, but rather only in due return for worthwhile goods or services. In an inflationary age, where international indexing and the legal enforcement of contracts are either in their infancy or of very shaky construction, this primary advantage of barter may more than compensate for its cumbersome awkwardness.

Throughout by far the greater part of man's development, barter necessarily constituted the sole means of exchanging goods and services. It follows from this that the historical development of money and finance from relatively ancient times onwards the substance of our study overlaps only to a small degree the study of barter as a whole. Consequently, we know more about barter's complementary coexistence with money than we do about barter in those long, dark, moneyless ages of prehistory, and thus we tend to derive our knowledge of barter from the remaining shrinking moneyless communities of more modern times. It is principally from these latter backward communities rather than from the mainstream of human progress that most accounts of barter have been taken to provide the basic examples typically occurring in modern textbooks on money. Little wonder then that these have tended not only to overstress the disadvantages of barter but have also tended to base the rise of money on the misleadingly narrow and mistaken view of the alleged disadvantages of barter to the exclusion of other factors, most of which were of very much greater importance than the alleged shortcomings of barter. Barter has, undeservedly, been given a bad name in conventional economic writing, and its alleged crudities have been much exaggerated.

As the extent and complexity of trade increased, so the various systems of barter naturally grew to accommodate these increasing demands, until the demands of trade exceeded the scope of barter, however improved or complex. One of the more important improvements over the simplest forms of early barter was first the tendency to select one or two particular items in preference to others so that the preferred barter items became partly accepted because of their qualities in acting as media of exchange although, of course, they still could be used for their primary purposes of directly satisfying the wants of the traders concerned. Commodities were chosen as preferred barter items for a number of reasons some because they were conveniently and easily stored, some because they had high value densities and were easily portable, some because they were more durable (or less perishable). The more of these qualities the preferred item showed, the higher the degree of preference in exchange. Perhaps the most valuable step forward in the barter system was made when established markets were set up at convenient locations. Very often such markets had been established long before the advent of money but were, of course, strengthened and confirmed as money came into greater use money which in many cases had long come into existence for reasons other than trading. In process of time money was seen to offer considerable advantages over barter and very gradually took over a larger and larger role while the use of barter correspondingly diminished until eventually barter simply re-emerged in special circumstances, usually when the money system, which was less robust than barter, broke down. Such circumstances continue to show themselves from time to time and persist to this day. In some few instances communities appear to have gone straight from barter to modern money. However, in most instances the logical sequence (barter, barter plus primitive money, primitive money, primitive plus modern money, then modern money almost exclusively) has also been the actual path followed, but with occasional reversions to previous systems.

Persistence Of Gift Exchange

One of the more interesting forms of early barter was gift exchange, which within the family partook more of gift than exchange but beyond that, as for example between different tribes was much more in the nature of exchange than of gift. Silent or dumb barter took place where direct and possibly dangerous contact was deliberately avoided by the participants. An amount of a particular commodity would be left in a convenient spot frequented by the other party to the exchange, who would take the goods proffered and leave what they considered a fair equivalent in exchange. If, however, after obvious examination, these were not considered sufficient they would remain untaken until the amount originally offered had been increased. In this way, the barter system, despite being silent was nevertheless an effective and competitive form of hard bargaining.

Competitive gift exchange probably reached its most aggressive heights in the ritualized barter ceremonies among North American Indians, whence it is generally known from the Chinook name for the practice, as 'potlatch'. This was far more than merely commercial exchange but was a complex mixture of a wide range of both public and private gatherings, the latter involving initiation into tribal secret societies and the former partaking of a number of cultural activities in which public speaking, drama, and elaborate dances were essential features. The potlatch was a sort of masonic rite, eisteddfod, Highland games, religious gathering, dance festival and market fair all rolled into one. The cultural and the commercial interchanges were part of an integrated whole. However it is clear that one of the main purposes of these exchange ceremonies was to validate the social ranking of the leading participants. A person's prestige depended largely on his power to influence others through the impressive size of the gifts offered, and, since the debts carried interest, the 'giver' rose in the eyes of the community to be an envied creditor, indeed a person of considerable standing. So much time and energy, so much rivalry and envy, coupled with a certain amount of understandable drunkenness and, for reasons about to be explained, of wasteful and deliberate destruction also, accompanied these proceedings that the Canadian federal government was eventually forced to ban the custom. It did this first by the Indian Act of 1876, but its ineffectiveness led to further amendments and a comprehensive new enactment some fifty-one years later. Although the potlatch system was fairly widespread over North America and varied from tribe to tribe, the experiences of the Kwakiutl Indians of the coastal regions of British Columbia may be taken as typical. A taped autobiography of James Sewid, chief councillor of the largest Kwakiutl village in the 1970s, contains vivid first-hand descriptions of potlatch ceremonies during the period of their final flourishes. According to Sewid, awareness of rank dominated his tribal society, and the major institution for assuming, maintaining and increasing social status was the potlatch, of which there were local, regional and tribal varieties in ascending order. After much feasting and many speeches, the public donations were ostentatiously distributed. A person would fail to attain any social standing without a really lavish distribution, and in the extreme cases chiefs would demonstrate their wealth and prestige by publicly destroying some of their possessions so as to demonstrate that they had more than they needed. Increasing trade with European immigrants in the 1920s at first considerably raised the material standards of the Kwakiutl and increased the number and wanton waste of the potlatches, so much so that the federal government felt compelled to react strongly.

The Revised Statutes of Canada 1927, clause 140, stipulated that 'Every Indian or other person who engages in any Indian festival, dance or other ceremony of which the giving away or paying or giving back of money, goods or articles of any sort forms a part . . . is guilty of an offence and is liable on summary conviction to imprisonment for a term not exceeding six months and not less than two months.' Sewid himself, as a boy, saw his relatives sent to prison for participating in the proscribed potlatches. In

Sewid's experience, these potlatch ceremonies would last for several days, and the competitive presents would include not only such traditional items as clothing, blankets, furs and canoes, but also copper shields and such twentieth-century luxuries as sewing machines, pedal, and motor cycles and motor boats. After reaching their high point in the mid-1920s the age-old potlatch ceremonials gradually died away the combined result of the new legislation, its stronger enforcement and, probably of still greater influence, the cultural penetration of Indian villages by teachers and entrepreneurs. It is rather ironic that by the time the clauses of the 1927 Act prohibiting potlatches were finally repealed in 1951, these age-old ceremonies were already on their last legs and to all intents and purposes ceased to exist by the end of the 1960s. Modern money and European cultures had however taken nearly three centuries to conquer this form of tribal barter in North America.

Having persisted for many hundreds of years this elaborate system of barter, more social than economic, at the first easily absorbed the various kinds of money brought in by the European conquerors, but after a final flourish in the inter-war period, rather suddenly slumped. Unfortunately, in trying to suppress the less desirable aspects of the potlatch, its good features were also weakened. The replacement of one kind of exchange by another, or of one kind of money by another, often has severe and unforeseen social consequences. In the case of a number of Indian tribes, the conflict of culture was particularly harsh and the ending of the potlatch removed some of the most powerful work incentives from the younger section of the communities.

One cannot leave the subject of competitive gift exchange without a brief reference to the most celebrated of all such encounters, namely that between the Queen of Sheba and Solomon in or about the year 950 BC. Extravagant ostentation, the attempt to outdo each other in the splendour of the exchanges, and above all, the obligations of reciprocity were just as typical in this celebrated encounter, though at a fittingly princely level, as with the more mundane types of barter in other parts of the world. The social and political overtones were just as inseparably integral parts of the process of commercial exchanges in the case of the Queen of Sheba as with the Kwakiutl Indians, even though it would be harder to imagine a greater contrast in cultures.

Money: Barter's Disputed Paternity

One of the most influential writers on money in the second half of the nineteenth century was William Stanley Jevons. His theoretical approach was enriched by five years' practical experience as assayer in the Sydney Mint in Australia at a time when money for most people meant coins above all else. He begins his book on Money and the Mechanism of Exchange (1875) by giving two illustrations of the drawbacks of barter, and it was largely his great influence which helped to condition conventional economic thought for a century regarding the inconvenience of barter. He first relates how Mlle Zélie, a French opera singer, in the course of a world tour gave a concert in the Society Islands and for her fee received one-third of the proceeds. Her share consisted of three pigs, twenty-three turkeys, forty-four chickens, five thousand coconuts and considerable quantities of bananas, lemons and oranges. Unfortunately the opera singer could consume only a small part of this total and (instead of declaring the public feast which she might well have done had she been versed in local custom) found it necessary before she left to feed the pigs and poultry with the fruit. Thus a handsome fee which was equivalent to some four thousand pre-1870 francs was wastefully squandered. Jevons's second account concerns the famous naturalist A. R. Wallace who, when on his expeditions in the Malay Archipelago between 1854 and 1862 (during which he originated his celebrated theory of natural selection) though generally surfeited with food, found that in some of the islands where there was no currency mealtimes were preceded by long periods of hard bargaining, and if the commodities bartered by Wallace were not wanted then he and his party simply had to go without their dinner. Jevons's readers, after having vicariously suffered the absurd frustrations of Mlle Zélie and Dr Wallace, were more than willing to accept uncritically, as have generations of economists and their students subsequently, the devastating criticisms which Jevons made of barter, without making sufficient allowance for the fact that those particular barter systems, however well suited for the indigenous uses of that particular society, had not been developed to conduct international trade between the Théâtre Lyrique in Paris and the Society Islanders, nor was it designed to further the no doubt interesting theories of explorers like Wallace. Obviously, whilst one should not take such inappropriate examples as in any way typical, nevertheless they show up in a glaringly strong light, as Jevons intended even if in an exaggerated and unfair manner the disadvantages appertaining to barter.

By far the most authoritative writer on barter and primitive moneys in the twentieth century was Dr. Paul Einzig, to whose stimulating and comprehensive account of Primitive Money in its Ethnological, Historical and Economic Aspects (1966) this writer is greatly indebted, as should be all those who write on these fascinating subjects. Unfortunately, most writers on money seem studiously to have avoided Einzig's most valuable and almost unique contribution, possibly because his lucid, readable style belies the quality, erudition and creativity of his work, and possibly also because his sharp attacks on conventional economists' treatment of barter were driven home with unerring aim. As he demonstrates:

There is an essential difference between the negative approach used by many generations of economists who attributed the origin of money to the intolerable inconvenience of barter that forced the community to adopt a reform, and the positive approach suggested here, according to which the method of exchange was improved upon before the old method became intolerable and before an impelling need for the reforms had arisen ... The picture drawn by economists about the inconvenience of barter in primitive communities is grossly exaggerated. It would seem that the assumption that money necessarily arose from the realisation of the inconveniences of barter, popular as it is among economists, needs careful re-examination.

One must not of course overplay the adaptability of barter, otherwise money would never have so largely supplanted it. The most obvious and important drawback of barter is that concerned with the absence of a generalized or common standard of values, i.e., the price systems available with money. Problems of accounting multiply enormously as wealth and the varieties of exchangeable goods increase, so that whereas the accounting problems in simple societies may be surmountable, the foundations of modern society would crumble without money. Admittedly the emergence of a few preferred barter items as steps towards more generalized common measures of value managed to extend the life of barter systems, but by the nature of the accountancy problem, barter on a large scale became computationally impossible once a quite moderate standard of living had been achieved and, despite the growing importance of barter in special circumstances in the last four or five decades, modern societies could not exist without monetary systems. A second inherent disadvantage of barter is that stemming from its very directness, namely the double coincidence of wants required to complete an exchange of goods or services. In pure barter if the owner of an orchard, having a surplus of apples, required boots he would need to find not simply a cobbler but a cobbler who wanted to purchase apples; and even then there remained the problem of determining the 'rate of exchange' as between apples and boots. In the same way for each transaction involving other exchanges, separate and not immediately discernible exchange rates would have to be negotiated for every pair of transactions.

In very simple societies exchanging just a few commodities the absence of a common standard of values is no great problem. Thus trading in three commodities gives rise at any one time to only three exchange rates and four commodities to six possible rates. But five commodities require ten exchange rates, six require fifteen and ten require forty-five. Obviously the drawbacks of barter quickly become exposed with any increase in the number and variety of commodities being traded. As the numbers of commodities increase the numbers of combinations become astronomical. With a hundred commodities nearly 5,000 separate exchange rates (actually 4,950) would be necessary in a theoretical barter system, while nearly half a million (actually 499,500) would be required to support bilateral trading for 1,000 commodities.4 Consequently, despite the undoubted 'revival' of bartering in recent years this must remain very much an exception to the rule of money as the basis of trade. Even in final consumption there are many thousands of different goods purchased daily, as any glance at the serried ranks of supermarket shelves will immediately convey but these represent only the final stage in the complex network of intermediate wholesale dealing and the multiple earlier processes in the productive chain. Retail trade, massive as it is in modern societies, is simply the tip of the iceberg of essentially money-based exchanges: a perusal of trade catalogues should convince any doubter.

What money has done for the exchange of commodities, the computer promises to do at least partially for information retrieval and the exchange of ideas and not before time. To give but one example from a relatively narrow and specialized field of human knowledge, Chemical Abstracts for the year 1982 gives 457,789 references. Perhaps nothing provides a more enlightening snapshot of the essence of money than the ability it gives us to compare at a glance the relative values of any of the hundreds of thousands of goods and services in which we as individuals, families or larger groups may be interested, and to do so at minimal costs. Of course there are still very many national varieties of money where prices are less certain, more volatile, where bilateral restrictions are not uncommon and where the costs of exchange are far from being negligible. The Financial Times publishes every week tables giving the world value of the pound and of the dollar, listing over 200 different national currencies. If these were each of equal importance then foreign exchange would involve arbitrage between some 20,000 different combinations. Luckily, as with 'preferred barter items', a few leading currencies, notably sterling throughout the nineteenth and early twentieth century, plus the American dollar and more recently the German mark, the euro and the Japanese yen, have provided the basis of a common measure of international monetary values. Every time a preferred commodity or a leading currency acts as a focus for a cluster of other commodities or currencies, so the progressive principle of the law of combinations works in reverse and thus greatly reduces the possible number of combinations. Internally money reduces all these to a single common standard, just as would the single world money system that reformers have dreamed about for generations in the past and probably for generations to come also. Even so, the world's major banks have been forced to install the most modern electronic computational and communications equipment to handle their foreign exchanges: a costly and speculative, but essential and generally quite profitable business.

Traditional condemnation of the time-wasting 'higgling of the market' (to use Alfred Marshall's phrase) which was inevitably associated with much African and Asian barter, even up to the middle of the present century, might well indicate a lack of awareness among critics of the fact that the enjoyable, enthusiastic and argumentative process of prolonged bargaining was very much the prime object of the exercise the actual exchange being something of an anticlimax, essential but not nearly as enjoyable as the preliminaries. What the European saw as waste the African saw as a pleasant social custom. However, given the spread of western modes of life the wasteful aspects of barter become more insupportable and unnecessarily curtail not only the size and efficiency of markets but also act as a brake on raising the living standards of the communities concerned. Specialization, as Adam Smith rightly emphasized, is limited by the extent of the market, and so is the mass production upon which the enviable standards of living of modern communities depend. However, the size of the market is itself crucially dependent upon the parallel development of money. Thus just as continued reliance on barter would have condemned mankind to eternal poverty, so today our lack of mastery of money is in large part the cause of widespread relative poverty and mass unemployment, while the enormous waste of potential output forgone is lost forever.

Among other disadvantages of barter are the costs of storing value when these are all of necessity concrete objects rather than, for example, an abstract bank deposit which can be increased relatively costlessly and can whenever required be changed back into any marketable object. Besides, a bank deposit earns interest, whereas, to reverse Aristotle's famous attack on usury, most barter is barren. Services, by their nature cannot be stored, so that bartering for future services, necessarily involving an agreement to pay specific commodities or other specific services in exchange, weakens even the supposed normal superiority of current barter, namely its ability to enable direct and exactly measurable comparisons to be made between the items being exchanged. In the absence of money, or given the limited range of monetary uses in certain ancient civilizations, it is little wonder the completion of large-scale and long-term contracts was usually based on slavery. Thus the building of the Great Pyramid of Ghiza, the work of 100,000 men, and a logistical problem commensurate with its immense size, was made possible at that time only by the existence of slavery (even though these slaves enjoyed higher standards of living than others). This is not to deny that some relics of bartering for services still exist in the tied cottages, brewery-owned public houses and company perquisites or 'perks' today. However despite the drawbacks in our use of money, particularly the recurrence of enormously wasteful recessions, caused partly by instabilities inherent in money itself, it is plain from these few revealing contrasts with money, that barter inevitably carries with it far greater intrinsic disadvantages. Thus, barter's stubborn survival into modern times and its occasional flourishes do not mean that it can play other than a comparatively very minor role in the complex interactions of our economic life as a whole.

In the uncrowded, predominantly agricultural communities which preceded modern times, it was possible to carry on a fairly considerable amount of trade and to enjoy a reasonably high standard of living since subsistence farming occupied such a large role, even when barter was the main method of exchange. However, this should not lead us to conclude that barter and a similarly extensive trade or a comparable standard of living would be possible in any major area of the modern world. Attention has already been drawn to the overpopulated areas of urban squalor in less developed countries, so that, despite the fact that agriculture is still the major occupation in most developing countries, the economies of such countries can no longer rely on a mixture of subsistence farming plus barter but are inescapably dependent upon their modern monetary systems, however inflationary. Their recent involvement with bartering in their international trade with the more advanced countries should therefore be seen in true perspective, as special cases arising from current pressures and not in any sense a return to the old pre-monetary methods of barter. For most people most of the time the economic clock cannot be turned back.

Modern Barter And Countertrading

Having thus differentiated between modern barter where the participants are fully conversant with advanced monetary systems and early barter where such knowledge was either rudimentary or non- existent, we may now turn to examine a few of the more salient examples of modern barter and to explain the reasons for this surprising regression. The many recurrent and the few persistent examples of barter in modern communities are most commonly though not exclusively associated with monetary crises, especially runaway inflation, which at its most socially devastating climax destroys the existing monetary system completely. Thus in the classic and well-documented case of the German inflation of 1923 the 'butter' standard emerged as a more reliable common measure of value than the mark. Towards the end of the Second World War and immediately after, much of retail trade in continental Europe was based on cigarettes virtually a Goldflake or a Lucky Strike standard, which also formed a welcome addition to the real pay of the invading soldiers. A most interesting and detailed account of the cigarette currency as seen from inside a German prisoner of war camp was published by R. A. Radford (1945, 189–201). Such inflationary conditions were widespread from western Europe through China to Japan at this time, but the world record for an inflationary currency belongs to Hungary. Its note circulation grew from 12,000 million pengö in 1944 to 36 million million in 1945. In 1946 it reached 1,000 million times the 1945 total until at its maximum it came to a figure containing twenty-seven digits. Its largest denomination banknote issued in 1946, was for 100 million 'bilpengos', which since the bil is equivalent to a trillion pengos, was actually for 100 quintillion pengos or P.100,000,000,000,000,000,000. This astronomical sum was in fact worth at most only about £1 sterling. Little wonder that in such circumstances the monetary system temporarily destroyed itself and people were forced to revert to barter, at least for use as a medium of exchange even if they continued to use their currency as a unit of account, though even here for the shortest possible space of time, until confidence in the new unit of currency, the forint, had been established.

The breakdown in multilateral trading in the Second World War was mended only slowly and painfully in the following decade. In the mean time, as Trued and Mikesell (1955) show, bilateral trade agreements, most of which included some form or other of barter, became very common. In fact, these authors concluded that some 588 such bilateral agreements had been arranged between 1945 and the end of 1954. Many of these involved strange exchanges of basic commodities and sophisticated engineering products, such as that arranged by Sir Stafford Cripps whereby Russian grain was purchased in return for Rolls Royce Nene jet engines (which were returned with interest over Korea). However, these awkward methods of securing international trade were first thought to be due simply to the inevitable disruption of the war and would fade away completely in time as the normal channels of peacetime trade were reopened. From the end of the 1950s to the 1970s this faith was justified, and it therefore occasioned some surprise when new forms of barter and 'countertrading' began to grow again in the 1970s and persisted strongly into the 1980s.

By 1970 a new growth in international barter was already becoming obvious, with the London Chamber of Commerce having noted some 450 such deals during the course of the previous year, a rate about twenty times the pre-war average. Already there were some forty companies in the City of London actively engaged in international barter. The Financial Times (11 May 1970), reporting on this new growth in barter, commented that 'We have moved on from the days in which beads were offered for mirrors to ones in which heavily flavoured Balkan tobacco is offered for power stations and when apples are offered for irrigation.' The same article reported that a conference on barter, arranged by the London Chamber of Commerce was heavily oversubscribed, with more than 300 representatives present, including clearing and merchant bankers, members of the Board of Trade and, of course, academics.

Most of the countries then involved in barter the eastern bloc, Iran, Algeria, Brazil and so on continued to figure prominently a decade or so later. Thus, the Morgan Guarantee Survey of October 1978 reported yet 'A New Upsurge' in barter and countertrade, 'an ancient custom that suddenly is enjoying new popularity'. The largest of the deals described was a $20 billion barter agreement between Occidental Petroleum and the Soviet Union. In a similar spirit, Pepsico arranged a counter-purchase agreement with USSR selling Pepsi-Cola concentrate to Russia in return for the exclusive right to import Soviet vodka. Levi Strauss licensed trouser production in Hungary to be paid for by exports to the rest of Europe, while International Harvester gave Poland the design and technology to build its tractors in return for a proportion of such production. 'Iran, short of hard cash but swimming in oil', said the same source, 'barters to the tune of $4 billion to $5 billion a year, ladling out oil for everything from German steel plants and British missiles to American port facilities and Japanese desalinization units.' It was estimated that some 25 per cent of East–West trade involved some degree of barter, with the proportion expected to rise to around 40 per cent in the course of the 1980s. Algeria, India, Iraq and a number of South American countries again figured prominently in these projections. Five years later the international interest in barter was still strong, as evidenced by the influential papers presented at a conference, 'International Barter – To Trade or Countertrade' held at the World Trade Centre, New York, in September 1983, dealing with the barter of agricultural commodities, of metals and raw materials, of the special role of trading houses assisting large western companies to trade with the less developed countries, and so on.

Among the many reasons for this rebirth of barter are first the fact that external trade from communist countries is normally 'planned' bilaterally, and therefore lends itself more naturally to various forms of barter than does multilateral, freer, trading. This is of course why the General Agreement on Tariffs and Trade sets its face sternly against bartering arrangements. Secondly, the international trading scene has been repeatedly disrupted by the various vertical rises in the price of crude oil since it first quadrupled in 1973. Thirdly the relative fall in the terms of trade for the non-oil Third World countries caused them greatly to increase their borrowing from European and American governments and banks, a proportion of this being in 'tied' form, and thus, as with eastern bloc trade, becoming more susceptible to bilateral bargaining. Fourthly the rise in the world inflationary tide, together with the monetarist response in the main trading nations, caused international rates of interest to rise to unprecedented levels and so raised the repayment levels of borrowing countries to heights that could not readily be met by the methods of normal trading. In this respect the recrudescence of barter is simply a reflection of what has become to be known since the early 1980s as the 'sovereign debt' problem facing the dozen or so largest international debtor countries, including especially Mexico, Brazil and Argentina, but also Poland, India and Korea. The fifth and fundamental cause (though these various causes are interactive and cumulative rather than separate) is the breakdown in the stability of international rates of exchange following the virtual ending of the fixed-rate Bretton Woods system after 1971. With even the dollar under pressure there was no readily acceptable stable monetary unit useful for the longer-term contracts required for the capital goods especially desired by the developing countries. In such circumstances the direct exchange of specific goods or services for other such goods or services, assisted by all the various modern financial facilities, seemed in certain special cases such as those just indicated, to be preferable either to losing custom entirely or to becoming dependent solely on abstract claims to paper moneys of very uncertain future value.

Modern Retail Barter

Most of the examples of modern barter given so far refer to wholesale trading or large-scale international projects. Barter however continues to show itself in the retail trade and small-scale level, not only in such self-evident examples as the swapping of schoolboy treasures but also in much more elaborate and organized ways. Of particular importance in this connection is Exchange and Mart, an advertising medium which has been published in Britain every Thursday since 1868. Jevons himself noticed it in its earliest years and was obviously puzzled that any such publication, partly dependent on serving such a long obsolete purpose as barter, should appear to have any use to anyone. He refers to Exchange and Mart as 'a curious attempt to revive the practice of barter' and quoted examples of advertisers offering some old coins and a bicycle in exchange for a concertina, and a variety of old songs for a copy of Middlemarch. 'We must assume', concluded Jevons, 'that the offers are sometimes accepted, and that the printing press can bring about, in some degree, the double coincidence necessary to an act of barter.' He would no doubt be surprised that the publication has lasted for well over a century and that on average each issue contains around 10,000 classified advertisements. However, well over 95 per cent of these are not barter items, though sufficient remain to testify to its original purpose. A few examples must suffice: 'Exchange land for car, 2½acres freehold land, Dorset, for low mileage 280 SL Mercedes Benz', 'Lady's Rolex 8363/8, exchange computer, word processor, etc.'; 'Council exchange, three bedroomed house, Coventry, for same Cornwall', obviously a very good swap for the advertiser; but then, possibly remembering the imperative pressures of double coincidence, he adds, 'all areas considered'. The example of council house exchanging is a good reminder of what happens in a constrained situation where the normal market forces cannot freely operate. In these circumstances barter offers a way out.

A further reason for the re-emergence of barter in recent years may be seen as a by-product of the so-called 'black or informal economy'. According to Adrian Smith 'the informal economy can be seen as one of the main trends in economic evolution today, going with the continuous shrinkage in terms of employment and value added, of the production of goods and the corresponding growth of recorded employment in the service sector'. A contributory factor was tax evasion. Smith estimated that the informal economy represented about 3 per cent of the economy of the USA, between 2 and 7½ per cent of that of UK, 10 per cent for France and as much as 15 per cent for Italy, though by the very nature of the 'hidden' economy such estimates could be hardly more than partly informed guesses. With regard to the importance of changes in employment in recent years the present writer has pointed out that 'In little over a decade from 1971 Britain has lost almost two million jobs from manufacturing a devastating change; while almost as significant has been the good news of a gain of around one-and-three-quarter million jobs in services . . . a sort of industrial revolution in reverse'. Such a massive switch has provided a wealth of opportunity for informal economic activities. Although only a very small proportion of the hidden economy would involve barter, the point to bear in mind is that, though small, it seems to be growing vigorously. We may conclude therefore by saying that although modern man cannot live by barter alone, it may still make life more bearable for a minority of hard-pressed traders and heavily taxed citizens in certain but increasingly limited circumstances.

Primitive Money: Definitions And Early Development

Perhaps the simplest, most straightforward and, for historical purposes certainly, the most useful definition of primitive money is that given by P. Grierson, Professor of Numismatics at Cambridge, viz., 'all money that is not coin or, like modern paper money, a derivative of coin' (1977, 14). Even this definition however fails to allow for the ancient rather sophisticated banking systems that preceded the earliest coins by a thousand years or more. Nevertheless, with that single exception, it serves well for distinguishing in a general way between primitive and more advanced money, whether ancient or modern, and in its clarity and simplicity is perhaps preferable to the almost equally broad but rather more involved definition suggested by Einzig, as 'A unit or object conforming to a reasonable degree to some standard of uniformity, which is employed for reckoning or for making a large proportion of the payments customary in the community concerned, and which is accepted in payment largely with the intention of employing it for making payments'.

On one thing, the experts on primitive money all agree, and this vital agreement transcends their minor differences. Their common belief backed up by the overwhelming tangible evidence of actual types of primitive moneys from all over the world and from the archaeological, literary and linguistic evidence of the ancient world, is that barter was not the main factor in the origins and earliest developments of money. The contrast with Jevons, with his predecessors going back to Aristotle, and with his followers who include the mainstream of conventional economists, is clear-cut. Typical of the latter approach is that of Geoffrey Crowther, formerly editor of The Economist, who, in his Outline of Money, begins with a chapter entitled the 'Invention of money' and insists that money 'undoubtedly was an invention; it needed the conscious reasoning power of Man to make the step from simple barter to money accounting. It was possibly such gross oversimplifications that caused Paul Samuelson, in an article on 'Classical and neo-classical monetary theory' to contrast 'Harriet Martineau. who made fairy tales out of economics' with those 'modern economists who make economics out of fairytales'.

The most common non-economic forces which gave rise to primitive money may be grouped together thus: bride-money and blood-money; ornamental and ceremonial; religious and political. Objects originally accepted for one purpose were often found to be useful for other non-economic purposes, just as they later, because of their growing acceptability, began to be used for general trading also. We face considerable difficulty in trying to span the chronological gap which separates us from a true understanding of the attitudes of ancient man towards religious, social and economic life, and similarly with regard to the cultural gap which separates us from existing or recent primitive societies. In both ancient and modern primitive societies human values and attitudes were such that religion permeated almost the whole of everyday life and could not as easily be separated from political, social and economic life in the way that comes readily to us with our tendency for facile categorization. To us the categories may seem sensible and justified and no doubt they help us to appreciate the role of money (or of other such institutions) when we relate them to methods of thought and social, religious, political and economic systems with which we are familiar. But there are limits to our ability to force ancient or recent primitive fashions into modern molds. In particular, primitive moneys originating from one source or for one use came to be used for similar kinds of payments elsewhere spreading gradually without necessarily becoming generalized. For example, money first used for ceremonial purposes, because of their prestigious role were frequently ornamental also, these purposes being mutually reinforcing. Mrs. A. Hingston Quiggin, in her readable and well-illustrated survey of Primitive Money give a number of examples 'to show how an object can be at the same time currency or money, a religious symbol or a mere ornament'. However, the penalty of widening the functions of primitive moneys from their original rather narrow group of roles lay in weakening their force in their main function. It was a matter of balancing the formidable powers of money in one narrow group of, say, religious and ceremonial roles against the greater usefulness which followed from extending the currency of the money at the cost of losing part of its original religious or ceremonial associations.

Because of this conflict a division arose (though it had long been latent) between the experts on primitive economies as to whether or not to exclude the whole body of relatively narrowly functioning primitive objects from being called 'money' at all. Some would argue that unless such objects can be seen to have performed a fairly wide variety of functions they should not really be classed even as primitive money. This view seems to be far too narrow and rules out much of the long evolutionary story of monetary development. For money did not spring suddenly into full and general use in any community, and primitive man commonly used a number of different kinds of money for different purposes, some of which are almost certainly older than others. Even today we have not arrived at universal money, nor even universal banking, and just as we buy houses by going to see a building society and insurance through the insurance agent coming to see us, so primitive men saw different moneys being naturally confined to different groups of uses. The origins of these were quite varied, and although we emphasize that many of the most important of these origins were non-commercial, they established concepts, attitudes and ideas which conditioned the growth in the use of a huge variety of different kinds of 'money' in ancient and modern primitive communities.

Loving and fighting are the oldest, most exciting (and usually separate) of man's activities, so that it is perfectly natural to find that payments associated with both are among the earliest forms of money. Thus 'Wergeld', a Germanic word for the compensation or fine demanded for killing a man, was almost universally present in ancient as in modern primitive societies. Our word to 'pay' is derived from the Latin 'pacare', meaning originally to pacify, appease or make peace with through the appropriate unit of value customarily acceptable to both parties involved. Similarly, payments to compensate the head of a family for the loss of a daughter's services became the origin of 'bride-price' or 'bride-wealth'. The pattern of payment for human services was sometimes broadened to include the purchase or sale of slaves, who for centuries acted as 'walking cheque-books'. Although there may be room to doubt the extent of the direct connections between the compensatory payments of wergeld and bride-wealth, a number of social anthropologists argue, with many supportive examples, that they were closely related both in the nature and scale of payments. Thus Grierson cites among a number of similar examples the custom of the Yurok Indians of California where wergeld was identical with bride- price. He admits, however, that such identities are not evident everywhere: one could hardly expect it.

Over the course of time, paying for injuring, killing, marrying and enslaving became elaborated into different values according to the customs of the community concerned, with the tribal chief or head of state intervening either to accept the payments or to lay down the law as to what was or was, not acceptable compensation. Tribute or taxation, ransoms, bribery and various forms of protection payments such as those which we later came to know as 'Danegeld', were all various means by which the early state became involved in the extension of the geographical area of the peaceful enforcement of law and hence confirmed the greater role for the monetary payments that such a peace made possible. As we approach the medieval period these laws, specifying the amount and types of indemnities, were encoded. Such codes, extending from the Celtic laws of Ireland and Wales eastward through those of Germanic and Scandinavian tribes to central Russia, exhibit basic similarities and, in contrast with the ancient Mosaic laws which demanded an eye for an eye and a tooth for a tooth, they provided peacemaking monetary alternatives. The role of the state in thus spreading the use of money has been stressed by generations of economists, but by none more than G. F. Knapp.

Knapp's State Theory of Money considerably influenced Keynes, through whose efforts the work was translated into English. Knapp was nothing if not forthright: 'Money is a creature of law . . . the numismatist usually knows nothing of currency, for he has only to deal with its dead body'. This view of the role of the state as the sole creator and guarantor of money, although useful as a corrective to the metallistic theories current at the end of the nineteenth century, nevertheless carries the state theory of money to an absurd extreme, a criticism of which the author himself appears to be aware since in his preface he defends himself with the plea that 'a theory must be pushed to extremes or it is valueless' surely a most dangerously dogmatic assertion. The main point at issue, however, is simply this, that right from the inception of money, from ancient down to modern times, the state has a powerful, though not omnipotent, role to play in the development of money. Yet neither ancient money nor, despite Sir Stafford Cripps's view to the contrary, even the Bank of England, is a mere creature of the state.

Knapp's pre-monetarist emphasis on the fundamental role of the state in the creation of money does at least consistently reflect the tendency of German economists in the late nineteenth and early twentieth centuries to extol the power of the state. Modern monetarists such as Friedman however, strongly uphold the supremacy of the market and at the same time seek, inconsistently, to minimize the role of the state except in monetary matters: an exception which fits ill with their basic philosophy. Whatever barriers the state or academics may erect within which to confine money, money has an innate ability demonstrated not only during recent decades but by thousands of years of history to jump over them. Experts on primitive and modern money disagree where to draw the line between money and quasi-money precisely because it is in the nature of money to make any such clear distinction impossible to uphold for any length of time. Money is so useful in other words, it performs so many functions that it always attracts substitutes: and the narrower its confining lines are drawn, the higher the premium there is on developing passable substitutes.

Economic Origins And Functions

Having emphasized the non-economic origins of money to the extent required to counteract the traditional strongly entrenched viewpoint, we may now more briefly examine its economic or commercial origins, since these require, at this stage, little elaboration. Money has many origins not just one precisely because it can perform many functions in similar ways and similar functions in many ways. As an institution, money is almost infinitely adaptable. This helps to explain the wide variety of origins and the vast multitude of different kinds of objects used as primitive money. These include: amber, beads, cowries, drums, eggs, feathers,5 gongs, hoes, ivory, jade, kettles, leather, mats, nails, oxen, pigs, quartz, rice, salt, thimbles, umiaks, vodka, wampum, yarns and zappozats, which are decorated axes to name but a minute proportion of the enormous variety of primitive moneys; and none of this alphabetical list includes modern examples like gold, silver or copper coinage nor any of the 230 or so units of paper currency.

Functions of money

1. Specific functions (mostly micro-economic)
2. Unit of account (abstract)
3. Common measure of value (abstract) 3 Medium of exchange (concrete)
4. Means of payment (concrete)
5. Standard for deferred payments (abstract)
6. Store of value (concrete)
7. e.g. the Quetzal used by the Aztecs as currency and adopted as the modern currency of Guatemala.
8. General functions (mostly macro-economic and abstract)
9. Liquid asset
10. Framework of the market allocative system (prices) 9 A causative factor in the economy

Controller Of The Economy

Because it appeared that, at some time or place, almost anything has acted as money, this misled some writers, including especially the French economist, Turgot, to conclude that anything can in actual practice act as money. One must admit that in any logical (not chronological) list of monetary functions, that of acting as a unit of account would normally come first. It follows from the fact that money originated in a variety of different ways that there is little purpose in the insistence shown by a number of monetary economists in analyzing which are the supposed primary or original and which are the supposed secondary or derived functions. What is now the prime or main function in a particular community or country may not have been the first or original function in time, while what may well have been a secondary or derived function in one place may have been in some other region the original which itself gave rise to a related secondary function. Here again there is exhibited a tendency among certain economists to compare what appears in today's conditions to be the logical order with the actual complex chronological development of money over its long and convoluted history. The logical listing of functions in the table therefore implies no priority in either time or importance, for those which may be both first and foremost reflect only their particular time and place.

Turning back now to the first function listed, it is easy to see that, since an accounting or reckoning unit is, of course, abstract, it has in theory no physical constraints. Theoretically one could easily make up any word and apply this as an accounting record. As a matter of fact in recent years the European monetary authorities co-operated in producing just such a unit and called it the European 'unit of account', later becoming the Ecu, a brief forerunner of the euro. There is an essential connection but not necessarily an identity between counting and measuring money.

Thus cowries, coins and cattle were (and are) usually counted, whereas grain, gold and silver were usually weighed: hence come not only our words for 'spend', 'expenditure', etc., from the Latin 'expendere' but also originally 'pound', as being a defined weight of silver. But acting as a unit of account is only one of money's functions and although anything picked at random, whether abstract or concrete, admittedly could act as such a unit and if a sensible choice, might do so admirably this would not necessarily mean that it could perform satisfactorily any or all of money's many other functions. Although acting as a unit of account or as a common measure of value which are two ways of looking at the same concept are both abstractions, it added greatly to the convenience of money if the normally concrete media of exchange and/or the means of payment carried the same names as, or were at least consistently related to, money's two abstract qualities of accounting and measuring. By that is meant that, for example, one's bank balance is kept in pounds (including subdivisions), that prices are quoted in pounds, that one is paid in pounds, and that one pays others for purchases or services also in pounds. But for around half the long monetary history of the £ sterling in Britain this was not the case: there was no such thing as a pound; it existed only as a unit of account. There are numerous similar examples.

As well as the specific functions of money listed, there are also a number of more general functions. All these various functions and the changing relationships between them will form the main subject of the remainder of our study, stemming from cowries to Eurocurrencies. However, a few further important aspects of money, not captured in the given categories, need to be at least hinted at in this introductory chapter, namely first the dynamic quicksilver nature of money or to vary the analogy, its chameleon-like adaptability. Money designed for one specific function will easily take on other jobs and come up smiling. Old money very readily functions in new ways and new money in old ways: money is eminently fungible.

Let us come now to the little matter of definition: what, after all is money? The form in which the question is put tends to indicate that the proper place for a definitive definition, as it were, is at the end rather than near the beginning of our study; but the dictates of custom would suggest the need at least for this preliminary definition: Money is anything that is widely used for making payments and accounting for debts and credits.

A METATHEORY OF MONEY

Money is the mechanism by which markets are most perfectly cleared, whereby the forces of demand and supply continually and competitively fight themselves out towards the draw known as equilibrium. As we have just seen with regard to barter, no other mechanism is nearly as good as money in this function of sending early and appropriate signals to buyers and sellers through price changes, so helping smoothly to remove excess balances of demand or supply. Markets are however, rarely perfect, and in practice even money cannot remove all the uncertainty surrounding them. There are three fundamental reasons for market uncertainty. First, the full information and correct interpretation necessary for perfect balance are costly; secondly, the aggregate flow of goods and services which form the counterpart to the total quantity of money changes over time in volume and trading velocity; and thirdly and most importantly money is by its very nature dynamically unstable in volume and velocity, in quantity and quality.

We shall see as our history of money unfolds that there is an unceasing conflict between the interests of debtors, who seek to enlarge the quantity of money and who seeks busily to find acceptable substitutes, and the interests of creditors, who seek to maintain or increase the value of money by limiting its supply, by refusing substitutes or accepting them with great reluctance, and generally trying in all sorts of ways to safeguard the quality of money. Although most consumers and producers are at some stage both debtors and creditors it is their net power that influences the value of money. What is most interesting in historical perspective is to analyse the long-term pendulum movements between the net forces of debtors, which cause the pendulum to swing excessively towards depreciating the value of money, and the net forces of creditors which act strongly the other way to raise the unit value of money or at least to moderate the degree of depreciation. While the historical record will confirm popular condemnation of the inflationary evils of an excessive quantity of money, it will also point to the more hidden but equally baneful effects when excessive emphasis on quality has severely restricted the growth of the economy.

Although monetary stability may be to the long-term advantage of the majority, there are always strong minorities who tip the net balance of power and who wish to increase or decrease the value of money. They thus help to push the pendulum into a state of almost perpetual motion. During all periods of history, the debtors are generally much poorer and always much more numerous than the normally more powerful and less numerous creditors, even though by definition the total of debts and credits is the same. In this context it is the distribution which matters, while it should be remembered that debtors can and often do include the most powerful of politicians and the most ambitious of entrepreneurs. For long periods of history the most important net debtor has been the single monarch or the composite state, each possessed with a varying degree of sovereign power to determine the supply of money, though never with complete control over the acceptability of money substitutes. Not surprisingly when the state becomes a net debtor the pendulum tends to widen its oscillations. An indebted monarch or government is usually able not only to reduce the real burden of its own debt, but can as a bonus consciously or unconsciously court popularity with the indebted masses by allowing the net pressures of indebtedness to increase the supply of money or the acceptance of substitutes and so lift some of the heavy burden of debt from the shoulders of the poor masses – and from many up-and-coming entrepreneurs. There is therefore a secular tendency for money to depreciate in value, a tendency halted or partially reversed whenever net creditors, such as large landowners, rich moneylenders and well-established bankers, are in the ascendancy or can bring their usually powerful influence to bear upon governments.

Corresponding therefore to our simple preliminary definition of money we have a simple theoretical framework for assessing changes in the value of money, namely the 'pendulum theory' or more fully, the 'oscillating debtor–quantity/creditor–quality theory'. At any given time, especially after drastic changes have taken place in monetary affairs, a whole host of theories may arise in attempts to explain the existing value of money. Given a wider historical perspective these temporary theories, whatever they are called, group themselves with little distortion into either debtor quantity or creditor quality theories. The pendulum theory brings these two apparently contradictory and divergent sets of theories together into a symbiotic union. It indicates why these temporary theories, like certain aspects of money itself, tend to rather extreme oscillations, and helps to explain why such opposite theories tend to follow each other in repeated alternations over the centuries, interspersed with the occasional long period of comparative stability.

The pendulum theory is therefore of particular relevance to the long perspectives of monetary history and yet may shine some light on current financial controversy, for it is within the vectors of that wider theory that the shorter-term, fashionable 'temporary' theories appropriate to the particular period in question play out their powerful but inevitably limited roles. In this sense the pendulum theory acts as a metatheory of money, i.e. a more general theory comprising sets of more limited, partial theories, which latter spring out of the special circumstances of their time. The enveloping pendulum or metatheory also explains why the usual theories of money, despite being so confidently held at one time, tend to change so drastically and diametrically (and therefore so puzzlingly to the uninitiated) to an equally accepted but opposite theory within the time span appropriate to historical investigation. The longer view given by the pendulum theory may also help to correct the dangerous 'short-termism' present in much current financial theory and practice.

The most recent, and therefore perhaps the most obvious, an example of the workings of the pendulum theory can be seen in the enormous swing from almost universal acceptance in theory and policy of the broadly based but temporary 'liquidity theory of money' held by the Keynesians to the later fashionable, widely based acceptance in theory and still more in practice of the very narrowly based monetarist theories of Milton Friedman and his followers. Another recent example of the age-old principle of the pendulum may be seen in the much discussed tendency of the external values of currencies to 'overshoot' their equilibrium values in the foreign exchange markets once they became free to move away from much of their fixed-rate anchors. The extreme volatility of rates of interest in much of the post-war period points to a third instance of the pendulum in vigorous 'overkill' action. In the chronology of oscillation, quality comes first; for if whatever is intended to act as money is not desired strongly enough to be held for that purpose, it will fail to be selected long enough to be imitated. Once the selection is confirmed by general acceptance then, sooner or later, depending on the society in question, quality faces competition from an increased quantity of substitutes. Monetary imitation is the most effective form of flattery. As quantity increases so quality generally falls, and if the process is speeded up, the currency may become completely discredited and useless, requiring replacement by a new monetary form which emphasizes its special quality; hence the periodic currency reforms which punctuate monetary history, followed by eventual backsliding.

It follows from the pendulum theory that the nearer the money supply is kept to its equilibrium position, the more moderate will be the policy measures, such as variations in the official rate of interest, required to re-establish equilibrium. Conversely, a wide swing away from equilibrium will require such strong counteracting policy measures, such as very large changes in interest rates, that dangerous 'overshooting' or 'overkill' will commonly result. A monetary stitch in time saves nine. Finally it is of the utmost significance to realize that because the monetary pendulum is rarely motionless at the point of perfect balance between the conflicting interests of creditors and debtors, so money itself is rarely 'neutral' in its effects upon the real economy and upon the fortunes of different sections of the community, for all sections are involved all the time in their daily lives. Monetary changes of any substantial weight could only be neutral if everyone had the same amounts, incomes, wealth, debts, expectations, etc., as everyone else: an impossibility. On this point Kindelberger quotes Schumpeter as 'doubting that money can ever be neutral'. This feature further enhances the importance of money in economic, social and political history.

Institutional Money Theories

German scholar Karl-Heinz Brodbeck in his most recent book "Money! Which Money? - Money as a figure of thought" gives a dual epistemological analysis of the monetary theories reviewed in the previous chapter. Similar to the distinction introduced here so far, for him, ideas about money originate from two different questions: one about the historical genesis of money, the other is concerned with the validity of money, which in German not only implies its legal or logical foundation but also value and purchasing power. To him, both questions have two clear sets of answers, which in some senses overlap. The metalists' theory answers to both the genesis of money, in terms of a spontaneous development as a solution to the unlikeliness of coinciding wants and needs in a barter scenario, and it also provides an answer to the question of validity with its adherence to the 'universal' value of precious metals. Chartalism provides the second popular answer to the genesis question as it views money as a creature of the state, which also implies an answer for the validity question as the state will always have to ensure the purchasing power of its money, with or without gold backing. For Brodbeck however, both questions, and the traditional answers, obscure, or even conceal a more central question: a philosophical inquiry into money as a social institution and the role that our intersubjective awareness and cognitive processes play in it.

His two questions about genesis and validity reflect the two readings of the question "Where does money come from?". And with the premise of social constructivism, his third question becomes a linguistic, psychological or behavioral one. Hence, asking about money as a social institution here takes on the form of an ontological inquiry into "What is the nature of money?". This question then becomes the background against which all other questions and most of the answers presented in the previous chapter can be situated. It also renders many of those answers unsatisfactory, particularly when recognizing the varied forms of 'money', both those that are unrelated to any material backing, and those redeemable in gold with no relation to the state and its powers. In this sense, an institutional theory of money would be not only a third, but a unifying concept from which the other theories can assume their practical or historical place without having to compete for universal truth.

Institutionalism has been a school of thought in economics since the early 20th century. However, despite this long history, the word has not fully shed its double lexicographic meaning, both in everyday and in expert use. On the one hand, which also reflects its use in everyday parlance, an 'institution' refers to an "organisation for a religious, educational, professional, or social purpose", whereas in the second, related but broader and less tangible meaning, it describes "an established law or practice". This ambiguity can also be found in the usage of the descriptor 'institutional' in theories of money that emerge particularly towards the end of the 20th century. This ambiguity introduces such a broad meaning to the idea of institutionalism that it can even be seen as such a self-evident and obvious framing, particularly in economics, that the distinction between institutional economics and any other form of economics would seem futile.

Thus, it is not surprising that precursors or implicit institutional theories can be traced back to many of the authors without them necessarily having described themselves or their theories as institutional. Economic historian Dudley Dillard describes those lineages in "Money as an Institution of Capitalism", and specifies that institutional theories of money do not simply see money as a neutral and negligible numeraire, but a relevant "strategic factor" that is shaped by rules and conversely also impacts on the complex of rules that make up other institutions.

Dillard argued that since Adam Smith there has been a "fault" line in economics between those who want to eliminate and relegate 'money' behind the veil of neutrality on "the great wheel of circulation", and those, starting with Thorstein Veblen, who challenge that view. With this second institutional position, 'money' is taken seriously for economic thought and modelling, a position then elaborated on by Wesley Mitchell and Minsky. Along with those authors Dillard also places Marx and Keynes into the lineage of institutional monetary economists. However, in quoting Minsky saying that "Monetary theory must be institutional economics" the self-evident nature of 'money as an institution' is stated as something so obvious that it does not seem to require further attention in ontological terms.

This can be said in particular about the elements of the institutional thought in Keynes and from thereon in neo-chartalist schools where "money was originally a social institution, although it had subsequently become a government one". This notion has also been present in the writings of Andre Orléan, Michel Aglietta and their colleagues in the French speaking world for more than 20 years, however their reception in English speaking countries, and consequently within broad academia in general, has been limited as only very few of their articles have been translated. Orlean's award winning book "The Empire of Value", originally written in 2011, is the only monograph that became available in English in 2014. Since at least 1992 Orléan has been describing money and finance as institutional phenomena in the context of state power with a special and broader interest in how such institutions come to be and can undergo change. Institutions to him are the "social force" that explains how behavioral dispositions, like our usage of money, come about, while "Common sense suggests that it is a matter of suspension of our faculty for engaging in individual critical thinking: we follow the monetary rule out of habit, confidence, or faith […]."

With reference to these writings by Orléan, Italian economist Luca Fantacci asserts that: "Money is not a thing, but an institution, an agreement within a community" echoing the working definition of complementary currency scholar Bernard Lietaer: "Money is an agreement within a community to use something as a means of payment" which carries the ontological idea of money being the result of a social process and not only an element therein. But Fantacci proceeds by positing state power as the facilitator of this social process because "[money] has to have an institutional sanction within a political context, such as a law establishing the relationship between unit of account and weight of pure metal, or a market in which they can be exchanged."

This is also reflected in the seminal legal treatise on 'money' already cited before in which the "institutional theory of money" is discussed as the modern third grand theory after metalism and chartalism. But again there is a practical bias towards state legislation native to the law faculty as it concludes that 'money' is only that which "is originated and managed by a central bank in a manner that preserves its availability, functionality, and purchasing power."

Towards the end of the 20th-century institutionalist theory advanced in a way that also helped to leave behind this limitation observed in traditional institutionalism in which 'money' is too easily presented as just another institution provided by the state. From the 1970s lines of inquiry that were focused on rules and norms that govern individual behaviour started to be called 'new institutional economics'. Advances in computing power and the ensuing opportunities to model economic behaviour have contributed to the increasing popularity and multidisciplinary attention to this 'new institutionalism'. This extended from the economic disciplines into schools of thought in sociology that took a similar analytical interest in the emergence and interaction of different social constellations. In this new or neo-institutionalism, the ambiguity of what an institution is was to a large degree resolved as the focus was no longer on the static organisation but the process that makes such organization (or any other structure) possible and the focus of institutional research was not the organization itself but "the rules of the game in a society or more formally [...] the humanly devised constraints that shape human interaction."

These constraints have been conceptualised and described by various authors with a number of terms such as rules, norms, permissions, conventions, codes, traditions, strategies, scripts, etc. often with overlapping and conflicting definitions of this terminology. However, at the heart of all these ways of describing an institution lies the essentially social constructivist assumption that the word refers to the collective effects of social interactions and intentional acts that establish behavioral constraints, explicitly or implicitly. For the philosophical underpinnings of neo-institutional thought John Searle and his concept of 'social facts' is often referenced, also in regards to 'money as an institution'. Curiously, 'money' was, next to 'government' and 'baseball', one of the examples Searle often used to illustrate his ideas. As his theories are given as foundational references both in the literature of institutionalism and monetary theory, the following will provide a brief overview of his theories and a brief critique of how they were found to be applied by different monetary authors.

When Searle wrote his first book on the matter, "The Construction of Social Reality" he had not been aware of the links and relevance it would have for the neo-institutional thinking in economics. But as he admits in a later edition, when he looked into it, he became aware of, as he put it, the "unclarity of what exactly an institution is" in the economic literature. For Searle institutions are systems that are capable of enabling what he calls 'institutional facts': ideas that would not exist if it was not for human interactions, as opposed to 'brute facts' which, in line with the notion of critical realism expressed earlier, acknowledge that some things exist regardless of us perceiving or describing them: "Mountains, molecules, and tectonic plates, for example, exist and would exist if there had never been any humans or animals."

Institutional facts on the other hand are created by what Searle calls "collective intentionality", which in turn relies on language to bring together the assumptions and perceptions of individuals to ascribe meaning to an object in the form of "X counts as Y in context C". To make X 'count' rests on the setting of norms and conventions, which in turn provides the conceptual and operational alignment of his theory to the neo-institutionalism found in economics. By their collective and construed nature 'institutional facts' are 'social' and 'observer relative', as they require humans to perceive and express them. And they are incremental or interlocking, meaning that one institutional fact might rely on previous such facts to exist. For example, the 'institutional fact' of marriage depends on the more basic facts of contracts, promises, the language they are uttered in and, ultimately, language per se as the most basic and necessary condition for all other institutional phenomena.

Searle refers to 'money' as an institution and continually illustrates the development of his theories with it: "In order that this piece of paper should be a five dollar bill, for example, there has to be the human institution of money" or "in order that the concept of "money" applies to the stuff in my pocket, it has to be the sort of thing that people believe is money. If everybody stops believing it is money, it ceases to function as money, and eventually ceases to be money". There are around 70 other passages in his 1995 book which use this example. In his later writings, the examples he gives help to highlight how his theory is related to the crude distinctions of Money and money introduced in the previous chapter. But a closer look at how Searle does this also highlights his conceptual limitations in regards to the understanding of contemporary money. A section from his 2005 paper "What is an Institution?" states: "the fact that a certain object is money is observer relative; money is created as such by the attitudes of observers and participants in the institution of money. But those attitudes are not themselves observer relative; they are observer independent. I think this thing in front of me is a 20 dollar bill, and, if somebody else thinks that I do not think that, he or she is just mistaken. My attitude is observer independent, but the reality created by a large number of people like me having such attitudes, depends on those attitudes and is therefore observer dependent. In investigating institutional reality, we are investigating observer dependent phenomena."

This description points to two related issues in regards to the framing of money and Money. One is that his description poses the question how the attitude towards a piece of paper in his hand is the first formed. The universality of social constructivism as it applies to phenomena outside of us but also to those concepts in our minds leaves this part of Searle's theory unsatisfactory for a theory that can describe both Money and money and the dialectic relationship between the two. The second issue is how Searle took as his departure point a physical representation of money: the bills in his hands or pockets. While his formula "X counts as Y" in general does not necessarily only apply to a material X. Sometime between 1995 and 2005 Searle seemed to have understood the need to disentangle his concept of 'money' from physical 'brute facts. It can here only be speculated whether monetary reform evangelists in attendance at his lectures or simply the changing realities of everyday payments accounted for the change in this thinking. But later in the paper cited above he writes:

"The paradox of my account is that money was my favorite example of the 'X counts as Y' formula, but I was operating on the assumption that currency [as in US Dollar notes and coins] was somehow or other essential to the existence of money. Further reflection makes it clear to me that it is not. You can easily imagine a society that has money without having any currency at all. [...] Money is typically redeemable in cash, in the form of currency, but currency is not essential to the existence or functioning of money."

Consequently he cites ideas of Barry Smith and expands his theory to include "what [Berry] calls 'free-standing Y terms', where you can have a status function [as in something counting as something else in a social context], but without any physical object on which the status function is imposed.

This conceptual extension is further explored and illustrated in his later book "Making the Social World - The Structure of Human Civilization". Here he calls this new version of institutional facts a "fallout" from other institutional facts because now no intentionality or deontology is imbued onto an object when those facts come to be. He gives various examples for this, starting with statistical findings of left and right-handed pitchers in baseball. These observations are facts and they are dependent on observers, but, different from other institutional facts, they are not required or construed by the rules of baseball and thus emerge without human intention. This example seems to match well what he describes as a "systemic fallout", or an unintended consequence. However, he later returns to the example of 'money', this time not the dollar bill but the description of how money in its dominant form is created when a banker extends an electronic loan to a client. But he makes sense of his new realizations about 'money' being possible without any material correlate (or what he had identified as cash or currency before) by relegating this kind of money to a mere 'fallout' as well. His explanation is that the creation of money was not in the bank's intention. "It is trying to loan Jones some money, not to increase the money supply."

This argument seems too simplistic and brings the concept of 'fallouts' in regards to money into question. Firstly, the intention of most banks would ultimately not be the extension of loans either, but the profit that a larger loan portfolio will provide. Furthermore, since extended bank balance sheets are today equivalent with an increased money supply, the intentionality of the banker can be summarised as 'making money'. This relationship between making money for the bank (profit) and making money for general circulation (money supply) are determined by laws, regulations and popular sufferance. What Searle fails to explain is how 'money' needs to be seen as an institution as a whole, not just the particular 'institutional fact' that turns a piece of paper or metal into money. Institutional theory needs to apply to all its practical forms, and all its socially construed levels, including Money the concept.

Regardless of those shortcomings, many monetary theorists have referred to Searle's concept of 'social facts', 'institutional facts' and 'collective intentionality' in their own portrayals of 'money as an institution'. In those there seem to be two non-exclusive ways in which the inconsistencies mentioned above do not appear as a problem for the respective authors or are resolved in light of the authors' presuppositions. The more obvious way is when the authors themselves are captivated by the physicality of some forms of money and can follow Searle in his bias.

The second condition under which Searle's philosophy seems to be an unproblematic theoretic foundation is the chartalists' starting point that money is adherent to the power of the state. Money is therefore seen as a pure virtual accounting unit that may or may not be 'imprinted' onto a physical medium of exchange, but in both cases, the chain of interlocking institutional facts that underlie the value that those units convey resolves to the power of the state. The analysis here highlights how the attitudes and concepts of individuals in regards to money, which here were found not be coherently explained in Searle's theory, are disregarded by these theorists. For the chartalist, those elements of an institutional ontology are outsourced to the political sciences and sociology. Also since there is always a state that can guarantee the value of money, institutional monetary theory does not have to cover that ground.

An example of the first, physical bias only, is Hidenori Suzuki, who in his Ph.D. thesis explored the way in which normative notions of value relate to markets. The empirical elements of his research do not require a more comprehensive monetary theory and, being intrigued by phenomena like credit cards (which he often refers to), he applies a realist stance to money in which its physical manifestations are given primacy and, in literal reference to Searle, counts them as 'brute facts'. A combination of both, the fixation on physical forms of money and a chartalist disposition can be observed in the Ph.D. theses of Stefano Sgambati (2013) and Georgios Papadopoulos (2015).

Sgambati follows the development of money from antiquity until today, trying to understand its historical changes, by tracing various epistemological standpoints and philosophical concepts. He concludes that it is the tradition of nomisma first found in Aristotle that is still valid today: "That is to say, we can only understand money if we consider its phenomenon in its intrinsic relatedness with the currency, for without the currency money cannot exist." In later publications, he questions the theories put forward in the chartalist tradition, but only when it comes to their relevance for the practical issues observed in a burgeoning financial sector and the power that shareholders hold over governments and their subjects. Papadopoulos clearly subscribes to both an institutionalist and chartalist outlook and also refers to Searle throughout his thesis. Yet when it comes to physical money he frames those as extra-institutional as his analysis "is moving away from the institutional structure of money and focuses on the objects that instantiate money, or currency, but also on the different technological devices that we use in our monetary transactions". Even with this contradictory notion, he keeps referencing Searle.

Finally, all of those three authors take reference to one of the most significant monetary theorist of the new Millenium. With his seminal 1996 paper "Money is a Social Relation" and a comprehensive book in 2004 "The Nature of Money: New Directions in Political Economy" Geoffrey Ingham made significant inroads towards what elsewhere was called for as "An alternative understanding of money not as a thing but as a social technology." For Ingham, 'money' is the result of societal processes "in the sense that it cannot be adequately conceptualised other than as the emergent property of a configuration (or "structure") of social relations." To conceptualise this, he repeatedly draws on the ideas found in Searle, but even in his later publications he only ever takes them from their initial elaboration from 1995. In so doing he proposes to fill the gap that the deductive and empiricist methodologies in economics left: a coherent ontology of money.

Describing 'money' as a social relation allows Ingham to follow the footsteps of Innes who stated that all money is some form of credit. In reference to Simmel, he can explicitly extend this definition to include all forms of money which are related to a commodity such as precious metal: "metallic money is also a promise to pay and [...] it differs from the cheque only with respect to the size of the group which vouches for its being accepted." With this, Ingham clearly lies outside of the group of authors that refer to Searle because of their common focus on the material phenomena that take on a new meaning as social facts: For him, money is not a thing. Moreover, Ingham has fervently defended this position, for example against Marxist economist Costas Lapavitsas in a published debate in the Economy and Society journal in 2005, where Lapavitsas maintains: "Much of the mystery and complexity of money arises because it is simultaneously a social relation [money of account] and a thing [monetary medium]."

Thus Ingham anchors himself firmly with the other faction of theorists who rely on Searle's focus on the normative power of the state:

"[Money] is a social relation based upon definite and particular social structural conditions of existence involving, among other things, an institutionalised banking practice and constitutional legitimacy of the political authority in which the promises of banks and the states to pay gradually became currency."

However, "Ingham insists that not all credit is money". Ingham does not entirely disregard credit systems that do not spring, in one way or another, from the authority of the state, but does not count phenomena like LETS (Local Exchange Trading Systems) and timebanks24 as 'money' and thus marginalizes their importance, both in practice and for theory: "unless a state loses power and legitimacy, these diverse media [of exchange] will remain near the bottom of the hierarchy of media to be found in all societies."

Different from this, for authors like Nigel Dodd, who are interested in how money is changing today and what it could become, the argument of macroeconomic irrelevance has no place in the aspiration of finding a theory that encompasses all monetary phenomena, ontologically and practically. This includes, but is not limited to, what was above called 'money as we know it' in its various contemporary forms, from cash to electronic bank balances, but also LETS, timebanks and the so called virtual currencies like Bitcoin. Dodd has pointed to this theoretical gap for many years, called for 'greater conceptual clarity' and attempted to provide a solution with his early theory of 'money as information'.

In his recent book, Dodd gives a strong exposee of the innate diversity that money possesses today, but instead of elaborating on his previous theory further he discusses Simmel's idea of 'perfect money' as a purely conceptual notion, that will never be found in any one of its implementations. In this sense "perfect money" is akin to the concept of Money that was proposed in the previous chapter. The aim of this thesis however is to provide a theory of the 'nature of money' that can apply equally to the concept of Money, and the multitude of real existing phenomena here called money and currencies as the instantiations of Money. In this latter regard any theory must also be applicable to all material as well as non-material implementations, while neither disregarding the physical manifestations nor giving them primacy. In line with Dodd's ambition, all the unconventional forms of money referred to as 'complementary currencies', including timebanks, LETS, (so called) Local Currencies, Bitcoin and Airmiles must have, at least on the theoretical level, equal importance with the Dollar, Euro and Yen. For this, the next two sections will supplement the notion of 'money as an institution', as found in the literature, by introducing the concept of 'discursive institutionalism' in order to explicitly enable a conceptual and practical engagement with all forms of 'money' and 'Money'. Finally, to enable a more coherent way to communicate about all these monetary phenomena, the existing, and the conceptual, an extension of the distinction between 'money' and 'Money' by the terms 'currency' and 'Currency' will be introduced.

Triangulation And Transdisciplinarity

The methodological approach of this thesis considers the questions of 'what is money' from three very different angles. Amongst the different influences that shaped this research, the strongest comes from the epistemological and heuristic openness of philosophical inquiries. However, the topic does require a certain engagement with economic and organizational perspectives, especially given the fact that

146

this research took place within the business school of the University of Cumbria. Furthermore, the strong focus on interdisciplinarity, critical social theory and social impact in the courses taught at the Institute for Leadership and Sustainability (IFLAS) strongly influenced my intellectual curiosity and shaped the final research programme of this thesis. In particular, it meant my approach to the topic of Money and currency was influenced by an awareness of both the importance of our monetary system for contemporary global challenges and a view that the current contribution of academia to progressive monetary reform or transformation appeared negligible. Therefore, throughout the doctoral research, my hope and intention has been to generate knowledge that can provide fresh grounds for academic input into the practical future of monetary systems.

Given this context, the following three 'analysis' chapters of this thesis rely on multiple, closely related but distinct methodological approaches rather than one single disciplinary thrust. The variety of methods will be combined to form a more textured picture than any single methodology could create given the broadness of the topic and its multifaceted and far-reaching nature. Therefore, the hypothesis of 'money as a discursive institution' will be tested in three different ways which is known as an 'triangulation' approach. This is deemed appropriate for complex and involved topics.

for which a single methodology might be prone to bias and 'tunnel-vision' effects. For instance, in my masters thesis about the implicit anthropological assumptions of F.A. von Hayek, his writings were analysed in relation to different schools of thought from the disciplines of economics, political science and psychology. However, where triangulation can just refer to the application of different methods to the same set of data and the same or very similar research questions, the analysis in this thesis will look at three distinct datasets (complementary currency, central bank publication, and law texts) with three different, but complementary, methodological approaches.

Consequently, this study represents what is increasingly referred to as 'transdisciplinary research. This idea is related to the better known concept of 'interdisciplinarity' as both combine the viewpoints, heuristics and methods from different disciplines. However, while no common definition of 'transdisciplinarity' has yet emerged.

Many scholars use the term to refer to a larger scientific program that is not only concerned with the production of knowledge but the scientific contribution to solutions of complex societal problems. Therefore, transdisciplinarity does not only combine insights from different disciplines, but creates and synthesises them into novel and innovative research programmes that in themselves cannot be situated within one of the employed original disciplines. According to Pohl and Hirsch Hadorn (2007), when the very nature of a problem is under dispute, transdisciplinarity helps to clarify the underlying questions and the systemic relevance, the appropriate norms and objectives to appraise the progress of a research programme and the transformational implementation pathways that stem from the findings.

Transdisciplinarity is hence applied in order to "a) grasp the complexity of problems, b) take into account the diversity of life-world and scientific perceptions of problems, c) link abstract and case-specific knowledge, and d) develop knowledge and practices that promote what is perceived to be the common good". The questions about the nature of 'money' asked in this thesis require a no less integrative methodological approach and the data and analytical engagement of the following three chapters fill the ambition of transdisciplinary research to the degree that the format and scope of a doctoral dissertation allows for.

Cultural historical activity theory will be employed to elucidate the diversity and discursive nature of the instantiations of Money that were introduced under the term 'complementary currencies' earlier. The 'grammar of institutions' methodology, a specific way to understand and analyze institutions, will be the principal methodology. It will be applied to a set of publications by the Bank of England to ascertain what the 'official' description or definition of 'money' by such an eminent actor is. Finally, a general legal analysis of the laws and statutes of the United States will be conducted to see what 'the law' has to say on the matter of 'money'. Finally, yet foremost, the stance and perspective of critical discourse analysis, which in itself calls for a transdisciplinary approach, provides the common paradigm for all three methodological approaches which makes 'critical reading' the smallest common methodological denominator that this thesis applies to three diverse, but related, datasets. Here the attribute 'critical' relates to all three ambitions that the word carries. Firstly, a conventional meaning of careful inquisitive questioning of literature, traditional views and theories. Secondly, an active awareness of the inescapable ideological bias that any discourse bears and the role that power and privilege play in disguising those biases, an idea that will be illustrated in the next section. And last, an acute sense of the urgency of the social and environmental context, as described in the introduction, that the topic under research here is undeniably part of - both in facilitating current crises but also in creating the conditions for systemic change. In light of the findings from the analytical chapters, the methodologies here described will be critically appraised (Implications).

Bank Talk

We have demonstrated how in the practice of complementary currencies the concept of Money is implemented in much more diverse forms and is more conceptually open than is commonly considered. The narrow homogeneity of conventional money can easily be illustrated with an image search on the term 'money' with the Google search engine. This homogeneity stretches across what is commonly called 'national currencies. Regardless of whether the generic US-centric search engine google.com or its UK site google.co.uk is used, the US Dollar is the dominant representative of 'money'. This narrow meaning will be challenged by the means of discourse and institutional analysis. In the first section, the importance of central bank communications in the establishment of a 'common image' of money is reviewed. In the second and third sections, one particular corpus of texts from the publications of the Bank of England will be analysed in relation to the statements about the nature of 'money' and 'currency' with an empirical application of the grammar of institutions. A subsection therein will focus on references to gold as one curious aspect of the Bank of England's framing of 'money'.

The framing of 'money' employed by financial regulators and central banks is a topic not only interesting for discourse analysis but also of practical relevance in regard to the legal and regulatory ambiguities that are revealed by the implementation of complementary currencies. The very language used by regulators to define 'money' has the power to "define potentials, sets of possibilities" which is the phrase Norman Fairclough uses to describe the attributes and importance of language in general. Or as a former governor of the Bank of England once said: "Habits of speech, not only reflect habits of thinking, they influence them too. So the way in which central banks talk about money is important."

Internal discrepancies in how authors of the Bank of England think and write about the terms 'money' and 'currency' are apparent even without much analysis. As a point of illustration, the Bank of England's Quarterly Bulletin from January 2014 titled "Money in the modern economy: an introduction" clearly defines "currency" in its glossary as "cash" or the "notes and coins" issued by a government. Yet, the term appears in other publications by the Bank of England in a way that is contrary to their definition. An earlier issue of their Quarterly Bulletin looked at the phenomenon of "local currencies", a term used in the field of complementary currencies.

The first apparent discrepancy here arises from the fact that local currency notes are obviously not issued by any governmental body and hence would not match the narrow definition offered in the 2014 Bulletin. Furthermore, most transactions in the described UK-based 'local currencies' happen purely electronically, via online banking and text messages, without any physical medium that would meet the concept of cash.

Subsequent publications by the Bank of England operate with the term 'digital currency' to describe specific complementary currencies like bitcoin which, given the aforementioned lexical definition, simply amounts to an oxymoron: nothing can be digital and at the same time physical. Of course, it can be argued that the usage of the term currency has evolved along with technology and the new exchange media that have gradually replaced the importance of cash. If this development was acknowledged openly and old definitions amended to respond to new and emerging phenomena, with a high degree of transparency and care towards the discursive context, the situation could be seen as fruitful and creative. For now, the stance of critical discourse analysis chosen for this research mandates a special attention to statements from powerful actors in any given context, even if they seem so commonplace, technical or even benign as the two examples above. Or, as monetary reform scholar Randall Wray insists, when it comes to analysing monetary discourse: "It is not so much the accuracy of the conventional view of money that we need to question, but rather the framing."

Here, the methodology of frame analysis will not be applied explicitly to the discourse of financial regulators, but an analysis of the "constituent statements" they make about the nature of money and currency and the relation between these two terms will be presented. This application of the grammar of institutions will not only demonstrate how money can be treated as a discursive institution, but also allows for a critical appraisal of the way that the concept of money is viewed and communicated by the Bank of England as one of the pre-eminent actors in the wider discourse of money. This demands acute attention and scrutiny because of the Bank of England's explicit communication strategy that was developed in 2014 and, at the time of researching this thesis, published as part of their strategic document "Vision 2020" (Bank of England, 2017a): "Communication at a central bank is an important policy tool. Our policies have maximum impact when they are heard and understood. Good communication therefore links directly back to the successful delivery of our mission. On external communications we will seek to attract a wider audience with a targeted, creative approach to content and analysis including key publications and speeches."

This reorientation towards wider non-expert audiences is a remarkably novel stance for central banks. To give an account of the historical approach of central banks towards transparent communications, Issing (2005, p. singles out the central bank of the United Kingdom saying: "There was a time when the Bank of England could almost be classified as the epitome of reticence vis-à-vis the public". This was not true only in the UK. Today, the communication efforts of central banks are seen as being on a par with their other, more obviously monetary or financial activities. In a play on words to 'open market operations' - the buying and selling of government bonds to regulate asset prices and the amount of money in the economy. speak of modern central bank communications as "open mouth policies" and hold them as being just as potent as their traditional policy tools.

With this change in practice a plethora of literature has emerged addressing the questions of how much and what kind of communication activities constitute "optimal communication policies" for central banks.

Some authors have taken an openly normative approach, particular in respect to the European Central Bank (ECB), which is seen as markedly less transparent than its sister institutions in other constituencies. Not publishing the minutes of ECB committee meetings and the voting behavior of its members is criticised as a symptom and indicator of the political complexities under which the ECB was created and the undemocratic nature of its operations. However, in the literature that analyses the discourse emanating from central banks, most attention is concerned with the use of language in regards to how they explain and announce the setting of interest rates, the analysis of their respective economies' performances, and optimistic or pessimistic predictions of economic growth. Nuances in the wording thereof in reports, at press conferences or speeches now affect the public's appraisal of the state of economic affairs and thus can be seen as an enactment of central bank "intention to shape pricing behaviour". Many people and institutions closely monitor every utterance from central banks because foreseeing their actions promises an advantage in gauging market developments. In the US, commentators have even coined the term "FED-watching" for the economic journalists' close observations of central bank communications, and former chairman of the FED Ben Bernanke was quoted saying: "it has not been uncommon in the past few years for financial markets to react more strongly to changes in the wording of the

[Federal Open Market] Committee's statement than to its decision about the target for the federal funds rate itself".

This genre that Karl calls "Bank Talk", to which the present analysis of the term money in Bank of England publications appears to contribute a fundamental element, has been identified to have strong performative elements with an "ontology and tendencies [...] akin to those of fiction". Holmes, having studied the communications of different central banks for over 15 years, even likens it to public drama, storytelling and ritual. A reference to discourse and discourse analysis is however found only in passing and never as an explicit methodological approach in this body of literature. Just one piece of research, Moretti and Pestre (2015), employs a specific quantitative discourse analysis methodology to the corpus of the annual reports of the World Bank between 1946 and 2012. Their paper, titled "Bankspeak" in reference to George Orwell's 1984 "duckspeak", analyses the prevalence of nouns, verbs, conjunctions and temporal words longitudinally and finds significant changes in the language and semantics of these reports over the decades. This leads them to conclude that "the style of the reports becomes much more codified, self-referential and detached from everyday language", giving a general verdict about the style of these reports as being: "All very uplifting - and just as unfocused". Remarkably, within a few years their paper acquired recognition and achieved publicity beyond most individual research publications. In 2016 the New York Times reported it, if only with an ironic undertone. And in 2017 the new World Bank chief economist himself took the "Bankspeak" findings seriously and demanded a maximum ration for the word "and" in all reports of his research division. The Guardian and The

Economist subsequently reported and speculated that this might have been cause for an unexpected change in his position within the bank, which made him lose all editorial control over its research outputs.

Bank Of England Communications

Returning to the Bank of England and the data here to be analysed, the above mentioned communication strategy is positioned on the Bank's own website as a natural component of its mission that has been outlined ever since the Bank received its charter in 1694. This mission is however only vaguely defined in the original charter and is currently expressed as: "[T]he Bank's mission is to promote the good of the people of the United Kingdom by maintaining monetary and financial stability." (Bank of England, 2017a) Illustrating what this means (and tying it more closely to the focus of this research), a current pamphlet distributed online and at the Bank of England Museum further explains: "Monetary stability means stable prices and confidence in the currency. [...] Maintaining confidence in the currency is a key role of the Bank and one which is essential to the proper functioning of the economy." (Bank of England, 2015a, p. 1). Therefore, the following analysis can be seen as a very close look at what "the currency" means in the Bank's own understanding, and how their communications might be employed to ensure our confidence in it. The selected texts are part of a particular interdiscursive genre, which spans the specialist economic and popular discourses about money.

Today, the Bank's website and the publications freely distributed at their on-site museum in London increasingly use a language and imagery that clearly speak to an audience much wider than economists, financial experts and politicians. The same style can be found in recent articles of their regular and fully referenced publication called the "Quarterly Bulletin". A blog page has even been launched in 2014 in which Bank staff can publish articles of academic quality which would previously have been considered working papers and bear the same disclaimers as to the arguments expressed therein representing nothing but the author's opinion. All these highlight the paradigm shift in central bank communications discussed above. In regard to the nature and concept of money, this new approach to publicity is directly relevant. As Holmes explains in his seminal book "The economy of words" communications are now part of the "search for new means by which monetary affairs could be anchored conceptually - not to gold or to regimes of fixed exchange rates by means of an evolving relationship with the public". In other words, in the perspective of discursive institutionalism descriptions of money are constitutive, not just descriptive, of what 'money' is. The following analysis demonstrates how institutional methodologies can be applied to ascertain this notion empirically.

CHAPTER 4

Perspectives On A Changing World Order

Observers of world affairs like to point to a defining moment or pivotal event to proclaim the end of one era and the beginning of another. Not surprisingly, the novel coronavirus pandemic has already spawned much speculation that the world will undergo profound change as a consequence, even that contemporary history will forever be divided between what happened BC (before coronavirus) and AC (after coronavirus). Historical eras, however, and certainly international orders the complex amalgam of rules, norms, and institutions that govern relations among states at any given time rarely, if ever, hinge on singular events. They, and the power relationships that undergird them, are simply too entrenched to change rapidly. For this reason, it is more accurate to identify transitional periods that span the rise and fall of specific international orders. In these periods, elements of the old order are still discernible, albeit functioning below their peak, while features of the new order are clearly emerging and playing a more influential role.

Just such a situation appears to exist today. The international order largely constructed by the United States in the aftermath of World War II is still very much in evidence for the basic reason that most states appreciate its benefits and thus abide by its rules, all on the understanding that America retains sufficient power and influence to enforce compliance. At the same time, the global distribution of power is inexorably shifting with the rise of new powers as well as influential nonstate actors, such as multinational corporations and transnational terrorist organizations. The United States is also growing more reluctant to bear the costs of world leadership, especially when it comes to using military force. China and Russia, along with lesser regional powers, have taken advantage of this reticence in recent years to assert their own interests and to undermine the United States' international standing and authority. Their actions have at times openly flouted the rules and norms of the U.S. led order without incurring a serious price, which has demoralized its supporters and emboldened its detractors.

In addition, the benefits of the U.S led order and, in particular, the many international agreements that the United States has championed to open up the world to the free flow of goods, services, ideas, and people, no longer look so promising not least to the many Americans whose livelihoods have suffered as a consequence. This shift has caused a public backlash against globalization not only in the United States but also in many Western countries that have manifested itself in more nationalist and inward-looking policies. As a result, the political will to defend, much less extend, the liberal international order is in short supply.

Where all this leads is by no means certain. It is still possible to imagine several alternative future orders arising from the current transitional period. One would be a world divided between states that subscribe to open market economies and democratic forms of governance and those that choose not to, likely led by the United States and China, respectively. Another would be an international system organized around rival trade blocs and associated political organizations, each dominated by the principal regional power. Both of these future orders could differ substantially, depending on whether relations between the constituent elements were essentially cooperative or highly competitive.

If previous transitional periods serve as any precedent, the actions of the major powers will likely determine which of these international orders or a different one emerges in the future. How the major powers have managed these consequential moments in the past is not encouraging, however. Since the beginning of the twentieth century, there have been three transitional periods: from approximately 1913 to 1920, from 1938 to 1947, and from 1988 to 1994. In two of these, catastrophic conflicts broke out (World Wars I and II), and the third experienced violent upheavals in the Balkans and the Middle East as well as in Africa and Asia. Efforts by major powers to create a robust, collective security arrangement in these transitional periods either collapsed or never lived up to their full promise (the League of Nations, the early "Four Policemen" proposal for the United Nations, and the vision of a "New World Order" after the 1991 Gulf War). Moreover, the international orders that followed while bringing relative peace and stability were flawed. Thus, the League of Nations system lacked the active involvement of the United States and the Soviet Union, the bipolar Cold War rested on the threat of mutual annihilation and came close to it on several occasions and the post–Cold War order revolved around the vagaries of U.S. hegemony.

Today, the signs are not promising that the major powers either comprehend the risks of the current transitional period or have a clear vision for a new international order that would be broadly acceptable and thus considered legitimate by most other states. If anything, mistrust and friction is steadily growing among them. The United States, China, India, and Russia are acquiring new strategic capabilities and exploiting new operational domains, specifically cyberspace and outer space, ostensibly to bolster deterrence and improve their national defenses. These preparations, however, can just as easily signal hostile intent and increase the scope for dangerous misunderstandings and unintended military escalation during acute crises. In short, the prospect of a war breaking out between two or more of the major powers, something that was generally considered to be risibly improbable just a few years ago, is no longer unimaginable.

Growing strategic rivalry among the major powers has also started to play out in many regions of the world as each increasingly maneuvers for influence and advantage. If the experience of the Cold War provides any guide, this competition could exacerbate local sources of instability and conflict. At the same time, the United Nations' ability to address, much less resolve, these and other threats to peace is declining as the organization becomes consumed by growing acrimony among the major powers and thus essentially as deadlocked as it was for most of the Cold War. Finally, cooperation on a host of critical global challenges and common security concerns particularly nuclear proliferation, transnational terrorism, public health threats, and the interacting effects of climate change, resource scarcity, and environmental degradation seems also likely to suffer. Those problems can be meaningfully tackled only through collective international action, which is unlikely to coalesce without impetus from the major powers. Despite a common interest in addressing those threats, increasing mistrust and antagonism will only make the task more difficult. The poor level of international cooperation on the COVID-19 outbreak certainly in its initial stages stands in stark contrast to what happened during the 2008–09 financial crisis and would appear to validate this fear.

It was with these concerns in mind that the Center for Preventive Action (CPA) at the Council on Foreign Relations launched the Managing Global Disorder project with the generous support of the Carnegie Corporation of New York. At the outset, CPA thought it valuable to get different perspectives on the state of the world from leading scholars in each of the major powers. Each scholar was asked to address a common set of questions about the current international order its current state, its likely future evolution, the risk of major war, and the prospects for cooperation on common security concerns and other global challenges. The answers, which were drafted before COVID-19, vary considerably, which is not surprising given their different vantage points.

Qingguo Jia from China argues that the post–World War II order is not ending but is clearly in "serious trouble" as a result of recent developments. Military conflict among the major powers, particularly between the United States and China, remains unlikely, however, given the shared incentives to avoid such a catastrophe. Their relationship will nevertheless grow more competitive. If the current international order is to be sustained for the benefit of all, the leading powers will need to work together to reform its working practices and institutions in a mutually satisfactory and sustainable way.

Nathalie Tocci from Italy is much less sanguine. She sees the liberal international order as "fraying" badly, and though the risk of war is not preordained, "potent drivers" are at work that make it more likely. The European Union (EU), she argues, needs to wake up to the evolving reality of growing rivalry among the major powers and develop a coherent and practical new strategy for defending EU interests and preserving the multilateral institutions of the current rules-based international order. The world will become more unstable and dangerous if the practice of multilateralism is replaced by narrow, nationalistic approaches.

Dhruva Jaishankar from India also views the world as in a transitional phase, but, unlike Jia and Tocci, sees it evolving in a more complex way with elements of unipolarity, bipolarity, and multipolarity coexisting uneasily. He shares Tocci's concern, however, that if current multilateral approaches to international problem-solving become "undermined, bypassed, or disregarded," then the risk of great power conflict will increase. The development of new and potentially threatening military capabilities, the trend toward economic "decoupling," and rising nationalism around the world are all concerning. To avoid the world growing more fragmented and dangerous, existing global governance institutions will need to adapt and new ones are created to accommodate rising powers.

Andrey Kortunov from Russia sees the world as entering a period of increasing volatility if the leading powers do not adjust to its new realities and new imperatives. In contrast to the other commentators, however, he sees the greater risk stemming less from great power competition and more from the uneven reach and benefits of globalization.

This is leaving many parts of the world further behind in terms of living standards and future prospects. Conflict in the future is more likely to occur, he believes, between states that are the winners and the losers of globalization the haves and the have-nots as well as within countries where the socioeconomic disparities are greatest. The major powers, he argues, should not only develop new crisis management mechanisms to lessen the ancillary risks of their growing rivalry but also work together to ensure that global institutions such as the United Nations, as well as various regional bodies, are able to manage these growing international schisms.

While each of these scholars views the world today and the challenges that lay ahead in different ways, they share a common belief that the opportunity to shape a new international order that is stable, inclusive, and beneficial to all still exists, though the window to do this is growing smaller. The experience of earlier transitional periods suggests that any effort to reform or create a new global order must be a collaborative undertaking. It cannot be imposed or established by any major power acting alone or even in concert with another. The same is true for managing the major challenges that humanity now confronts. Although the world seems destined to grow more competitive, congested, and contested in the coming years, the logic of major power cooperation is inescapable.

Such cooperation will be rendered more difficult, if not impossible, if the major powers grow increasingly fearful of each other's strategic intentions. Meaningful cooperation requires basic mutual trust and security, which will not arise spontaneously. The major powers will, therefore, need to provide active reassurance through formal agreement, where possible, and informally when this is not politically practical. The goal should be to create a stable and mutually beneficial understanding that accepts the reality of strategic competition as well as the imperative of coexistence. At a minimum, this objective will require a deeper appreciation of each country's core national security interests and a renewed commitment to the fundamental international principles of political sovereignty, domestic noninterference, and territorial integrity. In some areas, the major powers will also need to practice reciprocated restraint on activities deemed potentially threatening, as has been done in previous eras of major power competition.

The subsequent discussion papers in this series explore in greater depth how to promote a stable and mutually beneficial relationship among the major powers that can in turn provide the essential foundation for greater cooperation on pressing global and regional challenges.

The European Union

Nathalie Tocci

The liberal international order, within which the European project was established and is embedded, is fraying. This trend has been building up for more than a decade now. As Paul B. Stares argues, the world may have been living through a transitional period akin to those of 1913–20, 1938–47, and 1988–94. The novel coronavirus has exacerbated, accelerated, and increased everything from protectionism and great power rivalry to nationalism and ideological competition. As a result, the pandemic may represent the tipping point from the international liberal order to disorder. This reality should encourage Europeans to realize that rules-based multilateralism is not simply nice to have but essential, especially if they are to maintain their way of life in the years to come. No longer simply driven by the ideal of peace on the continent and the benefits of the single market, today the rationale for the European project is global. Nationalism driven by nostalgia, the closure of borders, and racism is being undermined by the creeping realization that size and clout matter more than ever. Only together can Europeans negotiate with China, stand up to Russia, rebuild bridges across the Atlantic, address global pandemics, govern migration, combat climate change, and embrace artificial intelligence and biotechnology while ensuring digital safety. Europeans have precious few alternatives to sticking together if they want a fair chance of thriving in the twenty-first century. For precisely this reason, Europeans will perish in a world in which the strong (and big) do what they can while the weak (and small) suffer what they cannot avoid. Just as Europeans are bound to one another internally through the European Union (EU), the most radical form of multilateralism worldwide, they also have a stake in the broader world, in which multilateralism is a defining feature. This bestows on the EU a new and global raison d'être, one that poses a unique danger if the EU fails to rise to the challenge but that also holds great promise to reenergize the European project.

THE END OF THE LIBERAL INTERNATIONAL ORDER

Today's historical juncture offers few certainties. However, the post–World War II liberal international order has certainly ended. The so-called liberal international order rose from the ashes of two world wars. With it came the emergence and consolidation of the United Nations, the proliferation of international organizations, the slow but steady affirmation of international law, and the mushrooming of regional cooperation and integration initiatives, of which the European Union has been the most successful example. It first crystallized in the West during the Cold War and was extended after the fall of the Iron Curtain and the collapse of the Soviet Union. It was an order some reviled and others embraced.

Some mourn, others applaud, and others are not yet willing to accept the end of the liberal international order. However, few if any would dispute that the distribution of power within the international system is changing dramatically. The distribution of power is complicated. Its complexity is derived from concomitant trends: a traditional shift of power away from a global hegemon the United States toward multiple power centers and a diffusion of power, driven first by globalization and now by the fourth industrial revolution. Power is not shifting simply from the West to the East but also beyond state boundaries, flowing across air, land, sea, space, and cyberspace. The institutions, rules, and regimes built on the previous configuration of power the liberal international order will inevitably change to reflect this profound shake-up of the international system. This does not mean that all of its features, including its rules, regimes, and institutions, will disappear. Some will change, others will wane, and others will acquire renewed salience. In other words, the international order or disorder that follows will be non-liberal; shaped by liberal democracies and illiberal or authoritarian states, it will likely feature structured global cooperation on some issues like climate change, and transactional or ad hoc approaches to other issues like digital governance.

THE RISK OF GREAT POWER CONFLICT

Proponents of realism are quick to point out that, in a sinister repetition of history, the world, and in particular the United States and China, are sleepwalking into a Thucydides's trap the theory that all rising powers inevitably clash with the predominant powers. Although falling into the trap has never been preordained, the structural under-pinnings of the power shift, coupled with misperception and miscommunication, have created potent drivers for conflict. This is not to say that history will repeat itself. However, the competition between the United States and China has morphed from commercial to technological rivalry and, during the COVID-19 crisis, has acquired ideological undertones. This competition could, in turn, result in a twenty-first-century military confrontation.

Liberal observers would be hard pressed to reach a fundamentally different conclusion as international institutions, rules, and regimes have been hollowed out and marginalized, or have collapsed outright. These weak or effectively moribund international institutions are no longer capable of creating a controlled setting for the peaceful management of conflict. Russia's violation of the Intermediate Range Nuclear Forces Treaty, which the United States met by withdrawing from the agreement, underscores both the fragility of institutional arrangements and how their unraveling heightens the risk of devastatingly violent conflict. Given that the United States is no longer willing and able to sustain an international order larger than itself and no other global actor is in a position to fully step into the void, the multilateral rules-based order is at risk. Multipolarity could eventually lead to strengthened multilateralism. But, in the slow and convulsed process of transition from a unipolar to a multi-, inter-, or nonpolar system, multilateralism is taking a hard hit, and, with it, the potential for the peaceful management of international relations has been reduced dramatically.

Constructivists, arguing that history is shaped not merely by objective, material forces, but by inter-subjectively defined identities and interests, are pessimistic as well. Because identities are constructed in mutually exclusive ways, the potential for violent conflict escalates. Whether one pits the West against Islam, liberal democracies against authoritarianism, cosmopolitans against nativists, or elites against the people, twenty-first-century constructs of identity have set the scene for violent conflict.

Some features of a twenty-first-century global confrontation can be discerned. From the Middle East to eastern Europe and from the Balkans to the Korean Peninsula, great power rivalry interlocks with and exacerbates regional power struggles, state fragility, and violent conflict. Other features, though arguably far more consequential notably the links between economic and technological rivalry and the risk of military confrontation; the trade-offs between public health, political rights, and economic development; or the nexus between climate change and mass displacement will be more difficult to predict.

ADDRESSING THE CHALLENGES: MULTILATERALISM AND THE EU'S ROLE

In this changing international environment, the EU has been imbued with a new sense of responsibility to sustain a rules-based multilateralism. Doing so requires both hard work and imagination. Part of the approach covers the well-trodden ground. The EU should invest more in the UN system, both politically and financially, and spur reform of the World Trade Organization (WTO), notably its dispute settlement system, and of other international financial institutions to make them more representative and legitimate. The EU should also defend and implement international agreements and law, particularly by supporting the Joint Comprehensive Plan of Action with Iran. It should support forms of regional cooperation in Africa, Asia, and Latin America, which are the building blocks of global governance. It should also better coordinate internally, both between member states and across institutions and policy fields.

However, these actions will be insufficient on their own. The EU should also support multilateralism in at least three ways. First, it should systematically transform its bilateral or interregional arrangements into multilateral agreements. This means bringing the multilateral agenda forward in all of its bilateral and regional relationships, as well as making multilateral cooperation more central to EU activities, particularly in promoting sustainable development. For example, in order to better address youth and migration issues, the EU is already working to expand its bilateral relationship with the African Union into a trilateral partnership with the United Nations. Similarly, the EU could leverage its trade policy, which includes its relationships with Canada (through the Comprehensive and Economic Trade Agreement), Japan, members of Mercosur, Mexico, and others, to create a coalition to reform the stalled WTO.

Second, European foreign policy should acknowledge that a fixed set of like-minded countries to which it can automatically and lazily turn no longer exists. From like-minded partnerships, the EU should shift to like-minded partnering, in which the EU, guided by its principled goals, pragmatically identifies and fosters the appropriate multilateral group of actors on any given geographical or thematic issue. The constellation of actors will invariably change from issue to issue and, occasionally, within the same issue area as time (and governments) go by. The group of partners on the Iranian nuclear deal is not the same as for the conflict in Ukraine. The multilateral coalition in favor of a progressive climate agreement in Paris in 2015 was not the same as for a more ambitious outcome in

Madrid four years later. Looking ahead, it remains to be seen whether the Group of Twenty (G20), which played a key role in the 2007−08 global financial crisis, will rise to the challenge of spurring post-COVID-19 economic recovery, or whether other multilateral formats will emerge instead. Principled and pragmatic partnering requires much more creativity in seeking out partners, a far greater capacity for listening to others, and more clarity and at times assertiveness on European interests and goals than was previously necessary.

Third, given the accelerated speed of politics in the digital age and the highly fluid nature of geopolitics, the EU should blend flexibility and inclusivity in its pursuit of effective multilateralism. This suggests the need for more frequent mini-lateral forums and contact groups to deliver multilateral results. The EU three (France, Germany, and Italy) format on the Iranian nuclear file and the International Contact Group on Venezuela are two examples. These are characterized by both an internal EU contact group (a subset of member states) and an international group of which the EU is a part. Such groups should be small enough to be agile and responsive but also large and varied enough to be representative. At the same time, to be legitimate, they should establish an institutional link to the larger multilateral setting, including both in internal EU features (connection between the European contact group and EU institutions) as well as in international settings (link between the international contact group and the United Nations).

The liberal international order is gone. But this does not mean that future generations will be relegated to a world of (seemingly) strong-men toying with the prospect of nuclear Armageddon as the planet is ravaged by climate change and technological progress races ahead, unchecked by shared norms and rules. A future international order could feature more challenges to norms and be less stable than the current international order. Yet it could also be more inclusive, more flexible, and ultimately more resilient. The liberal international order may not survive, but what follows is not predetermined; it does not have to mean the end of the open, liberal values at the core of the European project. To maintain these values, Europeans and others should invest much more in multilateralism and, above all, be willing to break and recast the comfortable mold created in the recent past.

Russia

Andrey Kortunov

Two distinct but overlapping international agendas shape the complex global environment. The first reflects the concerns of the twentieth and early twenty-first centuries; the second reflects new and emerging threats. The old world agenda is disintegrating quickly and the new one is yet to be set. As a result, the world has entered a period of increasing instability, volatility, and uncertainty. To minimize the risk of armed conflict and to shape the new agenda, major powers, regional organizations, and international institutions should focus on developing confidence-building measures in technical or regionally specific areas, such as arms control agreements, to build consensus and create acceptable dispute-resolution mechanisms. As consensus builds, new voluntary agreements on emerging challenges and on international rules, norms, and regimes should be developed. In this way, major powers and rising powers can work together to manage the risk of armed conflict and create a more inclusive system of global governance.

THE FUTURE OF WORLD ORDER

Globalization has shaped world affairs for many decades, but the dynamics of the globalization process have turned out more complicated and less linear than many experts anticipated in the late 1980s and early 1990s. It was assumed then that waves of globalization would spread mainly from the economic, political, and technological "core" of the Western world to the "periphery," or the residual rest. Large "semi-peripheral" countries such as Brazil, China, India, Russia, and others would become transmission mechanisms linking the "global core" to the "global periphery." Consequently, experts predicted that countries moving closer to the core (or, to the West) would embrace globalization, while resistance to globalization would increase as countries moved toward the periphery. These peripheral countries would also be more nationalistic and isolationist, and more likely to generate trade wars and conflict.

However, events of the early twenty-first century suggest that, in many cases, the waves of globalization are moving in the opposite direction from the global periphery to the global core. Rather than push for global interconnectedness, the West is trying to fence itself off from the periphery by implementing restrictions on migration, adopting protectionist policies, repatriating previously abandoned industries, and allowing the rise of nationalism. Although Western countries as a whole currently surpass non-Western countries in their involvement in the globalization process, the question of who will become the main driver of this process in the future remains open. The core could ultimately be less globalized than the periphery.

Turning back or even significantly slowing down globalization in the foreseeable future is not possible. Even the COVID-19 pandemic, which has imposed rigid restrictions on some specific avenues of globalization, including international travel, has at the same time opened new routes for bringing humankind together by, for example, boosting international online job opportunities. Among other things, the pandemic has graphically illustrated that the world is getting smaller, more crowded, more complex, and more fragile. In the aftermath of the immediate repercussions of COVID-19, the world and its constituent parts are likely to become more, rather than less, interconnected and interdependent. Once the global economy has overcome the current recession, transnational flows of finances, goods and services, ideas, and people will start growing again, pressures from common problems will likely increase, and the need to upgrade the current system of global governance will become increasingly urgent.

The process of globalization will remain fundamentally uneven, however, in terms of who benefits the most and how it affects culture, the economy, and society. Large parts of the world will likely remain excluded for a long time not only failing states, but also regions within successful states that lag behind or fail. Some countries with strong economic sectors will be leaders in globalization; others will likely continue to oppose it. The dynamics of the global financial market will outpace the dynamics of the global labor market; globalization of science will progress faster than the globalization of culture.

As a result, the primary battle of the future will not be a competition between a small group of major global actors, nor a competition between a broader group of states although a devolution of power in the international system will likely continue. The great divide in international relations will be between the winners and losers of the globalization process, those countries that can best adapt to an increasingly dynamic and less certain global environment. This divide already cuts across existing coalitions, blocs, continents, individual countries, and even cities; it will make the transition to a new system of global governance painful and protracted. Consequently, a period of instability, multiple crises, and political volatility at the national, regional, and global levels could last for several decades.

MANAGING THE RISK OF WAR BETWEEN GREAT POWERS

The process of globalization should gradually shift the focus of the international system away from traditional great power competition to tensions between the global core and the global periphery. Large-scale military conflicts within the core are unlikely. In 1914, leaders of great powers had efficient instruments for mobilizing their societies to fight a large-scale war in the middle of Europe. Today, such mobilization looks impossible, even in authoritarian countries such as China or Russia. Moreover, control over territory, natural resources, or even over trade routes is no longer as critical to great powers as it was one or two hundred years ago.

However, the risk of a direct military confrontation between major powers will by no means disappear. At least two sets of circumstances could lead to such a confrontation. First, a technical or human error, a mistaken assessment of an opponent's intentions, or an inadvertent escalation of a political crisis could trigger a conflict between major powers. To reduce the risk of triggering these circumstances, great powers should maintain open lines of political communication and participate in a broad range of confidence-building measures and various forms of military-to-military collaboration, among other steps. New formats for strategic arms control will emerge.

Second, a direct military confrontation could result from intense regional crises fought by proxies or from civil conflicts in places regarded as top security priorities by a great power, or several great powers. Here again, the importance of direct political communication and military-to-military communication on the ground as Russia and the United States do in Syria is evident. Future states may not recognize the concept of spheres of influence but will have to accept implicitly the notion of spheres of special sensitivity for the major powers. This acceptance could decrease the risk of a direct military collision between major powers.

ADDRESSING COMMON SECURITY CHALLENGES

Over time, the scale and the number of common security challenges will grow, as will public demands to turn these challenges into top foreign policy priorities for major powers. These challenges will increasingly compete with more traditional foreign policy agendas, including the remnants of great power competition. As a result, major powers will need to pursue parallel foreign policy tracks: the old track, inherited from the twentieth and the beginning of the twenty-first centuries; and the new track, reflecting emerging international realities of the twenty-first century.

Ideally, these tracks should be kept separate similar to U.S. policies during the Cold War, when strategic arms control policies with the Soviet Union were insulated from the rest of the relationship between the two superpowers. However, complete separation is not achievable: the nature of the new challenges will require a certain trust among major powers. The United States and the Soviet Union achieved only minimal trust during the Cold War, but that did allow them to sign historic arms control agreements. In applying this concept to conflicts today, major powers are unlikely to participate in any strategic interaction to fight international terrorism if they are also operating within the framework of a predominantly adversarial major power relationship.

Merging the needs of a new foreign policy track with the limitations derived from the old track will likely be one of the main obstacles to enhancing global and regional governance. Nevertheless, the new track should gradually gain priority. The new rules of engagement and the new models of interaction will grow from technical, specific, and incremental pockets of cooperation, and eventually expand to more sensitive political and strategic domains. The new track will likely produce fewer old-fashioned, legally binding agreements and new international institutions. Instead, states will accede to voluntary regimens, unilateral commitments, and public-private partnerships.

MANAGING REGIONAL DISORDER

Regional crises and conflicts will continue, mostly along the borders between the global core and the global periphery. The Middle East and North Africa will likely remain the most significant global generators of instability, but other explosive regions, such as sub-Saharan Africa and South Asia, are also likely loci of violent outbursts. Crises will stem from failures of regional economic and social development strategies; they will be aggravated by the continued growth of international radical networks, global problems such as climate change, and major power competition.

Given the diversity of regional conflicts, a standardized approach to mitigating or containing them is difficult to envision. In some relatively uncontroversial cases (Yemen), the United Nations could play the leading role in the quest for settlements. In other cases (India-Pakistan), the parties to the conflict are more likely to support direct interaction between the competing sides by encouraging cease-fires, confidence-building measures, and diplomatic compromises. Yet in other cases (Libya), external powers will likely focus on limiting the horizontal or vertical escalation of conflict situations.

An important dimension of conflict management will be conflict prevention. Its efficiency will depend to a large extent on the ability to link security and development needs in explosive parts of the world, to enhance the efficiency of technical assistance programs, and to develop the capacity of interested parties to react in a timely manner to natural and man-made disasters affecting fragile and failed states. At the same time, states will need to master the ability to regulate transborder migration flows and the global arms trade, and to curb the proliferation of international terrorism.

THE ROLE OF INTERNATIONAL AND REGIONAL ORGANIZATIONS

Practical alternatives to the United Nations are hard to imagine in the near future. Prospects for a less divided and more functional United Nations are similarly unrealistic. UN reform will continue to be an uphill battle as long as fundamental differences exist between major powers regarding the likely and desirable new global order. Consequently, the role of the United Nations in critical matters (strategic arms control, nonproliferation, and many regional crises) will continue to be limited, and major powers will continue to violate the UN Charter.

At the same time, the United Nations can play a more active role in shaping the new international agenda, including by establishing rules of engagement for new challenges and threats. Major power competition has not yet entered new domains of world politics (such as cyberspace), which could create opportunities for the United Nations, especially if it operates in cooperation with other international institutions, such as the Asia-Pacific Economic Cooperation, BRICS (Brazil, Russia, India, China, and South Africa), the European Union, the Group of Seven, and the Group of Twenty.

Ideally, the global security role of the United Nations should be complemented at the regional level by appropriate collective security organizations, which should receive a UN mandate for managing crises and instabilities in their respective regions. These organizations should have the legitimacy, resources, and institutional capacities to provide for peace and security at the regional level. However, in areas of particular concern (East Asia, Europe, and the Middle East), such an arrangement will likely be beyond reach for a long time. Therefore, the immediate goal should not be to unite divided regions but rather to manage existing divisions to bring down risks (Russia and the West in Europe, China and the United States in East Asia, Iran and the Sunni monarchies in the Gulf). Over time, management of regional confrontations could lead to reconciliation and, eventually, to the establishment of a regional collective security system.

The transition to a new international system will be long and quite dangerous. It will involve a period of increased instability, volatility, and uncertainty as nation-states and other global actors seek to impose order and maintain or gain advantages. As a result, risk management and cost reduction should be urgent priorities for major powers. Perhaps most important, however, these powers should focus on making a compelling case for enhancements and improvements to global governance. Future governance structures should incorporate elements of the old order but prioritize reconciling the needs of rising powers and emerging threats of the twenty-first century.

India

Dhruva Jaishankar

The international order has changed radically over the past three decades in ways that are clearly discernible but not easily conceivable. This shift is evidenced by the lack of a commonly recognized term to characterize the emerging international order, beyond the increasingly inappropriate post–Cold War, which describes what the order is not. Without question, the prevailing international order has been under considerable strain, and the novel coronavirus has stretched it almost to a breaking point. Governance of the global commons is being undermined, rival economic institutions are being created, and international security institutions are increasingly anachronistic. The risk of great power conflict has increased as deterrence, interdependence, and socialization have given way to low-risk offensive weapons, changing cost-benefit calculations, and rising nationalism. Domestic political constraints in the United States, the nature of China's rise, and the role of other actors (Europe, India, Japan, and Russia) mean that the emerging international system could quite possibly reflect elements of unipolarity, bipolarity, and multipolarity simultaneously.

China and India are often grouped together as the two rising powers in Asia, but their interests and objectives differ. India desires a multipolar world in which it can protect its interests and play a role in shaping the international order. It also seeks stronger multilateral mechanisms to better manage the instability that will inevitably result from multipolarity. As a result, India rather paradoxically finds itself as a rising but largely status quo–oriented power, one that seeks to reform the international order but not necessarily overturn it. By contrast, China seeks to both reform and overturn many aspects of the international order. Consequently, China and India often find themselves working together to improve representation at international organizations and create parallel structures even as they seek different substantive outcomes on such issues as freedom of navigation and overflight, internet governance, and the sustainable financing of infrastructure.

The emerging international order will likely include elements of a unipolar, bipolar, and multipolar world, states competing for influence across domains and regions even as they work through international institutions and regional coalitions. At the same time, questions about the future international order will revolve primarily around the relative power and orientation of the United States and China. A multipolar world is less stable than the alternatives. It involves more actors, and one actor shifting could upset the overall balance of power. However, for India, multipolarity would provide a way to secure its national interests without deferring to either the United States or China.

CHALLENGES FOR THE FUTURE INTERNATIONAL ORDER

The international order can be parsed into three elements. The first is the governance of the global commons, or domains outside the control of any single sovereign state. This extends to the management of international waters, the atmosphere, outer space, polar regions, and by some definitions cyberspace. The second is the governance of economic and trade exchanges between states. This could include multilateral lending, trade, immigration, regulations and standards, infrastructure financing, energy security, and international financial management. The third (and oldest) element of international order is the management of peace and security, including through arms control, international legal conventions, confidence-building measures, information exchanges, and military alliances and partnerships.

Achieving these objectives governing the global commons, facilitating economic exchanges, and managing international security has required numerous agreements, treaties, conventions, and international institutions. For example, managing the global commons required the UN Convention on the Law of the Sea (UNCLOS), the Paris Agreement, the Antarctic Treaty System, and the Outer Space Treaty. The World Trade Organization (WTO), the World Bank, the International Monetary Fund (IMF), the International Organization for Standardization, the Group of Twenty (G20), and many other such institutions support the international economic order. The security order has been based on the UN Security Council, Nuclear Nonproliferation Treaty (NPT), and alliances such as the North Atlantic Treaty Organization (NATO), among a multitude of bilateral, regional, and international agreements.

Of these three concepts, global governance has evolved the most since the end of the Cold War. UNCLOS has been imposed, an international climate change agreement has been finalized, and other such institutions have been strengthened. However, these agreements are under increasing stress, including from the world's second most powerful country, China. China has claimed territory in the South China Sea, tested anti-satellite systems at high altitudes, developed potential dual-use facilities in Antarctica, and created the Great Firewall to limit internet access. Of course, the United States has not helped matters either, failing to ratify UNCLOS and withdrawing from the Paris Agreement on climate change.

In speed and scale, China's rise and, to a lesser degree, India's, is without precedent. In U.S. dollars, the proportion of gross domestic product (GDP) between the United States, the big three European economies (France, Germany, and the United Kingdom), Japan, India, and China in 2000 was roughly 20–10–10–1–3. By 2018, it was 8–4–2–1–5. If the change between 2008 and 2018 is sustained for another decade, by 2028 it would be roughly 4–2–1–1–6. A great leveling of global economic power if not diplomatic and military strength is underway.

The international economic order faces obstacles, most notably stagnation at the WTO, both the Doha Development Round of negotiations and the hollowing out of dispute-resolution mechanisms. Moreover, in the absence of reform of the Bretton Woods institutions, China, India, and others have begun to create parallel structures. These include the Asian Infrastructure Investment Bank (AIIB) and the New Development Bank, which was created by Brazil, Russia, India, China, and South Africa (BRICS). The G20 parallels the Group of Seven, which once represented the world's seven largest economies. The international economic architecture is evolving to reflect the changing balance of power.

The greatest stagnation, however, concerns the international security order. Most associated institutions from the UN Security Council and NPT to NATO are relics of the Cold War. They reflect the priorities and power differentials of the 1940s or 1960s, and make decreasing sense today. The transition from the Cold War to the post–Cold War period was unusual in that it occurred without a major international conflict, which, though desirable, also limited opportunities to reset the international security order. More than any other area, the international security order of today is anachronistic. It can no longer dampen security competition, particularly in the Indo-Pacific and the Middle East.

THE RISK OF GREAT POWER CONFLICT

The risk of great power conflict increases in a multipolar world in which multilateralism is undermined, bypassed, or disregarded. Optimists could argue that the absence of overt great power conflict in the Cold War and immediate post–Cold War periods was made possible by the presence of nuclear deterrents, economic interdependence facilitated by globalization, and greater socialization and acculturation. In terms that international relations theorists understand, these broadly reflect realist, liberal, and constructivist explanations.

However, reasons to doubt the continuing validity of each of these factors in preserving peace between the great powers are sound. First, new technologies risk overturning the offense-defense balance to which the world has become accustomed. Shortened decision making times enabled by artificial intelligence and hypersonic weapons are already being combined with low-risk offensive capabilities enabled by cyber technologies and robotic warfare. Second, the limits of the pacifying effects of economic integration are already being exposed. Russia was willing to suffer major economic losses, including from energy exports to Europe, to annex Crimea. Pakistan has continued to perpetrate low-level conflict against India despite suffering mightily in economic terms. Third, a documented rise of nationalism in many major power countries risks reversing the integration and interdependence of states and the priorities of national leaderships. These trends, coupled with emerging multipolarity and an anachronistic security order, suggest the risk of great power conflict is higher than it has been since the end of World War II.

In sum, India is likely to face considerable adversity as it continues its rise. The notion of international order confronts major obstacles: an erosion of the governance of the global commons, competing economic structures, and vestigial security institutions. The drivers of great power competition, including low-risk and potent offensive weaponry, shifting cost-benefit considerations, and growing nationalism, are gradually supplanting drivers of great power cooperation nuclear deterrence, economic interdependence, and social exchanges. India cannot afford to be marginalized. Thus, even as India will seek a multipolar order one in which it has a seat and a say at the global high table it will also seek stronger multilateral arrangements to mitigate competition and instability.

ADDRESSING THE CHALLENGE

To successfully prevent and mitigate future conflict, other major powers will need to understand the compulsions driving China and India, the largest rising powers that express both common and divergent approaches to the international order. To better represent the changing balance of power, China and India each desire to increase their stakes in existing multilateral institutions. In the absence of such reform, they have cooperated to establish parallel institutional structures. Thus, they work together on climate negotiations, including at the Copenhagen Summit, within BRICS, at the AIIB, and on certain issues, such as the responsibility to protect, at the United Nations.

At the same time, China and India seek different outcomes on many issues. India's tepid support for a multilateral approach to internet governance, its more vocal backing for freedom of navigation and overflight, and its obdurate boycott of the Belt and Road Initiative on normative grounds signal a sharpening of differences with China. These differences arise in part because India is a democratic polity and China is not; their approaches to global governance are an outgrowth of their contrasting approaches to domestic governance. India has positioned itself as a status quo power. China is perceived as revisionist. These differences have roots in how both states were established: India became independent in a nonviolent struggle and the People's Republic of China was established as the culmination of a revolutionary movement. These factors perhaps explain why many observers tend to either conflate China and India, and in the process overlook the sharpening differences in behavior and outlook, or contrast the two, but express surprise about their cooperation at international institutions.

Managing this apparent paradox will require the established powers the United States, Europe, and, on some issues, Japan, Russia, and even China to make room for others while defending and upholding the norms that have served the international system so well since the end of the Cold War. However, established powers are unlikely to be comfortable with this approach given that they are naturally mistrustful of the behavior of rising powers and seek to protect their privileges and securities. As a result, the prospect of UN Security Council, IMF, NPT, or Asian Development Bank reforms remains remote.

The best that can be hoped for under these circumstances is for India and like-minded states to better manage the impulses of revisionist great powers. A few principles, if adhered to, would help manage such revisionism. First, these states should establish rules of reciprocity so that authoritarian states cannot take advantage of democratic openness without opening themselves up further. This could extend, for example, to investment regimes, openness to media, intellectual property, and educational and research and development cooperation. Second, these states should place a premium on economic sustainability and the mutual benefits of growth, which in turn will require restructuring trade and technology arrangements. Today, the role of sovereign states has created a distortive effect in market economies. A more level economic playing field will be necessary to sustain the economic dimensions of the international order. Third, these states should invest in military preparedness, particularly military technologies that can play a defensive or denial role, to resist territorial revisionism and mitigate competition. As part of this effort, these states should also initiate a new round of arms control arrangements to address a host of lethal emerging technologies. Overall, India and other like-minded states should manage a multipolar world by establishing and enforcing multilateral agreements to foster new norms and thereby revitalize, not replace, the international order.

China

Qingguo Jia

Recent tensions in China-U.S. relations appear to support the claim that the post–World War II international order is coming to an end. In its place is a return to the great power rivalry and beggar-thy-neighbor competition that characterized the pre–World War I era. Careful analysis, however, shows that the postwar order is in no way over. Instead, it is evolving. Despite serious challenges and innate problems, it will persist as long as the great powers and others pursue necessary reforms to accommodate their respective interests while also taking care of those of others. All countries would benefit from sticking to the prevailing international order and making it work.

THE ORIGINS OF THE CURRENT INTERNATIONAL ORDER

Emerging from World War II as the preeminent world power, the United States was instrumental in creating a new international order, primarily because it realized that shaping the rules, norms, and institutions of the new era would protect its global interests. Maintaining world order is, however, a costly business. As Paul Kennedy describes in his book The Rise and Fall of the Great Powers, great powers decline not because rising powers defeat them but because the cost of maintaining world order drains their resources. To avoid or postpone this, the United States did three things in the wake of World War II: preserved and enhanced its wartime system of military alliances, established a UN centered group of international institutions and mechanisms, and developed partnerships with other countries. Through these efforts, the United States effectively enlisted others to help maintain world order at minimal cost.

But ensuring that help entailed costs and constraints for the United States. These included providing and coordinating initiatives for international action; abiding by the rules and norms of various institutions, occasionally even at the expense of perceived U.S. interests; and dealing generously with allies and partners, including burden sharing within alliance arrangements and allowing access to markets. At times, the costs have seemed excessive to American voters, leading to demands for more contributions from others. However, successive U.S. administrations, until that of Donald J. Trump, had decided that the benefits out-weighed the costs and largely maintained the arrangement. In retrospect, the United States has benefited tremendously from such practices. Most telling, it has remained the preeminent global power for seven decades, despite the challenges of the Cold War and its aftermath.

THE ORDER IN CRISIS

This international order is now in serious trouble. The United States' willingness to maintain world order has significantly declined, particularly under the Trump administration. Although every previous U.S. president put U.S. interests first in foreign policy, the Trump administration has gone much further both in rhetoric and action often at the expense of other countries and, in the long run, of the United States. Moreover, it has turned away from its leadership responsibilities in world affairs and even taken actions that have undermined existing international institutions, including withdrawing from the UN Educational, Scientific, and Cultural Organization (UNESCO), the Trans-Pacific Partnership, and the Paris Agreement on climate change. The Trump administration has also challenged World Trade Organization (WTO) rules by taking unilateral actions against other countries on trade disputes. Although this is, not the first time the United States has pursued its interests at the expense of others or defied international institutions, the breadth and scope of the Trump administration's actions are categorically different. Given the pivotal role the United States plays in maintaining the world order, it can inflict significant damage and has done so.

The capacity of Western countries, which have been the strongest supporters of the current world order, to maintain that order has also declined sharply, especially since the end of the Cold War. Statistics show that the share of the world's gross domestic product of Group of Seven (G7) countries the United States, Canada, France, Germany, Italy, Japan, and the United Kingdom dropped from 68 percent in 1992 to 47 percent in 2015. It dropped again to 30.15 percent in 2018 and is projected to go down to 27.26 percent in 2023. Although the decline in military capabilities is more moderate, North Atlantic Treaty Organization (NATO) spending has also shrunk from two-thirds of global defense spending to little more than half in 2017. On top of this, the Trump administration's America First policy has strained the unity of the West. Since the end of World War II, the West's ability to maintain the world order has never been weaker.

Other major countries have become increasingly dissatisfied and frustrated with existing international arrangements as well. Russia begrudges NATO expansion; India is unhappy with the perceived inadequate international recognition of its status as a great power; and China is frustrated that its voice and interests have not received due to attention and respect. Those countries and others are seeking a change in the current international arrangement. China's efforts to assert its interests receive the most attention. As the leading rising power, China has created a number of initiatives to improve international cooperation, most notably through the Asian Infrastructure Investment Bank and the Belt and Road Initiative. These demands, given the sharply increased capabilities of the countries making them, have also strained the extant world order. For those and other reasons, the postwar world order is facing an unprecedented crisis.

PROBLEMS WITH THE EXISTING INTERNATIONAL ORDER

Some countries have lamented its decline, but the post–World War II order does have real problems. First, in the absence of effective checks against it, the United States has operated as the indispensable and for many years undisputed leader. This status has allowed it to abuse its power, at times even at the expense of its own interests as well as those of others, despite its professed good intentions. Washington has not always been prudent in conducting foreign policy, as evidenced by its decision to fight wars in Iraq and Vietnam, withdraw from international organizations, initiate trade wars despite WTO rules, and drag its feet in reforming international institutions. Power corrupts. This applies not only to domestic politics but also to international politics.

Second, the existing world order is excessively West-centric. Although Western countries do advocate certain worthy values, they do not have the right to dictate what other countries should do in their pursuit of political stability and economic development. Because every country faces a unique set of circumstances at home, the Western model does not always apply. That few developing countries have made it into the rank of developed countries over the past seven decades, despite the West's tremendous efforts from a position of strength to impose Western models, shows that this model has real problems in catering to the needs of developing countries.

Third, although the U.S.-led system of military alliances has been useful in helping, maintain peace and stability, it is also exclusive and divisive. By default it divides countries into allies and others. This approach has ensured alienation and suspicion on the part of the others and has provided a fertile ground for zero-sum interactions, making security cooperation difficult if not impossible.

Fourth, the existing economic order attaches considerable importance to efficiency, sacrificing equality. Under this order, the world has made great strides in liberalizing cross-border trade and investment, yielding an era of unprecedented prosperity. However, although a freer market has led to increased efficiency, it has also engendered greater inequality. Calls to address inequality are dismissed as calls for socialism and not taken seriously. Consequently, polarization is increasing both within and between countries, along with anti-globalization protests.

The Future Of World Order

Despite its flaws, the current world order is still the best that humankind has created. Through established institutions, states champion universally accepted values and principles such as sovereignty, nonaggression, nonintervention in the internal affairs of other countries, human rights, rule of law, free trade, and the principle of common and differentiated responsibilities. States generally observe international laws and norms in light of the values and principles espoused by these institutions. Platforms have been created that offer countries an opportunity to air their frustrations with international arrangements and discuss ways and means to address pressing global issues. Another world war has thus far been avoided and unprecedented prosperity has been achieved. As a result, few countries have completely rejected the world order, regardless of any grudges they have against it.

Most nations have a stake in the existing order and are therefore more likely to stick with it. Wealthy countries expect that their wealth will be protected and poor countries expect aid when they are desperate. Both strong and weak states expect international laws and norms to protect their interests, one-way or another. Most concerns are about perceived injustices in the distribution of benefits than about absolute losses. Some countries could be unhappy with a particular piece of an existing international arrangement but have no intention of overthrowing the world order as a whole in favor of a nineteenth-century arrangement (might is right). Thus, despite the U.S. withdrawal from some international institutions, most countries have chosen to stick with the existing order, whether by staying in institutions such as UNESCO and the Universal Postal Union or by observing the Joint Comprehensive Plan of Action and the Paris Agreement on climate change. Even rising powers such as China and India, which feel that the world order has not given their voices and interests adequate attention and respect, call for reform rather than replacement. For example, India wishes to be a permanent member of the UN Security Council and China hopes that its voting shares in the World Bank and International Monetary Fund will increase to reflect its growing economic clout.

Furthermore, although tensions between China and the United States are increasing, they will likely remain limited. Both are nuclear weapons states, both have stakes in the existing order despite unhappiness with aspects of it, and both are more or less interested in maintaining their shared economic relationship. Under these circumstances, neither fighting a war nor decoupling their economies is a realistic option. The relationship could become more competitive, but China and the United States have thus far continued to observe the Code for Unplanned Encounters at Sea in the South China Sea and to negotiate trade agreements, indicating that they know they should find a way to coexist. They are still cooperating on many issues, including pressuring North Korea to give up nuclear weapons, fighting international crimes, ensuring international aviation safety, and dealing with pandemic diseases such as COVID-19. Moreover, most other countries have a vested interest in a stable and constructive relationship between China and the United States and refuse to take sides.

Finally, given the United States' stake in the existing world order and that it can protect its interests only by maintaining that order, Washington will possibly have second thoughts about its current policies. After all, the Trump administration's policies thus far are an exception rather than the rule in post–World War II U.S. activities. A future administration could see things differently and adopt a watered-down version of traditional U.S. foreign policy.

The world order is evolving, but most established institutions and norms will likely remain. The United States will stay a leading power but could be less dominant. The West will continue to play a pivotal role but the world order will likely be less West-centric. When power is more diffuse, the world could be less efficient in addressing global challenges; at the same time, it could also adopt an approach that is more equal and consultative. The rising powers will likely have more power but also more responsibilities. Despite concerns about the decline of world order, countries can choose to transform it for the better.

To turn hope into reality, the major powers, especially China, and the United States, should take up their respective responsibilities. They should resist the temptation to blame each other for the problems of existing institutions. Instead, they should carefully assess these institutions and identify areas that need improvement. They should consult with each other on that basis and jointly find a way to reform the extant international order in a way that accommodates their respective interests without undermining the interests of others. As the COVID-19 pandemic shows, the world is interconnected and mutually dependent. The only way to effectively deal with global issues is to embrace collaboration and cooperation. For a better future, cooperation is not a choice; it is a necessity.

CHAPTER

THE GREAT RESET

"The Great Reset" is the World Economic Forum's term for a world after the pandemic. It is an initiative to establish a new form of capitalism, 'Stakeholder Capitalism', which essentially maintains that corporations have more expansive duties than maximizing profits for shareholders, and that the state has a bigger role to play in the economy. The Great Reset initiative is a call to rethink the world economic system, as long as the existing system has shown many flaws, unleashing one world economic crisis after another, (including the stumbling of many countries in treating the Corona virus). COVID-19 has been the excuse for the Great Reset's argument: The pandemic has exposed the dysfunctionality of existing institutional settings, and (exposed the flaws of neoliberal capitalism); therefore, the world needs an alternate social and economic reality, a major transformation, or Great Reset.

As such, there has been a heated disagreement between the Great Reset and Neoliberalism. As a matter of fact, the authors of the Great Reset (Schwab & Malleret, 2020) have disputed neoliberalism, that has been in place since the late 1970s and until now, and hold it responsible for a number of problems. Over the past fifteen years, the cracks in neoliberal capitalism have been increasingly evident, including the financial collapse, wage stagnation and antilabor practices, sexual discrimination, corporate personhood, tech monopolization, child labor and a world economy geared to efficiency rather than resilience and sustainability. However, the fault lines that were most commonly circulated by detractors of Neoliberalism were arranged into two main headings:

Inequality in income and wealth, (and extreme poverty): In many institutions, it is not unusual to find that the wage of the CEO is roughly half the number of its employees. In the United States for instance, "the gap between the income of the average CEO and that of the average U.S. worker is 325 to 1" (Boje D. M., 2017). Income gap between the ultra-rich and the other 99 percent has been applied also to states and governments, where wealth in general is concentrated in the hands of a very small number in each country. An Oxfam's report reveals that "42 people hold as much wealth as the 3.7 billion who make up the poorest half of the world's population (Elliott, 2018). Moreover, half of the world population, currently numbering 7.4 billion, live on less than $2.50 a day, and 80 percent live on less than $10 a day.

Neoliberalism has created catastrophic effects on the environment. The onset of melting ice, pollution of the oceans and seas, the disappearance of a great deal of forests, a turbulent and extreme climate (rains in the summer and heat in the winter) are examples of important consequences on the environment that are unsustainable to all nations. Consequently, the global economic system is locked into a pattern of environmental damage, where positive changes and innovations are offset by continued growth of material consumption and pollution. Avoiding this environmental damage and its dramatic consequences requires new ways of thinking and models of production and consumption that reduce pressures on the environment while increasing human wellbeing, social and economic value.

The Great Reset reimagines a radically different global economic system, that actually address global challenges like extreme poverty, inequality and climate change. The paradigmatic core of this reset is a shift from neoliberalism to an interventionist approach, which is complemented by a shift from shareholder to stakeholder management (Roth, The Great Reset. Restratification for Lives, Livelihoods, and the Planet, 2020). The Great Reset agenda would have three main components. The first would steer the market toward fairer outcomes. The second would ensure that investments advance shared goals, such as equality and sustainability. The third priority is to harness the innovations of the Fourth Industrial Revolution to support the public good, especially by addressing health, and social challenges.

So far, the Great Reset has entered the theoretical and intellectual economic arena, and has earned an audience of supporters, as well as enemies and detractors. And while it is being defended by its partisans, it is also being questioned by its detractors. Many voices, so far, have praised the great reset agenda for its potential to make people more receptive to big visions of change. But many also were skeptical of the new form of internet governance, as required by the great reset, which includes developing digital health passports and contact tracing apps, which can be tools for state surveillance. Detractors of the Great Reset warned of the excessive use of high technology, which will give rise to digital dictatorships, that will monitor everyone all the time. Another shortcoming was that Great Reset lacks the capacity to achieve change. Change is urgent, but the Great Reset fails to predict how things should or will change in the future, and fails to offer any specifics as to how the socio-political-economic overhaul could be achieved.

Away from this fray, I can say that the ideas of deliberately causing Great Reset, nurtured by the World Economic Forum initiative, are not new themes in contemporary discussions of social and economic crises. Long ago before COVID-19, there had been many calls to resolve inequality and to develop solutions to the socioeconomic crisis of neoliberal capitalism. Pope Francis has called for new world economic order, criticizing global capitalism. "We want change, real change, structural change," the Pope said, decrying a system that "has imposed the mentality of profit at any price, with no concern for social exclusion or the destruction of nature".

Alternative economic theories to prevent and manage economic crises and unemployment in advanced capitalist economies, have been found in a number of colloquium presentations, books published, and papers gathered by editors since several decades. Klaus Schwab himself, the mastermind of the 'Great Reset', has been calling for transforming the world economic order since 1971. I do not know how serious Klaus's calls for a new economic order was, but I know and I have heard a number of renewed academics and liberal economists, (long before the outbreak of COVID-19), offering strong critiques of neoliberal/finance capitalism, postulating the fading or even tumultuous demise of neoliberal capitalism, and calling for reflections and major actions to avoid an economic and social meltdown in the countries that intensely experience the effects of Neoliberalism (Boje D. M., 2017), I have heard my teachers, Europe's most educated scholars of management and economics, blaming neoliberal capitalism for destroying and distorting all other forms of capitalism, proposing a viable alternative, and developing solutions to the socioeconomic crisis of global capitalism. One such solution to the socioeconomic crisis of global capitalism, that preceded the announcement of the Great Reset, is present in the work of Henri Savall on a fresh form of capitalism: The Socially Responsible Capitalism.

The Theory Of Socially Responsible Capitalism (Src)

The SRC is a new form of capitalism, an alternative to prevailing macro-economic theories associated with neoliberalism and global capitalism. It is a viable and pertinent alternative to the contemporary economy, offering an alternative understanding of what is possible in capitalism, supporting a socially responsible capitalism. The socially and sustainably responsible capitalism is the theoretical and practical framework of the socio-economic theory of companies and organizations (SEAM); a framework that reconciles the two levels of analysis that have been excessively differentiated: the company and the social and economic environment.

The authors of the SRC were strongly inspired by the economic thoughts and the pioneering works of the

Spanish economist, Germán Bernácer (1883-1965) (Savall, Péron, Zardet, & Bonnet, 2017). Drawn from European economic thought, and developed by Henri Savall, the prominent French scholar at IAE Lyon, Université Jean Moulin in France, Socially Responsible Capitalism (SRC) is not an ideological approach that corresponds to the spirit of globally financialized neoliberalism or a post-Keynesianism that has been on the rise in some academic circles. Rather, since its foundation in 1979, the SRC objective has been to touch the deepest roots of economic problems, and define and build a macroeconomic framework that allows companies and organizations to improve economic and social performance. The SRC model aims at reengineering the economy and stimulate domestic production through the development of human potential.

The "Socially" segment is not to be confused with Socialism. The "Socially" element of the model instead refers to maintaining good working conditions. "SRC does consider the private property of the means of production means as well as the responsibility for the public policies to orchestrate the production of goods and services, to create necessary infrastructures and regulate their utilization. It recognizes democratically elected public powers, an eminent role in stimulating health, education, security, justice, and solidarity practices arbitrage".

The SRC is a synthesis of usual theories of economic thought, and includes elements common to other economic ideologies. It can be compared with other economic models, as "third ways" of capitalism (between laissez-faire economic liberalism and socialist economics), including Tony Blair's Third Way, French dirigisme, the Dutch polder model, the Nordic model, Japanese corporate capitalism, and the contemporary Chinese model.

The main elements of the SRC model are the followings:

- It approaches economic growth from a human resource perspective.
- It reconciles the two levels of analysis: The micro and the macro- economic framework.
- It proposes an innovative management techniques and tools (SEAM management) that allows companies and organizations to improve economic and social performance.
- The SRC economic model provides a dramatic and useful contrast to the rentier economic model.

Like all other economic theories, the SRC is questioned by its detractors and defended by its partisans. COVID-19, and the novel way of working (teleworking, working from home), challenged some philosophical and practical premises of SRC (SEAM) managing and leadership approach. The SRC (SEAM) management philosophy is subject to many questions about the relevance of its management approach to the working from home model (WfH). SRC (SEAM) management approach is about human interaction, connectivity, communication, sharing, and this is far more difficult or impossible with a virtual working environment. Another shortcoming is the narrow and limited perspective of the macro economic framework of the SRC. The SRC (SEAM) approach has focused on the question of corporate responsibility, which has already been widely researched and investigated, but not to concentrate on the somewhat neglected issue of the financial instruments, mechanisms and institutions that hold the keys to such socially responsible capitalism.

SRC VS GREAT RESET: OLD WINE IN NEW BOTTLE

The objective of this section (of this opinion paper), is to show that there are points of convergence in the agendas of the SRC and the Great Reset. As a matter of fact, the underlying principles of the SRC carries traces of the fundamental specifications of the Great Reset. The ideas of the Great Reset initiative are barely any smarter than the underlying principles of the SRC theory.

Income inequality

One objective of the Great Reset initiative is to force a more equitable distribution of global resources; to encourage companies to play a clear, responsible and specific role towards society and future generations. Reseters want an end to the profit-at-all-costs mentality. The idea of equitable wealth distribution has been trending for quite some time. It is, therefore, not new to scholars with backgrounds in a broad scope of discipline from management science and economics. In other words, the idea is not precisely unpopular in business and economics studies either.

With a similar outlook, The SRC prioritizes people over profit, and incorporates wealth redistribution in its socio-economic management. Under the pretext of SEAM management approach, corporate decisions are made in negotiation with labor and community stakeholders, in order to close the gap between the 1 percent and the 99 percent living on what is left over.

To address the problem of income inequality, the SRC proposes to change organizations, through socio-economic interventions in the way corporations operate, and in curbing the runaway speculative (gambler) markets. The SRC refutes the common belief that the sole purpose of work is profit; work is to serve employees and society as well as owners. Therefore, the SRC model challenges common premises of traditional business and management, that focuses solely on the profit. By employing SEAM management, the SCR helps to grow socially responsible organizations, that develop their people, contribute to the society, and bring together profit-oriented capitalism and care for human beings.

The Role Of The State

The Great Reset calls for "fairer outcomes" and the redirection of investment towards a more "sustainable future". And in order to do that, the state will have a bigger role to play in the economy. This means that instead of leaving the market completely to the rules of supply and demand, the state has to intervene, takes some taxes from the rich and spends them in the form of education, health care programs, and social insurance for the poor. Funds need to be invested in people for long-term jobs.

According to the World Economic Forum website, the Great Reset is an attempt to reassert the authority of governments over capitalism, and to make some kind of control so that life goes on. Klaus Schwab, one of the architect of the Great Reset, considers that to build a better society, we will require stronger and more effective governments. This proposal (bigger role for the state) logically found support from politicians, who found their role enhanced as a result. The magnitude of the current economic crisis, and citizen strong fears, justified the relevance of government intervention. Thanks to COVID-19, Keynes' propositions of a Welfare State that can help poor, and defenseless citizens found a favorable echo and a strong reception. We saw governments favoring the emergency call for the "Interventionist State", rolling out stimulus measures, to support businesses, households and the economy.

This proposal raises serious concerns about the future of freedom and democracy and it is believed to threaten Western society and the "liberal" economy. As a matter of fact, the return to a planned, centralized economy might be dangerous for political democracy. The state has an irreplaceable role to play in the development of socially responsible capitalism. But the SRC proposes a viable and dynamic role for the state in the economy, calling for more radical and more durable economic and financial policies than vain monetary manipulations or ineffective gesticulations. The state's role is carried out through its sovereign missions integrated into the reflexes of everyday life and the recurring operation of the economic and social systems. The servitude of the state mainly lies on the principle of a state which is respectful of the individual and private, associative and public social decentralized groups. "SRC is opposed to centralized forms of planned, distant, and bureaucratic management practices that control economic and social activities, sanctioned by history such as political, military or popular dictatorships". The state, in socially responsible capitalism, ensures the respect of everyone, in terms of freedom, dignity, and personal or collective development.

The method for achieving the state's mission is by democratic dialog, and in the frame of a hybrid economy system. SEAM concept of cognitive interactivity is an essential principle of social responsibility, which is based on the fact that all the actors from all over the company should have their say in the decision-making or implementation process, in the vicinity of their local territory. As well, the Socially Responsible Capitalism offers a new form of democracy, which is a non-elective democracy, that has to be lived and built every day in the reality of human relationships. As a matter of fact, the concept of daily and proximity democracy (which an element of SEAM management), contributes to, and reinforce both practical and political democracy.

Sustainability And Sustainable Development

There is an overwhelming global trend towards sustainability in almost every economic sector. But it is important to know that integrating sustainability and sustainable development into economic sector is something not new. Various efforts were being conducted already, and the Great Rest initiative "is a rebranded, tightened-up version of the UN's decades-old "Sustainable Development" agenda ("Agenda 21"). The same policies and ideas are contained in "The Green New Deal," which was defeated in 2019 in the US Congress". The Great Reset encourages one to think about policy frameworks to deal with both people and the planet; to design policies to align with investment in people and the environment.

The SRC likens sustainable development to a long-term metamorphosis; the development of sustainability is built on the internal organizational energies, and it takes place inside the enterprise. "Sustainably responsible capitalism energizes everybody the individual, team, company, territorial organization (local, regional, national, and international) through the decentralized creation of companies, associations, jobs, products (goods and services), artistic activities, and cultural and spiritual activities". The notion of sustainability, in socially responsible capitalism, is intrinsic to the notion of individual and collective responsibility. This latter should not be ephemeral and has to be maintained by day-to-day practices, in the proximity of actors.

The authors of Socially Responsible Capitalism, address the problems of unsustainability, and they start with fundamental socioeconomic reform of companies, government agencies and nonprofit organizations. They assume that a new form of organization is possible, one that builds the human potential of workers and incentivizes workers to achieve innovation and efficiency, while developing sustainable strategies. The authors of Socially Responsible Capitalism start from fundamental reforms of socioeconomic practices of companies and propose to curtail runaway speculation markets that have all but drained productive markets of their capacity to build viable companies capable of anything like sustainable business practices.

The socially responsible capitalism refuses the destruction of the environment. But we must not create regulatory shackles that demotivate management and damage our entrepreneurial activities. In other words, we must not be allowed to "kill the goose that laid the golden egg". Environmental concerns should not lead to speculation or corruption and then forgetting our entrepreneurship model but on the contrary, one must answer to the challenge of these environmental dramas by taking into account the innovative spirit that belongs only to humankind. The SRC maintains that policies must prioritize planet over profit. But there should be a balance between the necessity to foster an entrepreneurial risk-taking environment to create a vibrant economy and the need for a balanced yet rigorous regulatory environment. For if we want to ensure a vibrant economy, we must not reduce the business community's appetite for risk and enterprise. Everything possible must be done to prevent the regulatory environment from becoming a burden that causes managements and boards to retain lawyers and accountants to oversee their activities curtailing their enthusiasm for growth and willingness to take appropriate risk. Finally, I think that with a global consensus emerging on the need to collectively address the challenges posed by climate change, there is a heightened need to proactively apply ecological policies to reap the benefits and complete the transition to a green economy. Such transition is an opportunity to create high quality jobs in emerging sectors, and to build resilience against the adverse impact of climate-related events, which disproportionately affect those already at risk.

The Place And Importance Of Technology

The third priority on the agenda of The Great Reset is to permeate digital technology in every aspect of citizens' life. As we entered the Fourth Industrial Revolution, plainly both business and industry have moved profoundly to more virtual and distant operations. Moreover, working from home has brought about a lot higher dependence on technology for many people. In the SRC, technology is not end in itself. The legitimacy of technology is proved when it serves humanity because this is its raison d'être. Socially responsible capitalism favors the mastering of technology. But it proposes a human-centered rewiring of the relationships between the individual and the technology-driven corporate world. It maintains that humanity and technology are not in conflict and it emphasis the importance of remaining human in a technology-driven world. In this regard, human concerns are not separate from technological advances at all, but integral for organizations looking to capture the full value of the technologies they've put in place.

The New Path Forward

COVID-19 can pave the way for major transformation processes in the world economic order. But the biggest question put forward is how? What transformation we may experience in the coming period? What are some of the milestones of the new world economy?

The author of this paper attempts to extrapolate what lies ahead from three angles:

1. The author resorts to economic lessons gleaned from historical pandemics to help grasp what lies ahead.
2. The author uses the SRC theory as a basis for identifying some elements better suited to new form of capitalism.
3. The development of guidelines for a new global economy was reinforced by the professional and academic experience of the author of this paper.

Augmentation Of The Importance Of Human Potential

The first assumption better suited to the needs of future economies is that:

In the post-pandemic era, and more than ever before, human capital will continue to be the most important factor, the primary factor, that creates economic value. Firms will be under pressure to pay less attention to shareholders and more to workers. This premise is partially derived from economic lessons gleaned from historical pandemics.

The history of previous epidemics shows that there were always gains on the human resources side, at the expense of fixed capital. The Black Death that ravaged Europe from 1347 to 1351, workers discovered for the first time in their life that the power to change things was in their hands. Barely a year after the epidemic had subsided, textile workers in Saint-Omer (a small city in northern France) demanded and received successive wage rises. Two years later, many workers' guilds negotiated shorter hours and higher pay, sometimes as much as a third more than their pre-plague level. Similar but less extreme examples of other pandemics point to the same conclusion: labor gains in power to the detriment of capital.

The above-mentioned premise is also based on the SRC focal tenet of putting human beings at the heart of action to enable the production of sustainable economic value. The pandemic had an impact on the journey of sustainability. The deep disruption caused by COVID-19 globally has offered societies an enforced pause to reflect on what is true of value and sustainable. Changing course will require a shift in the mindset of business and economic leaders, to make the kind of institutional changes and policy choices that will put sustainable deployment on a new path towards greater focus and priority on the well-being of all citizens, where the notion of development of human potential evolves. One implication of COVID-19 is to hear statements that institutions and territories need to do more with less. In the future, converting intangible assets to tangible results necessitates an innovative way of management thinking and requires a macro mechanism, which revolves around the optimization of human resource potential.

Measurement Of Hidden Cost Of Economic Activity – Measurement Of Value-Added Destruction

Another assumption better suited to the needs of future economies is that:

The measurement and the monitoring of the determinants of value creation, including the human resources, will be a driver for the true health of the future economies. The GDP indicator is incomplete and erroneous, because it only considers a limited view of value creation. It disregards the value potentially destroyed through certain types of economic activity. It omits the value created through work carried out in the household. Certain types of financial products, which through their inclusion in GDP are captured as value creating, are merely shifting value from one place to another or sometimes even have the effect of destroying it.

For these reasons, Klaus Schwab has been calling in his new Book for an updated GDP that reflects the real situation of the economic reality. And the reality here means the value-added destruction, waste, hidden costs. (Schwab & Malleret, 2020). The true health of an economy will need to be better measured and monitored, including the determinants of productivity, such as human capital and innovation ecosystems, which are critical for the overall strength of a system. Furthermore, the capital reserves upon which a country can draw in times of crisis, including human capital will need to be tracked systematically.

The SRC theory is very relevant in this regard. "In matter of economic policy, the main issue for socio-economic theory is helping to explain macroeconomic performance, by focusing on each citizen's responsibility in national economic value creation" (Buono & Savall, 2015). The academic and practitioner efforts, by ISEOR, to create a measurement framework for the value of human capital, can be praised in this regard.

Indeed, ISEOR's research focuses on misused human potential, (unemployed, under-employed or over-employed) insofar as such a state of affairs leads to relationship conflicts and sources of value losses whatever the organization typology studied, and entails a plethora of hidden costs. ISEOR's research team has created an indicator called the hourly contribution to value-added on variable costs (HCVAVC). The objective of this indicator is the measurement of human capital and the factors which contribute to the sustainable development of human capital through time.

This economic productivity indicator is different from physical productivity because it measures the individual responsibility in value creation. This indicator takes into account not only the physical productivity from all the actors and support functions, but also of the negotiation ability of the company within its environment. This global productivity indicator of an organization measures effectiveness and efficiency of human potential (HP) which, all things being equal, constitutes the primary value creation factor, composed of human energy, competencies, and behaviors.

The HCVAVC could be qualified as nano-GDP because it is measuring the individual contribution of a person to his own prosperity, to his company's prosperity, and his own nation. The GDP and HCVAVC isomorphism shines the spotlight on the link between the person, the organization, and the national territory by focusing on different scales of economic responsibility. Two studies, within the context of ISEOR's academic and practitioner efforts, can be inspirational to see concrete method to measure value-added from a macroeconomic perspective. The first one by (ABJEAN, BONNET, ROCHAT, & SALMERON, 2017), that demonstrates the monetary value of the Intangible Investments in Qualitative Development of Human Potential (IIDQPH), by setting up socio-economic dashboards and tested it, using the ISEOR qualimetric research-intervention method in two examples of integration structures in the Lyon region. The second study was an evaluation in monetary value the hidden performance, and the unrealized human potential in the technology and innovation sector in Lebanon.

Humanizing Technology

Without a doubt, the use the use of technologies and digitization in operations will increase. However, there is a significant challenge related to the extending reach of technology into our lives: overuse and ill-use of technology.

For optimal output, the following premise might be relevant:

Adapting the workforce to the requirements of automation, digitization, and other technologies. During lockdowns, technology emerged as an inevitable reality. Many of the tech behaviors that we were adopted during confinement will through familiarity become more natural. Moreover, the demand of robots, machine learning, internet of things, big data, artificial intelligence, augmented reality, and all similar new digital tools and technologies will be more prominent for the quality of life and well-being of the individual. COVID-19 showed that technology can augment work, but it does not replace what is needed, from humans.

The belief that the basis for an increase in productivity is to be found in mechanization and automation betrays a pessimistic view of human ability. Robots have shown their performance, if work is not organized along lines that make for much greater human involvement. Organizations will have an opportunity to push the envelope in the ways they integrate teams of humans and technology. Organizations shall evolve their thinking about technology from taking a purely substitution view (replacing humans with technology) to using technology as an augmentation or collaboration strategy. The latter view can allow organizations to not only streamline costs, but to also create value and ultimately, provide meaning to the workforce as a whole. Technologies will continue to be necessary for the success of organizations.

However, humans and technology will be more powerful together than either can be on their own.

Controlling Infodemic And Building Trust

In tomorrow's world, the concept of societal trust will be more-timely, because building trust will bring progress and prosperity. One implication of the existing ecosystem is the proliferation of fake news, misinformation, disinformation, and alternative facts. The proliferation of fake news is contributing to mistrust of the media also. In the past, before the pandemic, people chose media that reinforced their views among the most trusted; however, today with the lack of quality information and the challenges of misinformation and disinformation, trust in all news sources, including both traditional and social media, has hit record lows. People are viewing media as biased and unethical, and instead of promoting democracy, social media is undermining it.

This "epidemic of misinformation," has fueled a culture of institutional mistrust. Trust across institutions was broken, and people quit trusting societal structures. Trust is a foundation for financial prosperity. Scholars have found that it is unimaginable for countries to prosper without trust since it is the powerhouse for economic development. The economist J. Arrow once wrote, "Virtually every commercial transaction has within itself an element of trust [and] ... much of the economic backwardness in the world can be explained by the lack of mutual confidence". Building trust cannot be a single act. This will require a more adjusted trust balance between businesses and governments. In addition, media should be required to modify its image as the "arbitrator of truth." It is important of rebuilding the world's social and economic systems with more equity. Building "trust equity" in governments, in the economic system and among citizens, can be achieved by making institutions worthy of trust. The battle for trust will be fought on the field of ethical behavior, such as media autonomy, its relationship with capital, level of governance, ethical codes and sphere of influence, which have been increasingly questioned in recent years.

Creative Destruction Vs. Building Without Destruction

Global capitalism favored creative destruction over government intervention and economic growth over social welfare. But in 2020 the process of creative destruction did, not take place in the typical manner. The new economic system might favor the SRC entrepreneur over the Schumpeterian entrepreneur of creative destruction. The SRC model proposes the entrepreneur, who is doing start-ups and building industry after industry. This is not the Schumpeterian entrepreneur of creative destruction but rather a purveyor of the continuous improvement of human potential. The Schumpeterian model of entrepreneurship incorporates conflict, discord, demolition, undermining, and challenge, while the SRC's model raises the status of communication, unity and harmony that entrepreneurs may need to innovate and create new solutions. And the use of these values does not diminish their potential for achievement, creativity and innovation?

The SRC "propose a framework based on a socially, economically and sustainably responsible regenerated capitalism, built on an entrepreneurship spirit, tending to behavioral exemplarity that emphasizes social responsibility" (Buono & Savall, 2015). The SRC entrepreneurs use their dreams and passions as fuel to create extraordinary value for customers, team members, suppliers, society and investors for the whole gamut of stakeholders.

The Dynamic And Viable Role Of The State
— Rethinking the role of the state the epidemic has made the state playing a conservative role, and this has been particularly clear in the supportive and recovery measures taken by the public authorities. But welfare pension and aid programs are insufficient and surely unsustainable in the long run. Governments which attempt to bolster social safety nets and support businesses found that these efforts may not be enough to build for the future in unprecedented times. It is therefore necessary to have a social ideology that is in the direction of public policies of investment, productivity, education, employment and living wages that give substantivity to a social justice regime. The mission of the state, as created by the SRC theory is very relevant in this regard. One aspect of a state's purpose, in the SRC, is to contribute to the smooth operation of society as a whole. The principle of solidarity is at the heart of this mission, and define the scope of business responsibilities in the long term. Another aspect of the state's mission in SRC is that development planning cannot be a purely intellectual or technical exercise. This is apparent in the concept of decentralized synchronization, where the political authority must be closely involved in the definition of development objectives and in the selection of methods of implementation. Here the involvement of all parties concerned is paramount and decentralized planning should be organized in such a way as to involve all the actors.

Part of this robustness, as suggest by the SRC, will be achieved through bigger government interventions in the functioning of the economic system and social dynamics.

Globalization Vs. Nationalism

In difficult times like these, it is crucial to ask the hard questions. Even if the answers haven't been found yet. Is COVID-19 going to push the global economy toward more globalization or localization? In my opinion, globalization is in flux, and in 2020, we witnessed the partial retreat from globalization and the rising of nationalism. Every nation is trying to move towards certain forms of self-sufficiency, and a reduction in global output. The stagnation of globalization means that more multinationals will have to operate as federations of national businesses and will be unable to reap the full efficiency gains from being run as a single globally integrated organization.

And as the size of government expands everywhere locally, the levels of regulation and taxes will inevitably rise. Each state will be striving to serve the interests of its population before planning to support other countries in need. Separating the "national" from the "international" is impossible in the global economy. Every action even if its motive is "national" will have universal effects, and I think this is the key to understand what is happening today between China and America.

CHAPTER

What Is Digital Transformation?

Digital transformation is the use of new and fast changing digital technology to transform business activities, competencies, and business models. Virtually all modern electronics, such as computers and mobile phones, are digital i.e., they use information in the form of numeric code. Due to the widespread use of digital technology in our daily lives, the term "digital transformation" is often used interchangeably with "technological advancement". Many of the most visible new technologies are based on or intertwined with digital platforms, such as Google's search engine, the social platforms of Facebook or Twitter.

The digital transformation of the banking industry can be broadly summarized in two dimensions: technologies utilized and services impacted. Some popular technologies that have been used in the banking industry include the cloud, artificial intelligence (AI), big data analytics, blockchain, mobile technology, and robo advisors. Meanwhile, banking services affected include payments, lending, asset management, and communication. For example, an increasing number of banks are migrating to cloud technology to reduce onsite infrastructure management, AI-powered chat boxes that mimic human conversation and messaging applications are currently being tested to replace the unpopular call centers, and robot advisory platforms are being developed to provide consumers asset management solutions, which are often cheaper with transparent cost structures.

The History of Digital Transformation: How have Banks Performed?

Digital technology has evolved alongside the development of the computer and the internet. The shift to digital technology from mechanical and analogue electronic technology started as early as the 1940s and led to the adoption of digital computers and digital record keeping. In the 1970s, the home computer was introduced, but it was not used widely until the 1990s. While only 8 percent of U.S. households owned a personal computer in 1984, by 2000, 51 percent of U.S. households owned a computer. In the same period, the internet, developed in the 1960s and 1970s, became one of the most prominent applicatios of digital technology. Wider internet usage, however, did not happen until the 2000s, once computers had become a common household appliance. In late 2005, the internet was used by a population reached one billion. Another key development in diffusing digital technology has been the rapid rise of mobile technology. Over the past decade, mobile devices such as smart phones and tablets have replaced the use of computers. By the end of 2010, 3 billion people worldwide were using cellphones, and by 2015, tablet computers and smartphones had exceeded personal computers in internet usage. The wide-spread use of mobile devices and intrinsic advantages of a global network has led to an explosion of mobile-based innovations influencing all aspects of human lives. One prominent example is mobile-based payments.

As digital technology has advanced, banks have often been leaders in adopting these new technologies. Citibank installed the first ATM machine in 1977, but customers only started using ATMs on a regular basis in the 1980s. Similarly, online banking was piloted in the 1980s by Chemical Bank but was not used widely until the 2000s with more widespread internet usage. However, banks' leadership in adopting newer technologies has weakened since the Global Financial Crisis (GFC). While banks have been busy repairing balance sheets and adopting stricter regulations, digital innovation has become a low priority. In contrast, major industries such as retail, travel, communications, and mass media have undergone revolutionary changes in their technological platforms. With computer and internet proliferation, a younger generation of customers has quickly adapted to newer technology and are demanding higher quality and more digital-based services. However, incumbent banks have often struggled to meet this new demand. The gap between customer expectations and services that banks could offer was quickly picked up by new entrants: fintechs and bigtechs. The increasing use of digital technology has led to higher demand for bank digital services, particularly demand from non-corporate bank clients. Since 2015, fintech and bigtech companies have expanded rapidly, backed by the swift adoption of newer technologies. Within a few years, innovation in financial and business services has greatly increased and spread globally. Although some leading global banks have identified digitalization as one of their business priorities, maintaining a competitive edge remains challenging. Some European banks aspire to offer innovative payments on a par with those of new competitors (EBA, 2020). However, half-century old technological platforms are still widely used in the banking system, and such legacy systems inhibit banks from embracing innovation to thrive in the twenty-first century digital economy. The latest technological adoption in financial services, led by non-bank new entrants, has the potential to fundamentally disrupt the banking industry (BIS, 2017). For example, financial service platforms built by big techs, without the overhead of physical branches, could leverage parent companies' technology and data to streamline retail banking by offering more convenience and better pricing. To maintain market share, some leading global banks are accelerating their digital transformation to provide better and more digital-based customer services. However, these digitalization efforts are often considered futile.

Banks' Digital Transformation: Implications

Empirical studies on the implications of new technology usage in the financial sector are limited. A few studies have examined linkages between information, communication and technology (ICT) investment and bank performance. For example, Casolaro, and others (2007) analyzed the effects of ICT investment in the financial sector using micro-data from a panel of 600 Italian banks over 1989–2000 and found that the shift of both the cost and profit frontiers, as well as efficiency gains, are strongly correlated with ICT capital accumulation. Studies on the impact of a specific ICT technology are even more limited. For example, in a survey, Frame and White (2004) could only identify eight studies six of which use the same data on ATM diffusion.

To assess the impact of digitalization, the experience of SWIFT adoption could be a useful reference. Scott and others (2017) studied 6,858 banks in 29 countries in Europe and the Americas to examine the impact of the adoption of SWIFT, a network-based technological infrastructure, on bank performance. They found that SWIFT adoption has a large impact on profitability in the long term. Initial investment can be costly, including investment in internal and external hardware, software, services, and new staff with information technology skills.

However, recurrent costs in the medium to long term are expected to be lower, especially as newer, more flexible development technologies are adopted and banks spend less on inefficient legacy systems. The new technology would also allow banks to enhance their operational efficiency with fewer operational personnel and branches. For example, online distribution channels reduce investment in branches, branch staffs, and back-office departments. More recent evidence largely supports the role of digitalization as a means to boost bank profitability. Although cross-country academic studies have been lacking, abundant work has been done by private consulting firms and banks. Citi (2019) has estimated that digitalization could cut banks' operational cost by 30 percent to 50 percent mainly due to fewer branches and employees, but revenues would also decline for all banks by 10 percent 30 percent due to enhanced competition and transparency. A recent survey by Accenture (2019) suggested that digital maturity is associated with increased profitability: digital advanced banks have, on average, experienced an overall increase of return on equity (ROE) of 0.9 percent between

2011 and 2017, while less digitally advanced banks have seen an ROE decline of 1.1 percent, and this divergence of profitability is expected to widen in the following years.

Nevertheless, the benefits from digitalization could vary by the size of banks and their business models, foretelling a possible more concentrated banking industry. Digital transformation calls for large initial investment, which could be unaffordable for smaller banks or unprofitable banks. Local banks with smaller and more concentrated customer bases could also be slow in adopting new technologies, and thus find their market shares encroached by digitally advanced international competitors. Consequently, the banking industry could become more concentrated with large banks, especially if the industry exhibits increasing returns to scale.

One social benefit of financial technology advancement is enhanced financial inclusion. For example, mobile wallets in Africa have granted millions without a banking account access to financial services. In regions where banks remain the dominant financial service supplier, such as in Europe, a more digitally advanced banking industry could potentially enhance efficiency, reduce service costs, and extend customer reach. Karlan and others (2016) reviewed behavior of credit, savings, insurance and payments and found that digital financial services significcnatly enhance client well-being both directly and through enabling a broader ecosystem. However, for some bank employees, and less digitally capable customers, bank digitalization may foreshadow difficult times ahead. Ernst and Young (2019) 15 studied the impact of three technolgy trends Robotic Process Automation, Advanced Analytics, and AI on the future financial service workforce, and identified 40 out of the 121 job roles as highly impacted, with the potential for convergence or displacement. In addition, as digitalization is often accompanied with branch closings and transitioning to more IT advanced customer interface, those customers who are less prone to adopting new technology or live in remote areas may find themselves with no access to customer services. As reported by the Financial Times (FT, 2019): "bank branches in the U.K. are closing at an 'alarming' rate,' many people, especially those living in the rural areas, could be shut out of vital financial services."

The Digital Transformation Of Banks: A Global Comparison

i. Data

Cross-country databases on the digitalization of the financial industry are unavailable, but alternative databases could serve as a proxy. This study uses the Global Findex database (GFd) that has been produced by the World Bank every three years since 2011 (more details of the GFd data, its caveats, and other alternative database IMF FAS). Among a few hundreds GFd indicators, only one qualifies as a proxy for the level of bank digitalization: used a mobile phone or internet to access a financial institution account in the past years (% of 15+ with a financial institution account). This indicator focuses on banks' digital services rather than all the financial institutions that also include non-bank firms. In addition, by controlling the number of the adult population (15+) with a financial institution account, this indicator is not influenced by access to finance. However, data for this indicator is available for only 2017, and a sample of 139 countries. Despite its limitation, this indicator might be the best available indicator for cross-country comparison on bank's digitalization.

Digital Currency Areas

In a digital world, economic interactions will occur within the borders of what we term a "digital currency area" (DCA). The areas will form endogenously and may or may not be governed by national boundaries. We define a digital currency area as a network where payments and transactions are made digitally by using a currency that is specific to that network. By "specific," we mean that it possesses either one or both of the following characteristics:

1. The network uses its own unit of account, distinct from existing official currencies. As an example, Facebook has recently announced the launch of Libra. It is designed to be a digital representation of a basket of existing currencies and therefore will define a new unit of account. Hence, these types of DCAs arise through full currency competition.

2. The network operates a payment instrument, a medium of exchange, that can only be used inside, between its participants. So, even if the network still uses official fiat currencies as unit of account and to back the payment instrument, that instrument cannot serve for transactions and exchanges outside the network. Typically, that is the case for some large issuers of e-money when their systems are not interoperable with others. Today, the main example is China, where both Tencent and Ant Financial

have developed such networks with hundreds of millions of users, but with no mutual connection or interoperability. These DCAs are typically examples of reduced currency competition, in which the new currencies are not denominated in their own unit of account.

The amount of economic activity in DCAs will likely dwarf that in many national economies. For example, as of 2019, the Alipay network reached 870 million users, and quarterly trade volume reached RMB 47.2 trillion ($7 trillion). Tencent, the second-largest payment provider in China, is not far behind. Obviously, a DCA is very different from an OCA as defined in the massive literature following Mundell (1961)'s contribution. An OCA is typically characterized by geographic proximity and the ability of participants to dispense of the exchange rate as an adjustment tool. In turn, that implies some commonality of macroeconomic shocks and Brunnermeier, James and Landau (2019) were the first to introduce this concept, a sufficient degree of factor mobility. The design of OCAs is focused on the monetary authority's ability to smooth shocks, to the extent that they are symmetric across agents in the OCA, and ability to improve risk sharing, to the extent that markets in the OCA are incomplete.

By contrast, DCAs are held together by digital interconnectedness. The focus is not on the role of the monetary authority; indeed, the currency's issuer may be under a legally binding convertibility arrangement that ties its hands. Rather, DCAs aim to take advantage of the mutually complementary activities and data linkages that arise in a digital network's ecosystem. A payment function allows these connections to be fully exploited. The unique technology underlying network-based digital payment systems allow for stronger ties than those created by traditional digital payments. Network users in DCAs can make direct, peer-to-peer transfers using mobile applications, whereas until recently digital transfers using credit or debit cards were limited to transactions.

When participants share the same form of currency, whether or not it is denominated in its own unit of account, strong monetary links develop. Price transparency is greater inside the network, price discovery is easier, and conversion to other payment instruments is less likely and sometimes technically impossible. These monetary links further create an incentive to accumulate balances in the network's currency. This holds true regardless of whether the DCA is associated with a multifaceted platform or a more specific digital network, such as a messaging service.

Paradox of digital currency areas. One might think that the potential of DCAs to expand across national borders would lead to the emergence of global digital currencies. However, DCAs may be limited in their scope by regulatory frameworks. The digital networks associated with DCAs may treat data, and users' privacy in particular, in quite different ways. To the extent that jurisdictions such as Europe, the U.S., and China use different regulatory frameworks to approach privacy issues, it may be that certain digital payment networks are viable only within a restricted set of jurisdictions. In fact, it may be impossible to use some digital currencies within certain jurisdictions. This could be the ultimate paradox of digitalization. Digitalization has the ability break barriers and cross borders. But, because of its many inseparable dimensions, it may ultimately lead to an increased fragmentation of the international financial system.

Digital Dollarization

Digitalization can provide new paths to internationalize existing currencies and transform international monetary relations. There are, schematically, two ways through which a currency can internationalize: by becoming a global store of value, as a reserve instrument; or by being used for international payments, as a medium of exchange. Historically, the two roles have progressively converged. However, different paths and strategies are conceivable for a currency to gain international status and use in the 21st century. Analyzing the current dominant position of the dollar in the international monetary system, some economists emphasize its function as a reserve asset in its role as store of value, based on the size, depth, and liquidity of US financial markets. Others give more importance to its role in the denomination and settlement of international trade and transactions.

The distinction becomes relevant and important in a digital environment. Becoming a reserve asset is demanding as, in particular, it implies full and unconditional capital account convertibility. However, the theory that international status can be achieved through trade suggests that digital networks may be another device to internationalize a currency. The theory emphasizes a complementarity in invoicing decisions: merchants whose purchases are invoiced in a currency will want to invoice in the same currency in order to ensure they can make those purchases. Digital networks are particularly effective at opening new possibilities for trade and proliferating a medium of exchange beyond national borders. The closed nature of platform ecosystems further incentivizes invoicing in the platform's currency. A country that is home to large digital networks could therefore find new ways for its currency to gain international acceptance by exploiting the integrating effects of a DCA. Digitalization may thus serve as a powerful vehicle to internationalize some currencies as media of exchange.

Symmetrically, other countries may be exposed to more intense currency competition from foreign currencies through cross-border payment networks. Existing cross-border systems are currently pure infrastructures. They use domestic currencies as the medium of exchange and unit of account. However, that may change. As the example of Libra shows, private networks may be created that would give access to new and specific units of account to people in many countries. Even official currencies may progressively penetrate other countries' economies if supported by a strong digital network. Cross-border effects also may be significant. Within large networks, the same digital instruments of payments may easily be used in several jurisdictions. If so, they may have the effect of promoting the use of a specific unit of account outside of the country where it is legal tender.

Importantly, while small economies (especially those with high or unstable domestic inflation) are susceptible to both traditional and digital dollarization by a stable currency, economies that are economically or socially open to large DCAs will be uniquely vulnerable to digital dollarization.

The same is true for smaller countries as they do not provide the same scale of network externalities, large networks can offer. That is, even economies with stable currencies could be digitally dollarized if their citizens find themselves often transacting with users of a digital platform with its own currency. As the importance of digitally delivered services increases and social networks become more intertwined with the ways in which people exchange value, the influence of large digital currencies in smaller economies will grow.

CHAPTER 7

Central Bank Money And Actual Performance

Concepts of Central Bank Money

Central bank money refers to the liability of the balance sheets of central banks namely, money created by a central bank to be used by fulfilling the four functions of money described earlier. Cash used to be the most important means of payment in the past. The amount of outstanding coins issued is much smaller than the amount of outstanding central bank notes in circulation due to the smaller units, so coins are used only for small purchases. Meanwhile, the development of the banking system and technological advances have given rise to interbank payments and settlement systems where commercial banks lend to each other. A central bank manages interbank payments and settlement systems through monitoring the movements of reserve deposit balances at the central bank. The amount of cash is issued based on the quantity demanded by the general public, which is associated with transaction demand (normally proxied with nominal gross domestic product [GDP]) as well as the opportunity cost (normally a deposit rate paid by the commercial bank to the general public). Thus, a central bank supplies cash passively in response to changes in demand. A central bank provides commercial banks with cash by withdrawing the equivalent amount from their reserve deposit accounts; commercial banks then distribute the acquired cash to the general public on demand through windows of bank branches and/or ATMs.

Reserve deposits can be decomposed into required reserves (the amount set under the statutory reserve requirement system) and excess reserves (the amount in excess of required reserves). Banks use reserve deposits to lend to each other in the interbank market. In normal times, when the effective lower bound is binding, the central bank pays a (positive) interest rate on excess reserves (IOER), and this IOER forms a floor for the short-term market-determined interest rate corridors (while the ceiling is formed by a discount rate charged by the central bank when lending to commercial banks against collateral). The floor in the market interest rate can be established because no commercial banks should be willing to lend to each other at a rate below the IOER.

Both cash and reserve deposits are the safest and most liquid financial instruments held by commercial banks. Reserve money (base money or the monetary base [M0]) is comprised of cash and reserve deposits. Cash is regarded as legal tender by governments and central banks for all debts, public charges, taxes, and dues in their respective economies. The value of cash is stable in an economy where a central bank successfully conducts monetary policy in accordance with the price stability mandate (mostly at around 2% in advanced economies) and, thus, avoids substantially high inflation or serious deflation. The value of reserve deposits is also stable and is equivalent to cash in a one-to-one relationship.

Differences In Features Between Cash And Reserve Deposits

While both cash and reserve deposits constitute central bank money, they have different features. For example, cash is physical money, while reserve deposits are digital currency. Digital currency is a type of currency available in digital form, in contrast with physical, visible cash. Moreover, cash is used mainly among the general public (thus called "retail central bank money"), is available 24 hours a day and 365 days a year and is usable anywhere within an economy where the legal tender status prevails. By contrast, reserve deposits are available only to designated financial institutions, such as commercial banks (thus called "wholesale central bank money") and are used for managing the real-time interbank payments and settlements system. Wholesale central bank money is not necessarily available 24 hours a day or 365 days a year, depending on the computer network system managed by each central bank. With technology advances, central banks have been making efforts to improve systems for enabling faster and more efficient transactions.

From the perspective of users (the general public), the most important difference between cash and reserve deposits is that cash is anonymous and cash transactions are non-traceable since transactions cannot be monitored or traced by the central bank that issued the cash. In contrast, all the transactions based on reserve deposits are traceable by the order of the time sequence of transactions made, since they are a digital representation of money that enables the recording of all footprints. Reserve deposits are non-anonymous since they are based on an account-based system that uses an owner register so that information such as the ownership of money in the respective accounts and the amount of money transfers from one account to the other is available fully to a central bank. In addition, cash provides a peer-to-peer settlement form, while reserve deposits are non-peer-to-peer settlements as transactions between commercial banks are intermediated by a central bank. Because of anonymity and non-traceability, cash is often preferred by the general public who wish to maintain privacy but is often used for money laundering and illegal activities and tax evasion purposes. Cash handling costs are quite high when considering not only the direct fees (i.e., cost of paper and design fees to prevent counterfeiting) but also the security and personnel cost associated with the maintenance of cash provision and payment services by commercial banks, shops, firms, and individuals.

From the perspective of an issuer (a central bank), the most important difference between cash and reserve deposits is the presence or absence of an interest rate. Cash is an interest-rate free instrument, while a positive or negative interest rate can be applied to reserve deposits. It is known that a negative interest rate policy can be a monetary policy tool under the effective lower bound, as has been adopted, for example, by the European Central Bank (ECB), the Bank of Japan, and Sweden's Riksbank. A negative interest rate policy can be applied by a central bank to the IOER and can be more effective if commercial banks pass the increased costs (arising from the negative interest rate) on to their retail bank deposits held by the general public to maintain interest margins and profits. This is likely to happen when the general public no longer utilizes cash (so mainly uses private sector money or bank deposits) and, thus, is unlikely to substitute cash with bank deposits in order to avoid a negative interest rate charged on bank deposits.

Actual Performance Of Central Bank Money In Advanced And Emerging Economies

The performance of central bank money is examined by focusing on cash and reserve deposits separately. Cash is likely to rise as economic activities (proxied by nominal GDP) grow, reflecting transaction demand. Reserve deposits also tend to rise when greater economic activities are associated with the deepening of the banking system and, hence, an increase in bank deposits. Thus, this paper measures cash and reserve deposits by dividing these data by GDP in order to examine the trend excluding the direct impact coming from greater economic activities.

It is shown cash in circulation as a percentage of nominal GDP for the period 2000–2017 in advanced economies (the eurozone, Japan, Sweden, and the US). The ratio of cash to nominal GDP declined steadily in Sweden since 2008, suggesting that Sweden has progressed to become the most cashless society in the world. It is interesting to see that the Swedish cash-nominal GDP ratio continued to drop even after a negative interest rate policy was adopted on the repo rate (namely, the rate of interest at which commercial banks can borrow or deposit funds at the central bank for seven days) from February 2015 (–0.1% initially in February 2015, deepening to –0.25% in March 2015, then further to –0.35% in July 2015 and to –0.5% in February 2016 before increasing to –0.25% in January 2019 as part of normalization). This indicates that substitution from bank deposits to cash did not happen in Sweden despite a negative interest rateIn contrast, the cash-nominal GDP ratios have risen over time in the eurozone, Japan, and the US. These rising trends were maintained before and after the massive unconventional monetary easing namely, quantitative easing in the three economies and the negative interest rate policy in the eurozone and Japan. Japan's cash-GDP ratio has been always higher than those of the eurozone and the United States, suggesting that cash is more frequently used in Japan as a means of exchange and store of value. This may reflect that Japan's inflation has remained more or less stable at around 0% or in the moderately negative territory since the late 1990s. Japan's preference for cash may also reflect its long-standing low interest rate since the Bank of Japan implemented a series of monetary easing after the collapse of the stock and real estate bubbles in the early 1990s. It is also interesting to see that cash is growing fast in the US, even after the monetary policy normalization that has taken place since December 2015 with a continuous increase in the federal funds rate.

Regarding reserve deposits, we exhibits the ratios of reserve deposits to GDP for the period 2000–2017 in the same four economies. These ratios in the four economies have risen after the global financial crisis of 2008–2009, perhaps reflecting the quantitative easing tool adopted in the presence of the effective lower bound (i.e., large-scale purchases of treasury securities and other financial assets). The US currently faces a decline in the ratio because the Federal Reserve has begun to reduce its balance sheets by reducing the amount of reinvestment on redeemed bonds from October 2017—after having recorded a peak in

October 2014 when the process of "tapering", or a gradual decline in the amount of financial asset purchases, was completed so that the amount outstanding of reserve deposits reached the maximum of around $2.8 trillion. The European Central Bank (ECB) initiated net purchases of financial assets from June 2014 and introduced a large-scale asset purchase program in March 2015 but completed net purchases in December 2018 after conducting tapering. From 2019, a full reinvestment strategy will be maintained so that the size of the ECB's balance sheet will remain the same. Sweden adopted quantitative easing in 2015–2017 and has since continued to engage in a full reinvestment strategy to maintain the amount of holdings of government bonds. Currently, therefore, the Bank of Japan is the only central bank among advanced economies to continue asset purchases and, thus, expand reserve deposits and the balance sheet although the pace of net purchases dropped substantially since a shift from the monetary base control to the yield curve control in September 2016. In the case of emerging economies (India and the PRC), Figure 3 shows their cash-GDP ratios for the period 2000–2017. The ratios in the two economies have not risen like in the eurozone, Japan, and the United States, even though the amount of cash in circulation has grown rapidly in line with GDP (reflecting transaction demand). In particular, a declining trend in the ratio in the case of the PRC is noticeable, and this is likely to reflect a shift in the money held by the general public from cash to bank deposits or other cashless payment tools in line with the deepening of the banking system and an increase in the number of depositors at commercial banks, as pointed out later. A sharp drop in the ratio in India in 2016, meanwhile, reflected a temporary decline in cash after the government suddenly implemented a currency reform. India's government banned the Rs100 and Rs500 notes and instead introduced a new Rs500 note and issued new Rs2,000 notes for the first time. This currency reform was meant to fight corruption and anti-money laundering/illegal activities but created severe disruptions to economic activities by creating serious cash shortages. While the cash ratio recovered somewhat in the following year, it appears that the ratio was lower than the past trend, suggesting a moderate shift from cash to bank deposits or cashless payment tools. Meanwhile, reserve deposits in these two economies have remained stable (data are available only from 2007 in the case of the PRC), and this makes sense since the central banks have not conducted quantitative easing like those in advanced economies. To summarize, central bank money grew rapidly during the period 2000–2017 in the selected advanced economies because of an increase in cash in circulation, with the exception of Sweden. In addition, central bank money expanded significantly as a result of the adoption of large-scale asset purchases as part of unconventional monetary easing tools in the face of the effective lower bound. Meanwhile, cash in emerging economies has grown rapidly but does not show a rising trend when cash is measured in terms of nominal GDP. India's cash-GDP ratio remained stable until 2016, suggesting that India's cash growth is associated with transaction demand. The 2016 currency reform created a sudden decline in the ratio. The ratio since then has recovered but appears to be lower than the previous trend. The declining trend is more visible in the case of the PRC, and this appears to reflect a shift in the payment tool used by the general public from cash to bank deposits or other cashless payment tools (such as Alipay or WeChat Pay), which has contributed to the banking sector deepening as the prepaid system is linked to bank accounts. Reserve deposits in the emerging economies have remained stable due to a lack of an unconventional asset purchasing program. Overall, central banks in both advanced and emerging economies have continued to issue ample central bank money for various reasons.

Actual Performance Of Bank Deposits In Advanced Economies And Emerging Economies

The performance of private sector money is assessed based on the performance of bank deposits. Bank deposits may rise when economic activities expand as firms and individuals may increase access to bank accounts and increase the number of those accounts. Like central bank money, therefore, bank deposits are measured as a percentage of nominal GDP to examine the trend after excluding the direct impact of economic activities. We exhibits the ratios of bank deposits to nominal GDP in the same advanced economies (the eurozone, Japan, Sweden, and the US) for the period 2000-2015. Japan's ratio has remained the highest among the four economies, suggesting that Japan's financial system is bank-dominant with ample deposits held by individuals and firms. About half of households' financial assets have been allocated to bank deposits in Japan, and this ratio has remained roughly the same even after the retail deposit rate dropped significantly to nearly 0% as a result of quantitative easing or yield curve controls (Shirai 2018a, 2018b). The eurozone faces the second highest ratio, mainly reflecting the large bank deposits held by German individuals. Like Japanese individuals, German individuals are highly risk averse, so about 40% of their financial assets are allocated to cash and bank deposits. In contrast, Sweden faces the lowest ratio, suggesting that the financial system is less bank dominated, and commercial banks are more dependent on wholesale financing (rather than retail deposits).

All the four economies have experienced a rising trend with regard to the ratio of bank deposits to nominal GDP, especially after the global financial crisis. This rising trend does not appear to reflect a deepening of the banking system. It is refered to that the percentage of respondents who reported having an account (by themselves or together with someone else) at a bank or another type of financial institution or reported personally using a mobile money service in the past 12 months in the periods of 2011,2014, and 2017. We indicate that these ratios remained roughly the same over the period, suggesting that the banking systems were already well-developed and deepened a long time ago in these economies so that most of the general public already had access to bank accounts and other cashless payment tools. As a result, a large increase in the number of deposits (a sign of banking sector deepening) did not take place during the period surveyed. Namely, the rising trend in the bank deposits-nominal GDP ratio appears to reflect other factors, such as amplified risk-averse behavior and the resultant shift from risky assets (such as stocks, investment trusts, and funds) to safer assets. Bank deposit growth may also have happened as part of money creation driven by unconventional monetary easing although the growth rates of bank deposits (hence, the monetary base) were much smaller than those of reserve deposits in the four economies suggesting a decline or sluggish money multiplier effect. In the meanwhile, emerging economies may have different developments. Bank deposits as a percentage of nominal GDP steadily increased in India over the period 2011–2015. The ratio also increased in the PRC despite fluctuations during 2000– 2015. This may reflect deepening of the banking system in the two economies so that the general public significantly gained access to bank accounts or mobile payment services in 2011, 2014, and 2017. The increased use of digital wallets using mobile phones may have contributed to an increase in the number of depositors and increased access to the banking system. Given that their reserve deposits nominal GDP ratios remained the same, an increase in the bank deposits nominal GDP ratio indicates that money creation activities were greater than those in the advanced economies.

Private Sector Money And Digital Tokens

In addition to existing central bank money and private sector money, there is newly emerging private sector money in the form of digital tokens (or crypto assets, crypto currencies, encrypted currencies, or virtual currencies). These tokens are generally issued by independent "miners" (or nodes) based on the DLT, which records transactions between two parties and shares the information among any participants in the DLT network and synchronizes the transaction data in an electronically distributed ledger in a traceable and unfalsifiable way. The innovative nature of this technology lies in the mechanisms in which the process to verify transactions (such as the payment or transfer of digital coins) is conducted by unknown, independent third parties (namely, nodes) without relying on a central manager or register (such as a central bank or a commercial bank that manages the system). Blockchain is a type of distributed ledger where each transaction between two parties is proven to be true using encryption keys and digital wallets; then, the numbers of the transactions are recorded on a new electronic distributed ledger, which is then connected through a chain (using hash functions) to previous, proven distributed ledgers using the proof-of-the-work process in such a way that makes the falsification of transaction data difficult.

The most famous private sector digital coin is bitcoin, the first digital token based on the blockchain technology introduced in 2008 by Satoshi Nakamoto. There are currently over 2,000 digital coins, whose features vary substantially. These tokens have their own units of account that are universal across countries using the same tokens, with systems that enable instantaneous cross-border transfers of token ownership. Those tokens can be exchanged for some goods and services in many countries.

One of the attractive features of digital tokens is their similarity to cash, since peer -to-peer transactions can be made instantaneously and are available 24 hours a day, 365 days a year. All the transactions are anonymous, like cash, but are technically traceable, in contrast with cash. Unlike cash, meanwhile, digital tokens are digital money, so a positive or negative interest rate can be applied. Although this interest rate-bearing feature makes digital tokens superior to cash, one distinct feature of cash over digital tokens is the relative ease of verifying peer-to-peer transactions. This is partly because cash is designed by a central bank (or a government in the case of coins) in a way that is not easily falsified, and partly because cash recipients (such as commercial banks, shops, and individuals) just need to check carefully whether cash received is authentic, while digital tokens require more complicated verification approaches.

Central banks and regulatory authorities around the world so far do not regard these private digital tokens as "money" and have called for greater caution by the general public in using or investing in them because of the extreme volatility in their values and their limited use as a medium of exchange. Also, consumers and investors are not well-protected since a regulatory framework is almost non-existent. Nonetheless, the DLT has the potential to apply to many different fields, not only for payment and settlement systems but also for promoting trade finance, insurance, and other fintech services; tracking producers of industrial/agricultural products and commodities; and the ownership of real estate and precious metals. As the technology evolves day to day, and various new digital tokens have been issued with diverse features, DLT could conquer technical and legal problems in the future, such as 51% attack and double spending problems; scalability; substantial energy consumption; substantial volatility in the values; vulnerability to cyberattacks; potential anti-money laundering and illegal activities, etc.

According to CoinMarketCap, the size of the market capitalization of existing digital coins is estimated to have reached about $113 billion by the end of January 2019, of which bitcoin accounted for about 54% of the total market capitalization. The size of digital coins remains much smaller than central bank money and private sector money since their use as a payment tool remains limited. Moreover, money creation is not permitted by digital token exchanges and developers (since a banking license is necessary and no financial authorities have issued a license so far). Thus, they have generated little threat to both central banks and commercial banks issuing traditional money.

There has been an interesting development by the Swiss Financial Market Supervisory Authority (FINMA). In February 2018, FINMA published guidelines regarding the regulatory framework for initial coin offerings (ICOs). An ICO refers to a mechanism in which investors transfer funds in the form of cryptocurrencies to the ICO organizer and in return receive a quantity of blockchain- based digital tokens that are created and stored in a decentralized form (either on a blockchain specifically created for the ICO or through a smart contract on a pre-existing blockchain). In December 2018, furthermore, the Swiss Parliament permitted the FinTech license for fintech financial services providers (a company limited by shares, a corporation with unlimited partners, or a limited liability company, in addition to the requirement that a company has its registered office and conducts its business activities in Switzerland) to accept public deposits of up to SwF100 million under the conditions that those deposits are not invested and paid an interest rate. FINMA has begun to accept license applications from 2019. This means that fintech companies are not allowed to engage in money creation using digital coins but are given greater opportunities to expand their businesses.

Central Bank Digital Currency Proposals And Prospects

The emergence of private sector digital tokens issued to the general public has prompted intensive debates over whether they could become money in the future. In addition, another heated debate has risen about whether central banks should issue their own digital tokens. The idea of central banks issuing digital tokens nowadays called central bank digital currency (CBDC) proposals can be classified into "retail CBDC" (issued for the general public) and "wholesale CBDC" (issued for financial institutions that hold reserve deposits with a central bank). CBDC could be a new interest-bearing liability for central banks.

Four Proposals On Central Bank Digital Currency

It is interesting to find that the International Monetary Fund (IMF) has begun to examine the potential innovative nature of digital coins (crypto assets) and has supported CBDC proposals more positively. Christine Lagarde, Managing Director of the International Monetary Fund, for example, urged central banks to consider CBDC in November 2018 since they could satisfy public policy goals, including financial inclusion, security/consumer protection, and privacy in payments.

In my view, the ideas on CBDC discussed around the world can be classified into proposals related to "CBDC, not based on DLT" and those related to "CBDC proposals based on DLT". The CBDC proposals could be further differentiated between those targeting the general public (namely, "retail CBDC") and those targeting financial institutions (namely, "wholesale CBDC"). Figure 10 summarizes all the CBDC proposals by classifying them into the following four types: (1) account-based retail CBDC without DLT, (2) value-based retail CBDC without DLT, (3) retail CBDC based on DLT, and (4) wholesale CBDC based on DLT. The first two proposals are currently being examined by Sweden's Riksbank. All of these CBDCs are digital currencies, as described in detail below.

Motivations Leading to the CBDC Proposals

Before investigating the proposals, it is important to examine the reasons why some central banks have found it important to examine these four proposals. There are mainly six reasons. First, central banks find it necessary to provide safe, liquid payment instruments to the general public just like central banks have been doing for financial institutions using reserve deposits for a long time. This is relevant to the first two proposals (1) and (2) without recourse to DLT and seriously considered by Riksbank. Given that the large majority of the general public in Sweden no longer uses cash, Riksbank has found it important to provide a safe, liquid payment instrument equally to both the general public and financial institutions for the sake of fairness in a democratic society. This reflects the concerns that private sector issuers may take advantage of their privileged positions, possibly by increasing fees and lending interest rates and misusing the information obtained from tracking transactions if the general public solely depends on private sector money. Also, if a number of private sector issuers or cashless payment providers go bankrupt as a result of systemic financial crises, the general public may suffer substantially without proper payments and settlements systems and encounter large losses. As a result, the payments and settlements systems, as well as the financial systems, may become less stable and safe.

It is indicated that central bank notes in circulation have dropped to around 1% in Sweden as well as Norway, while those in terms of GDP have exhibited a declining trend in Australia, Denmark Sweden, and Norway in selected advanced economies. According to Riksbank's survey, only 13% used cash for paying their most recent purchase in 2018, down from 39% in 2010. Sweden is more enthusiastic about the idea of retail CBDC than Norway and has already published the first e-krona report in September 2017 and the second e-krona report in October 2018 and announced its intention to experiment with the e-krona project in the foreseeable future in the 2018 report.

Second, some economies especially in emerging economies wish to reduce the cost of printing and managing cash and contain the associated crimes by promoting cashless payment tools. The third proposal (retail CBDC based on DLT) is relevant to this motivation. Substantial money has been spent in each economy, not only on direct paper and design fees (spent so as to reduce counterfeits) but also on the personnel and transportation costs needed to handle cash (at central banks, commercial banks, and shops, and at the individual level) as well as on the security fees paid to reduce robbery, tax evasion, and illegal activities, etc. DLT has the potential to reduce cash handling costs since all the transactions can be made using a digital representation of money and are traceable. The informal or shadow economy is large in many emerging economies, so the governments find it difficult to tax economic activities and cope with illegal and unreported activities. Thus, a shift in central bank money from cash(physical money) to digital currency is one way to shift the economy from being informal-based to formal-based so that the economy becomes more tax-based, transparent, and efficient. DLT enables anonymity, but CBDC might reduce the possibility of executing unreported transactions and crimes.

Third, financial inclusion is another important motivation for some emerging economies regarding retail CBDC proposals based on DLT in recent years. There is still a large number of low-income people or people living in rural areas who are unbanked and without access to commercial banks and the internet and, thus, use cash as their main payment method on a daily basis. Retail CBDC might promote digitization of the economy and, thus, economic and social development.

Fourth, the use of DLT, such as in the third and fourth proposals, may promote a technological environment and foster the fintech sector. Many emerging economies are keen on developing global financial centers in their cities and regard fostering the fintech sector as one of the most promising routes for fulfilling this objective. While those economies may find it difficult to develop banking systems and capital markets that are comparable to those in advanced economies, fintech services are new and innovative, and the general public may be more eager to use them given that the banking system and capital markets are still in the early processes of development. These emerging economies may have a greater chance of success in DLT and associated fintech development, as seen in the recent rapid-growing activities in the Shenzhen area in the PRC.

Fifth, shifting from cash to digital currency through issuing retail CBDC may enhance the effectiveness of monetary policy (such as a negative interest rate policy under the effective lower bound) because of limiting the scope of cash substitution that could emerge to avoid a negative interest rate. This motive could be fulfilled in the case of the first, second, and third proposals.

Sixth, the efficiency and financial stability gains are feasible, especially with regards to the fourth proposal (wholesale CBDC). Wholesale CBDC has the potential to improve the existing wholesale financial systems including interbank payments and settlement systems, delivery versus payment systems, and cross-border payments and settlements systems—by speeding up and rationalizing the clearing and settlement processes and possibly reducing the associated cost of transactions and cost of developing/upgrading computer systems. The wholesale financial system could be more stable as a result of limiting the chances of data manipulation and removing a single point of failure problems from the system and the resultant disruption to the systems. Moreover, wholesale CBDC may be able to technically broaden the eligible financial institutions that have access to reserve deposits and, thus, improve the efficiency of the wholesale financial systems—such as insurance firms, pension funds, and other nonbank financial institutions that are normally not eligible to have accounts with a central bank.

First And Second Proposals: Cbdc Without Distributed Ledger Technology

Sweden's Riksbank has been the only central bank so far that has been actively considering the first two proposals over the past two years under the so -called "e-krona" project. The first proposal (so-called "account-based retail CBDC") is the issuance of a digital currency to the general public in the form of directly providing an account at the Riksbank. This is similar to retail bank deposits issued by commercial banks since all the receipts and payments of money are recorded in the same way.

The second proposal (so-called "value-based retail CBDC") is the issuance of a digital currency for which the prepaid value can be stored locally on a card or in a mobile phone application (digital wallets).

All the transactions of both e -krona proposals are traceable since an underlying register enables the recording of all transactions and identification of the rightful owner of the digital e-krona. This technical feature is regarded as important among central banks to preventing money laundering and criminal activities. Under the value-based system, a register examines whether a payer has the sufficient amount of e-krona to transfer, and all cards and digital wallets must be registered so that both payers and payees can be identified in the same manner that users of private sector bank cards and "Swish" (a fast mobile payment system) can be identified. Thus, transactions under the two proposals are non-anonymous because all transactions are identified. One exception of non-anonymity is the case of a prepaid e-krona card, where e-krona are already stored and, thus, can be used as cash and handed over from one user to another. This is allowed as long as the payment amounts to less than €250 (to be lowered to €150 by 2020), as set by the European Union (EU), on the condition that there is no suspicion of money laundering or terrorist financing according to the legislation on money laundering.

For the first and second proposals to be practically implementable for online purchases or in physical shops, Riksbank has stressed the need to develop e-krona payments and a settlement platform for the general public that contains the underlying register for e-krona by interacting with a number of other systems and entities, including commercial banks and other firms. Riksbank plans to experiment with the second proposal first since a value-based CBDC is classified as e-money in Sweden's existing financial regulation and, thus, is consistent with the mandate of promoting a safe and efficient payments system so that experimentation can be legally feasible in the current legal framework. On the other hand, the first proposal is more complicated since Riksbank may need the Parliament to revise the existing central bank act (Sveriges Riksbank Act) in order to provide Riksbank with the clear mandate to issue an account-based retail CBDC. Riksbank may need to prepare for drawing up proposals for the amendments before conducting any experimentation.

Most of the central banks, including Norway's Noregs Bank, have not expressed interest in these Swedish proposals so far. This is mainly because of concerns that commercial banks may suffer a loss in retail deposits from their accounts to those of a central bank and, thus, lose the financing sources of loans needed to extend credit to firms and individuals. This concern, however, can be mitigated if a central bank pays a lower interest rate to the general public (and financial institutions) than commercial banks do to their retail customers. Another concern is that bank runs may be exacerbated in the event of a crisis by a shift in deposits from commercial banks to the central bank, thereby deepening banking crises. In addition, central bank notes in circulation have continued to rise in most countries except for Sweden and Norway, although those in terms of GDP have dropped in some economies as mentioned before. Thus, there is no urgent reason for other central banks to examine the possibility of account-based and value-based CBDC proposals at this stage.

As for monetary policy, it is possible for Riksbank to technically impose a positive or negative interest rate on the first and second e-krona proposals. In Sweden, however, such an interest rate can be applied to account-based e-krona from a legal standpoint but not to value-based e-krona since the latter is regarded in legal terms as "e-money" and, thus, should be a non-interest-bearing instrument according to the E-money Directive.

Third Proposal: Retail CBDC Based On Distributed Ledger Technology

Under the third proposal (retail CBDC based on DLT), CBDC has the features of anonymity, traceability, availability 24 hours a day and 365 days a year, and the feasibility of an interest rate application. The proposal is relatively popular among central banks in emerging economies, mainly because of the motivation to take the lead in the rapidly emerging fintech industry, to promote financial inclusion by accelerating the shift to a cashless society, and to reduce cash printing and handling costs. Some countries, including Ecuador, India, Israel, Uruguay, Lithuania, the Marshall Islands, Tunisia, and the PRC, have expressed interest and/or conducted experiments in some cases, although enthusiasm at the Reserve Bank of India appeared to have, waned in 2019.

Cases Of Countries That Have Considered Or Experimented With The Third Proposal

Ecuador

The Central Bank of Ecuador, which adopted the US dollar as legal tender in 2000, was a frontrunner in terms of issuing retail CBDC (called "dinero electrónico") in 2014 as an additional payment instrument supplementing the US dollar. The central bank allowed users to open accounts with their identification numbers and transfer money between US dollar and digital token accounts via a mobile app. The government pressed for this initiative as it could save the cost of replacing old US dollar notes with new ones (about $3 million) and, thus, contribute to economic growth and reducing poverty. However, the retail CBDC initiative turned out to be unsuccessful because of the limited number of users using retail CBDC to purchase goods and services or make payments. Hence, the initiative was terminated by deactivating the underlying accounts in 2017. This reflected the fact that many citizens trusted the US dollar more than the new digital token.

Uruguay

The first and sole practical experiment conducted so far in the world was the case of the Central Bank of Uruguay in 2017–2019 as a six-month pilot study on instantaneous payments and settlements systems using retail CBDC (called "e-Peso"). Using 20 million pesos and converting them to digital currency, the project involved about 10,000 mobile phone users (not necessarily required to connect to the internet), 15 enterprises (such as shops and gas stations), ANTEL (a state-owned telecommunications provider), and a few fintech firms and payment solutions providers. No commercial banks were involved in this study. Users were required to download an app from the website of the national payments company Red Pagos to create a digital wallet and then register it by entering their personal information and creating a PIN code to have access with no charge. Each user (or firm) could charge up to 30,000 pesos (200,000 peso) with e-pesos in the digital wallets, which could then be used to pay bills, receive payments, or transmit money in an easy and secure way so that the e-pesos were secured in the digital wallets even if the phones or the passwords for the digital wallets were lost. All the transactions were anonymous, traceable, and safe so that double-spending and falsification were prevented. The pilot study was completed without any technological difficulties, and the Central Bank of Uruguay concluded that issuing retail CBDC benefited from lower costs, financial inclusion, the prevention of crime and tax evasion, and customer protection, although the experiment was performed on a limited scale. No clear initiatives for actual implementation have been announced.

Lithuania

The Bank of Lithuania (Lithuania's central bank) examined the retail DLT-based CBDC proposal in 2018 by involving domestic and foreign fintech firms as part of initiatives to develop the fintech industry. The central bank has examined issuing a collector coin using DLT since 2018. Since Lithuania has adopted the euro as legal tender, the central bank is not allowed to issue retail CBDC for wider use as legal tender. Thus, it announced a plan to issue digital collector coins along with physical collector coins commemorating the 200th anniversary of independence from the Russian Federation in 2018. While the central bank holds the view that financial institutions should not engage in crypto asset services, the first international blockchain center in Europe was established and the central bank announced its plan to create a blockchain sandbox platform service (so-called LBChain) in 2018 with the expected launch in 2019. The issuance of the first collectible digital coin to the general public for limited use is likely to happen in 2019. The digital coins can be exchanged among people and also exchanged for euros at the central bank.

People's Republic of China

The People's Bank of China (PBOC), the central bank of the PRC, established the Institute of Digital Money in 2017 and has been examining the possibility of issuing CBDC along with the renminbi through commercial banks in a so-called two -tiered system. Yao Qian of the PBOC wrote a report (Qian 2018) in Chinese in 2017 that a digital currency could be integrated into the existing banking system, with commercial banks operating digital wallets for the retail CBDC and the general public able to conduct peer-to-peer transactions like with cash. The report indicated that the digital coins would use a distributed ledger in a limited way to periodically check the ownership and that the ownership of digital coins could be verified directly by the issuing central bank. The report concluded that blockchain technology is not suitable for this purpose due to scalability problems. There are several reasons why the two-tiered system is prioritized in the PRC. First, it is relatively easy to replace cash since the PBOC supplies cash to the general public on demand through commercial banks. Second, the existing banking system is unlikely to be overturned, so commercial banks have incentives to provide CBDC to the general public—if a deposit rate paid by a central bank is lower than the interest rate paid by commercial banks (Qian 2018). The PBOC has not yet announced any clear plans to conduct a practical experiment.

Tunisia

Tunisia's initiative was promoted directly by the government, so it may not be accurate to regard the initiative as a CBDC initiative. Tunisia took the lead in issuing retail DLT-based digital tokens for its government initiative. La Post—a Tunisian governmental financial institution, but not categorized as a bank—has issued a blockchain-based digital token called "e-Dinar" (a digital version of the Tunisian dinar) since 2015 as a part of the government's e-Tunisia initiative, with support from a Switzerland-based software company and local fintech firms. This is so far the first and only successful case of a digital coin being issued by a governmental body or a central bank in the world. The digital tokens are currently listed on global crypto asset exchanges and can be used in Tunisia to transfer funds, pay for goods and services online, pay for salaries and bills, and manage official identification documents with limited costs using virtual accounts and transferring funds between virtual accounts and a postal account, and between different virtual accounts, etc. New digital tokens are issued in a decentralized manner through the proof-of-stake process by miners—the process developed to cope with bitcoin's energy-intensive proof-of-work process that requires a large number of calculations—with simple mechanisms that validate a new block. The issuer also claims that the number of tokens could be sufficient for all residents across the globe despite the maximum number set. The anonymity of transactions is maintained. So far, the digital token appears to have not yet been actively utilized to the extent envisaged in Tunisia.

The Marshall Islands

Another initiative led by a government is in the Marshall Islands, where the US dollar has been the official currency as legal tender since 1982, and no central bank exists. In 2018, the government floated the idea of introducing its own blockchain-based digital token called "sovereign" (SOV) as a second legal tender supplementing the US dollar. The parliament passed the Sovereign Currency Act in February 2018 to authorize the issuance. The digital token is to be issued in a decentralized manner by third parties through initial coin offerings (ICOs) with the cap set to 24 million tokens in order to avoid inflation, with support from a fintech startup company in Israel. The main motivation behind this initiative is to prepare for a scheduled decline in grants provided under the US Compact Trust Fund (established by the US government to compensate Marshallese citizens affected by nuclear tests conducted near the country) after 2023 and acquire new revenue sources. Thus, the issuing of ICOs by the government is being considered as an additional revenue source. Nevertheless, the IMF warned vehemently about the issuance of the SOV since it might elevate the anti-money laundering activities through a sole domestic bank existing in the country that already faces the risk of losing its last US dollar correspondent banking relationship with a US-based bank as a result of heightened due diligence by banks in the United States (IMF 2018). The introduction of the SOV may incur reputational risk due to the risk of deteriorating relationships further with foreign banks and the greater risk of money-laundering and terrorist financing. Moreover, criticism on the retail CBDC proposal has emerged and intensified in the Parliament because of the risk of losing the country's reputation after the passage of the Sovereign Current Act. However, Hilda Heine, the President of the Marshall Islands, managed to survive a no-confidence vote (split 16-16 votes) in November 2018, so the government plans to issue the SOV after satisfying the requirements imposed by the IMF, the US, and Europe.

Venezuela

Venezuela is the only country that has issued a government-sponsored digital coin. The digital coin (called the "petro") was issued in 2018 and is backed by a barrel of oil from the country's substantial oil reserves. The digital coin is complementary to the bolivar as legal tender. The main purpose of issuing a digital coin is to circumvent the financial sanctions imposed by the US on the grounds of corruption and human right violations and to obtain funds from abroad by attracting foreign investors in the face of severely disrupted economic and financial conditions—not targeting the general public. US President Donald Trump has reacted to this initiative by prohibiting transactions using the digital coin. The government has already required distributors of oil products and air carriers to set up digital wallets used to pay and receive funds in petro in 2018 and plans to use the digital coin in its oil exports in 2019. Due to insufficient information, it is not clear whether the digital coin has actually been issued and is functioning. Some media report that investors in the petro have only received petro certificates, not digital coins.

Viewpoints Of Advanced Economies On Retail CBDC Based On DLT

In sharp contrast to emerging economies, central banks in advanced economies including the Federal Reserve, Bank of Japan, Bundesbank, European Central Bank, and Swiss National Bank are not enthusiastic about DLT-based retail CBDC (for example, see Cœuré [2018]). This reflects the fact that existing retail payments and settlements systems have become more efficient, faster, and available for 24 hours a day and 365 days per year, so there is no strong case for promoting the proposal, and the potential benefits from using retail CBDC may not be as large as previously thought. Second, the use of cash is not yet declining in many advanced economies with the exception of Sweden and Norway. Third, almost all citizens are banked in advanced economies, so financial inclusion is not an urgent issue that should be tackled by a central bank. Fourth, many central banks do not wish to create competition between central bank money and private sector money and impose hardships on the existing baking system or amplify the resultant financial stability risk. Finally, central banks in advanced economies are generally more cautious on retail CBDC than those in emerging economies, perhaps because of fear of losing reputation in case of unsuccessful implementation of the initiative. Limited public interest and support for the proposal is also another factor discouraging these central banks from actively considering the proposal.

For these reasons, central banks in Australia, Denmark, and Norway, whose cash in circulation as a percentage of GDP has been dropping, have not made a decision to promote retail CBDC at this stage after carefully examining the pros and cons over the retail CBDC proposal and feasibility. Their retail payments and settlements systems are already highly efficient, immediate, and convenient, so they prefer existing private-sector money issued by traditional financial institutions Bank of Israel 2018; Mancini-Griffoli et al. 2018). The central bank in Israel also issued a report in November 2018 regarding retail DLT-based CBDC (called "e-shekel") and concluded that the actual implementation should be postponed until other major central banks in advanced economies take the lead, although several potential advantages were identified. The Federal Reserve also does not support the retail CBDC idea (called "Fedcoin") proposed by Koning (2014, 2016). Under the proposal, the digital token will be supplied on demand along with cash and reserve deposits, and their conversion can be undertaken at par to each other by the Federal Reserve Banks. The total amount of central bank money will remain unchanged since Fedcoin will be created (or destroyed) by destroying (creating) cash or reserve deposits.

Fourth Proposal: Wholesale CBDC Based On Distributed Ledger Technology

The fourth proposal (wholesale CBDC) is the most popular of the four proposals among central banks because of the potential to make existing wholesale financial systems faster, inexpensive, and safer. The Bank of International Settlements (BIS) also shares the view that wholesale CBDC could potentially benefit the payments and settlements system.

Some experiments have been already conducted or examined by central banks since 2016 such as those in Canada (called "CADcoin" under Project Jasper), Singapore (Project Ubin), Japan-Euro Area (Project Stella), Brazil, South Africa (Project Khokha), and Thailand (Project Inthanon). Among these central banks, those in Canada, Singapore, South Africa, Thailand have experimented with the proposal by involving a number of private sector financial institutions, fintech firms, consultants, and/or technology firms. The main purpose of these experiments was to promote the central bank's understanding of the DLT systems and their applicability in the existing wholesale financial markets, such as real-time gross settlement systems, delivery versus payment systems, cross-border interbank payments and settlements systems, etc.

The two frontrunner central banks are the Bank of Canada and Monetary Authority of Singapore, which launched a series of wholesale CBDC initiatives in 2016–2017 in the areas of interbank payments and settlements systems (real-time gross settlement systems) and delivery versus securities systems, etc. Both Canada and Singapore have concluded that their experiments successfully transferred digital tokens on a distributed ledger in real time and in reasonable volumes. Nevertheless, these central banks have not taken further steps toward actual implementation because of the view that the current technology has not yet been sufficiently advanced to cope with the issues related to the protection of privacy. Also, these central banks have the view that the process of verifying transactions could be faster and most cost-efficient if the verifier can be centralized (either through a group of selected commercial banks or a central bank), but then this approach would end up being similar to the existing centralized system (not necessarily becoming superior to the existing system). In addition, their current wholesale payments and settlements systems are already efficient enough, so no strong advantages can be expected from the CBDC initiative.

Subsequently, the Bank of Canada, Bank of England, and Monetary Authority of Singapore worked jointly together with some financial institutions based on Project Jasper and Project Ubin to assess whether wholesale CBDC could enhance cross-border payments and settlements by improving the access, speed, and transparency of payments. The three central banks published a joint report in November 2018 and concluded that further work on implementation and policy challenges would be required by both industry and regulators despite significant room expected for improvement in the cross-border payments space.

Regarding securities clearing and settlement systems, the Deutsche Bundesbank and Deutsche Börse jointly developed a DLT-based securities settlement platform that enables the delivery-versus-payment settlement of digital tokens and securities. Meanwhile, the Federal Reserve has not shown strong interest in issuing wholesale CBDC, mainly because of the view that the financial system is already efficient and sufficiently innovative.

CHAPTER

The Marshall Plan and the Present

Between 1948 and 1951, the United States undertook what many consider to be one of its more successful foreign policy initiatives and most effective foreign aid programs. The Marshall Plan (the Plan) and the European Recovery Program (ERP) that it generated involved an ambitious effort to stimulate economic growth in a despondent and nearly bankrupt post-World War II Europe, to prevent the spread of communism beyond the "iron curtain," and to encourage development of a healthy and stable world economy. It was designed to accomplish these goals by achieving three objectives:

1. the expansion of European agricultural and industrial production;
2. the restoration of sound currencies, budgets, and finances in individual European countries; and
3. the stimulation of international trade among European countries and between Europe and the rest of the world.

It is a measure of the positive impression enduring from the Economic Recovery Program that, ever since, in response to a critical situation faced by some regions of the world or some problem to be solved, there are periodic calls for a new Marshall Plan. In the 1990s, some Members of

Congress recommended "Marshall Plans" for Eastern Europe, the former Soviet Union, and the environment. Meanwhile, international statesmen suggested Marshall Plans for the Middle East and South Africa. In the 21st century, there continue to be recommendations for Marshall Plan-like assistance programs for refugees, urban infrastructure, Iraq, countries affected by the Ebola epidemic, the U.S.-Mexican border, Greece, and so on.

Generally, these references to the memory of the Marshall Plan are summonses to replicate its success or its scale, rather than every, or any, detail of the original Plan. The replicability of the Marshall Plan in these diverse situations or in the future is subject to question. To understand the potential relevance to the present of an event that took place decades ago, it is necessary to understand what the Plan sought to achieve, how it was implemented, and its resulting success or failure. This report looks at each of these factors.

Formulation Of The Marshall Plan

The Marshall Plan was proposed in a speech by Secretary of State George Marshall at Harvard University on June 5, 1947, in response to the critical political, social, and economic conditions in which Europe found itself at that time. Recognizing the necessity of congressional participation in development of a significant assistance package, Marshall's speech did not present a detailed and concrete program. He merely suggested that the United States would be willing to help draft a program and would provide assistance "so far as it may be practical for us to do so." In addition, Marshall called for this assistance to be a joint effort, "initiated" and agreed by European nations. The formulation of the Marshall Plan, therefore, was, from the beginning, a work of collaboration between the Truman Administration and Congress, and between the U.S. Government and European governments. The crisis that generated the Plan and the legislative and diplomatic outcome of Marshall's proposal are discussed below.

The Situation In Europe

European conditions in 1947, as described by Secretary of State Marshall and other U.S. officials at the time, were dire. Although industrial production had, in many cases, returned to prewar levels (the exceptions were Belgium, France, West Germany, Italy, and the Netherlands), the economic situation overall appeared to be deteriorating. The recovery had been financed by drawing down on domestic stocks and foreign assets. Capital was increasingly unavailable for investment. Agricultural supplies remained below 1938 levels and food imports were consuming a growing share of the limited foreign exchange. European nations were building up a growing dollar deficit. As a result, prospects for any future growth were low. Trade between European nations was stagnant.

Having already endured years of food shortages, unemployment, and other hardships associated with the war and recovery, the European public was now faced with further suffering. To many observers, the declining economic conditions were generating a pessimism regarding Europe's future that fed class divisions and political instability. Communist parties, already large in major countries such as Italy and France, threatened to come to power.

The potential impact on the United States was severalfold. For one, an end to European growth would block the prospect of any trade with the continent. One of the symptoms of Europe's malaise, in fact, was the massive dollar deficit that signaled its inability to pay for its imports from the United States.6 Perhaps the chief concern of the United States, however, was the growing threat of communism. Although the Cold War was still in its infancy, Soviet entrenchment in Eastern Europe was well under way. Already, early in 1947, the economic strain affecting Britain had driven it to announce its withdrawal of commitments in Greece and Turkey, forcing the United States to assume greater obligations to defend their security. The Truman Doctrine, enunciated in March 1947, stated that it was U.S. policy to provide support to nations threatened by communism. In brief, the specter of an economic collapse of Europe and a communist takeover of its political institutions threatened to uproot everything the United States claimed to strive for since its entry into World War II: a free Europe in an open-world economic system. U.S. leaders felt compelled to respond.

How The Plan Was Formulated

Three main hurdles had to be overcome on the way to developing a useful response to Europe's problems. For one, as Secretary of State Marshall's invitation indicated, European nations, acting jointly, had to come to some agreement on a plan. Second, the Administration and Congress had to reach their own concordance on a legislative program. Finally, the resulting plan had to be one that, in Marshall's words, would "provide a cure rather than a mere palliative."

The Role Of Europe

Most European nations responded favorably to the initial Marshall proposal. Insisting on a role in designing the program, 16 nations attended a conference in Paris (July 12, 1947) at which they established the Committee of European Economic Cooperation (CEEC). The committee was directed to gather information on European requirements and existing resources to meet those needs. Its final report (September 1947) called for a four-year program to encourage production, create internal financial stability, develop economic cooperation among participating countries, and solve the deficit problem then existing with the American dollar zone. Although Europe's net balance of payments deficit with the dollar zone for the 1948-1951 period was originally estimated at roughly $29 billion, the report requested $19 billion in U.S. assistance (an additional $3 billion was expected to come from the World Bank and other sources).

Cautious not to appear to isolate the Soviet Union at this stage in the still-developing Cold War, Marshall's invitation did not specifically exclude any European nation. Britain and France made sure to include the Soviets in an early three-power discussion of the proposal. Nevertheless, the Soviet Union and, under pressure, its satellites, refused to participate in a common recovery program on the grounds that the necessity to reveal national economic plans would infringe on national sovereignty and that the U.S. interest was only to increase its exports.

CEEC formulation of its proposal was not without U.S. input. Its draft proposal had reflected the wide differences existing between individual nations in their approach to trade liberalization, the role of Germany, and state controls over national economies. As a result of these differences, the United States was afraid that the CEEC proposal would be little more than a shopping list of needs without any coherent program to generate long-term growth. To avoid such a situation, the State Department conditioned its acceptance of the European program on participants' agreement to;

1. make specific commitments to fulfill production programs,
2. take immediate steps to create internal monetary and financial stability,
3. express greater determination to reduce trade barriers,
4. consider alternative sources of dollar credits, such as the World Bank,
5. give formal recognition to their common objectives and assume common responsibility for attaining them, and
6. establish an international organization to act as coordinating agency to implement the program.

The final report of the CEEC contained these obligations.

Executive And Congressional Roles

After the European countries had taken the required initiative and presented a formal plan, both the Administration and Congress responded. Formulation of that response had already begun soon after the Marshall speech. As a Democratic President facing a Republican-majority Congress with many Members highly skeptical of the need for further foreign assistance, Truman took a two-pronged approach that greatly facilitated development of a program: he opened his foreign policy initiative to perhaps the most thorough examination prior to launching of any program and, secondly, provided a perhaps equally rare process of close consultation between the executive and Congress.

From the first, the Truman Administration made Congress a player in the development of the new foreign aid program, consulting with it throughout the process (see text box). A meeting on June 22, 1947, between key congressional leaders and the President led to creation of the Harriman, Krug, and Nourse committees. Secretary of Commerce Averell Harriman's committee, composed of consultants from private industry, labor, economists, etc., looked at Europe's needs. Secretary of Interior Julius A. Krug's committee examined those U.S. physical resources available to support such a program. The group led by Chairman of the Council of Economic Advisers Edwin G. Nourse studied the effect an enlarged export burden would have on U.S. domestic production and prices. The House of Representatives itself formed the Select Committee on Foreign Aid, led by Representative Christian A. Herter, to take a broad look at these issues.

Before the Administration proposal could be submitted for consideration, the situation in some countries deteriorated so seriously that the President called for a special interim aid package to hold them over through the winter with food and fuel until the more elaborate system anticipated by the Marshall Plan could be authorized. Congress approved interim aid to France, Italy, and Austria amounting to $522 million in an authorization signed by President Truman on December 17, 1947. West Germany, also in need, was still being assisted through the Government and Relief in Occupied Areas (GARIOA) program.

State Department proposals for a European Recovery Program were formally presented by Truman in a message to Congress on December 19, 1947. He called for a 4¼-year program of aid to 16 West European countries in the form of both grants and loans. Although the program anticipated total aid amounting to about $17 billion, the Administration bill, as introduced by Representative Charles Eaton, chairman of the House Committee on Foreign Affairs, in early 1948 (H.R. 4840) provided an authorization of $6.8 billion for the first 15 months. The House Foreign Affairs and Senate Foreign Relations Committees amended the bill extensively. As S. 2202, it passed the Senate by a 69-17 vote on March 13, 1948, and the House on March 31, 1948, by a vote of 329 to 74. The bill authorized $5.3 billion over a one-year period. On April 3, 1948, the Economic Cooperation Act (title I of the Foreign Assistance Act of 1948, P.L. 80-472) became law. The Appropriations Committee conference allocated $4 billion to the European Recovery Program in its first year.

By restricting the authorization to one year, Congress gave itself ample opportunity to oversee European Recovery Program implementation and consider additional funding. Three more times during the life of the Marshall Plan, Congress would be required to authorize and appropriate funds. In each year, Congress held hearings, debated, and further amended the legislation. As part of the first authorization, it created a joint congressional "watchdog" committee to follow program implementation and report to Congress.

The Organization For European Economic Cooperation

A European body, the Organization for European Economic Cooperation (OEEC), was established by agreement of the participating countries in order to maintain the "joint" nature by which the program was founded and reinforce the sense of mutual responsibility for its success. Earlier, the participating countries had jointly pledged themselves to certain obligations (see above). The OEEC was to be the instrument that would guide members to fulfill their multilateral undertaking.

To advance this purpose, the OEEC developed analyses of economic conditions and needs, and, through formulation of a Plan of Action, influenced the direction of investment projects and encouraged joint adoption of policy reforms such as those leading to elimination of intra-European trade barriers.

At the ECA's request, it also recommended and coordinated the division of aid among the 16 countries.

Each year the participating countries would submit a yearly program to the OEEC, which would then make recommendations to the ECA. Determining assistance allocations was not an easy matter, especially since funding declined each year. As a result, there was much bickering among countries, but a formula was eventually reached to divide the aid.

Programs

The framers of the European Recovery Program envisioned a number of tools with which to accomplish its ends. These are discussed below.

Dollar Aid: Commodity Assistance and Project Financing

Grants made up more than 90% of the ERP. The ECA provided outright grants that were used to pay the cost and freight of essential commodities and services, mostly from the United States. Conditional grants were also provided requiring the participating country to set aside currency so that other participating countries could buy their export goods. This was done to stimulate intra-European trade.

The ECA also provided loans. ECA loans bore an interest rate of 2.5% starting in 1952, and matured up to 35 years from December 31, 1948, with principal repayments starting no later than 1956. The ECA supervised the use of the dollar credits. European importers made purchases through normal channels and paid American sellers with checks drawn on American credit institutions.

The legislation funding the first year of the ERP provided that $1 billion of the total authorized should be available only in the form of loans or guaranties. In 1949, Congress reduced the amount available only for loans to $150 million. The Administrator had decided that loans in excess of these amounts should not be made because of the inadvisability of participating countries assuming further dollar obligations, which would increase the dollar gap the Plan was attempting to close. As of June 30, 1949, $972.3 million of U.S. aid had been in the form of loans, while $4.948 billion was in the form of grants. Estimates for July 1949 to June 1950 were $150 million in loans and $3.594 billion for grants.

The content of the dollar aid purchases changed over time as European needs changed. From a program supplying immediate food-related goods—food, feed, fertilizer, and fuel—it eventually provided mostly raw materials and production equipment. Between early 1948 and 1949, food-related assistance declined from roughly 50% of the total to only 27%. The proportion of raw material and machinery rose from 20% to roughly 50% in this same time period.

Project financing became important during the later stages of the ERP. ECA dollar assistance was used with local capital in specific projects requiring importation of equipment from abroad. The advantage here was leveraging of local funds. By June 30, 1951, the ECA had approved 139 projects financed by a combination of U.S. and domestic capital. Their aggregate cost was $2.25 billion, of which only $565 million was directly provided by Marshall Plan assistance funds.25 Of these projects, at least 27 were in the area of power production and 32 were for the modernization and expansion of steel and iron production. Many others were devoted to rehabilitation of transport infrastructure.

Counterpart Funds

Each country was required to match the U.S. grant contribution: a dollar's worth of its own currency for each dollar of grant aid given by the United States. The participating country's currency was placed in a counterpart fund that could be used for infrastructure projects (e.g., roads, power plants, housing projects, airports) of benefit to that country. Each of these counterpart fund projects, however, had to be approved by the ECA Administrator. In the case of Great Britain, counterpart funds were deemed inflationary and simply returned to the national treasury to help balance the budget.

By the end of December 1951, roughly $8.6 billion of counterpart funds had been made available. Of the approximately $7.6 billion approved for use, $2 billion was used for debt reduction as in Great Britain and roughly $4.8 billion was earmarked for investment, of which 39% was in utilities, transportation, and communication facilities (electric power projects, railroads, etc.), 14% in agriculture, 16% in manufacturing, 10% in coal mining and other extractive industries, and 12% in low-cost housing facilities. Three countries accounted for 80% of counterpart funds used for production purposes—France (half), West Germany, and Italy/Trieste.

Five percent of the counterpart funds could be used to pay the administrative expenses of the ECA in Europe as well as for purchase of scarce raw materials needed by the United States or to develop sources of supply for such materials. Up to August 1951, more than $160 million was committed for these purposes, mostly in the dependent territories of Europe. For example, enterprises were set up for development of nickel in New Caledonia, chromite in Turkey, and bauxite in Jamaica.

Technical Assistance

Technical assistance was also provided under the ERP. A special fund was created to finance expenses of U.S. experts in Europe and visits by European delegations to the United States. Funds could be used only on projects contributing directly to increased production and stability. The ECA targeted problems of industrial productivity, marketing, agricultural productivity, manpower utilization, public administration, tourism, transportation, and communications. In most cases, countries receiving such aid had to deposit counterpart funds equivalent to the dollar expenses involved in each project. Through 1949, $5 million had been set aside for technical assistance under which 350 experts had been sent from the United States to provide services and 481 persons from Europe had come to the United States for training. By the end of 1951, with more than $30 million expended, over 6,000 Europeans representing management, technicians, and labor had come to the United States for periods of study of U.S. production methods.

Although it is estimated that less than one-half of 1% of all Marshall Plan aid was spent on technical assistance, the effect of such assistance was significant. Technical assistance was a major component of the "productivity campaign" launched by the ECA. Production was not merely a function of possessing up-to-date machinery, but of management and labor styles of work. As one Senate Appropriations staffer noted, "Productivity in French industry is better than in several other Marshall-plan countries but it still requires four times as many man-hours to produce a Renault automobile as it does for a Chevrolet, and the products themselves are hardly comparable." To attempt to bring European production up to par, the ECA funded studies of business styles, conducted management seminars, arranged visits of businessmen and labor representatives to the United States to explain American methods of production, and set up national productivity centers in almost every participating country.

Investment Guaranties

Guaranties were provided for convertibility into dollars of profits on American private sector investments in Europe. The purpose of the guaranties was to encourage American businessmen to invest in the modernization and development of European industry by ensuring that returns could be obtained in dollars. The original ERP Act covered only the approved amount of dollars invested, but subsequent authorizations broadened the definition of investment and increased the amount of the potential guaranty by adding to actual investment earnings or profits up to 175% of dollar investment. The risk covered was extended as well to include compensation for loss of investment due to expropriation. Although $300 million was authorized by Congress (subsequently amended to

$200 million), investment guaranties covering 38 industrial investments amounted to only $31.4 million by June 1952.

How Programs Contributed To Aims

The individual components of the European Recovery Program contributed directly to the immediate aims of the Marshall Plan. Dollar assistance kept the dollar gap to a minimum. The ECA made sure that both dollar and counterpart assistance were funneled toward activities that would do the most to increase production and lead to general recovery. The emphasis in financial and technical assistance on productivity helped to maximize the efficient use of dollar and counterpart funds to increase production and boost trade. The importance to future European growth of this infusion of directed assistance should not be underestimated. During the recovery period, Europe maintained an investment level of 20% of GNP, one-third higher than the prewar rate. Since national savings were practically zero in 1948, the high rate of investment is largely attributable to U.S. assistance.

But the aims of the Marshall Plan were not achieved by financial and technical assistance programs alone. The importance of these American-sponsored programs is that they helped to create the framework in which the overall OEEC European program of action functioned. American aid was leveraged to encourage Europeans to come together and act, individually and collectively, in a purposeful fashion on behalf of the three themes of increased production, expanded trade, and economic stability through policy reform.

The first requirement of the Marshall Plan was that European nations commit themselves to these objectives. On an individual basis, each nation then used its counterpart funds and American dollar assistance to fulfill these objectives. They also, with the analytical assistance of both fellow European nations under the OEEC and the American representatives of the ECA, closely examined their economic systems. Through this process, the ECA and OEEC sought to identify and remove obstacles to growth, to avoid unsound national investment plans, and to promote adoption of appropriate currency levels. Thanks to American assistance, many note, European nations were able to undertake recommended and necessary reforms at lesser political cost in terms of imposing economic hardship on their publics than would have been the case without aid. In this regard, some argue that it was Marshall Plan aid that enabled economist Jean Monnet's plan of modernization and reform of the French economy to succeed.

However, contending with deeply felt sensitivities regarding European sovereignty, U.S. influence on European economic and social decisionmaking as a direct result of European Recovery Program assistance was restricted. Where it controlled counterpart funds for use in capital projects, American influence was considerable. Where counterpart funds were simply used to retire debt to assist financial stability, there was little such influence. Some analysts suggest the United States had minimal control over European domestic policy since its assistance was small relative to the total resources of European countries. But while it could do little to get Europe to relinquish control over exchange rates, on less sensitive issues the United States, many argue, was able to effect change. On a few occasions, the ECA did threaten sanctions if participating countries did not comply with their bilateral agreements. Italy was threatened with loss of aid for not acting to adopt recommended programs and, in April 1950, aid was actually withheld from Greece to force appropriate domestic action.

As a collective of European nations, the OEEC generated peer pressure that encouraged individual nations to fulfill their Marshall Plan obligations. The OEEC provided a forum for discussion and eventual negotiation of agreements conducive to intra-European trade. For Europeans, its existence made the Plan seem less an American program. In line with the American desire to foster European integration, the OEEC helped to create the "European idea." As West German Vice-Chancellor Blucher noted, "The OEEC had at least one great element. European men came together, knew each other, and were ready for cooperation." The ECA provided financial assistance to efforts to encourage European integration (see below), and, more importantly, it provided the OEEC with some financial leverage of its own. By asking the OEEC to take on a share of responsibility for allocating American aid among participating countries, the ECA elevated the organization to a higher status than might have been the case otherwise and thereby facilitated achievement of Marshall Plan aims.

The Sum Of Its Parts: Evaluating The Marshall Plan

How the Marshall Plan Was Different

Assistance to Europe was not new with the Marshall Plan. In fact, during the 2½-year period from July 1945 to

December 1947, roughly $11 billion had been provided to Europe, compared with the estimated $13 billion in 3½ years of the Marshall Plan. Two factors that distinguish the Marshall Plan from its predecessors are that the Marshall Plan was the result of a thorough planning process and was sharply focused on economic development. Because the earlier, more ad hoc and humanitarian relief-oriented assistance had made little dent on European recovery, a different, coherent approach was put forward. The new approach called for a concerted program with a definite purpose. The purpose was European recovery, defined as increased agricultural and industrial production; restoration of sound currencies, budgets, and finances; and stimulation of international trade among participating countries and between them and the rest of the world. The Marshall Plan, as illustrated in the preceding section, ensured that each technical and financial assistance component contributed as directly as possible to these long-range objectives.

Other aspects of its deliberate character were distinctive. It had definite time and monetary limits. It was made clear at the start that the U.S. contribution would diminish each year. In addition to broad objectives, it also supported, by reference to the CEEC program in the legislation and, more specifically, in congressional report language, the ambitious quantitative targets assumed by the participating countries.

The Marshall Plan was also a "joint" effort. By bringing in European nations as active participants in the program, the United States ensured that their mutual commitment to alter economic policies, a necessity if growth was to be stimulated, would be translated into action and that the objective of integration would be further encouraged. The

Marshall Plan promoted recognition of the economic interdependence of Europe. By making Congress a firm partner in the formulation of the program, the Administration ensured continued congressional support for the commitment of large sums over a period of years.

Further, the Marshall Plan was a first recognition by U.S. leaders of the link between economic growth and political stability. Unlike previous postwar aid, which was two-thirds repayable loans and one-third relief supplies, Marshall Plan aid was almost entirely in the form of grants aimed at productive, developmental purposes. The reason for this large infusion of grants in peacetime was that U.S. national security had been redefined as containment of communism. Governments whose citizens were unemployed and unfed were unstable and open to communist advancement. Only long-term economic growth could provide stability and, as an added benefit, save the United States from having to continue an endless process of stop-gap relief-based assistance.

The unique nature of the Marshall Plan is perhaps best emphasized by what replaced it. The Cold War, reinforced by the Korean War, signaled the end of the Marshall Plan by altering the priority of U.S. aid from that of economic stability to military security. In September 1950, the ECA informed the European participants that henceforth a growing proportion of aid would be allocated for European rearmament purposes. Although originally scheduled to end on June 30, 1952, the Plan began to wind down in December 1950 when aid to Britain was suspended. In the following months, Ireland, Sweden, and Portugal graduated from the program. The use of counterpart funds for production purposes was phased out. To attack inflation, which resulted from the shortage of materials due to the Korean War, the ECA had begun to release counterpart funds. In the fourth quarter of 1950, $1.3 billion was released, two-thirds of which were used in retiring public debt.

Under the Mutual Security Act of 1951 and subsequent legislation, although in lesser quantities and in increasing proportions devoted to defense, aid continued to be provided to many European countries. In the 1952-1953 appropriations, for example, France received $525 million in grants, half of which was for defense support and the other as budget support. The joint nature of the Marshall Plan disappeared as national sovereignty came to the fore again. France insisted on using post-Marshall Plan counterpart funds as it wished, commingling them with other funds and only later attributing appropriate amounts to certain projects to satisfy American concerns.

Accomplishments Of The Marshall Plan

To many analysts and policymakers, the effect of the Marshall Plan policies and programs on the economic and political situation in Europe appeared broad and pervasive. While, in some cases, a direct connection can be drawn between American assistance and a positive outcome, for the most part, the Marshall Plan may be viewed best as a stimulus which set off a chain of events leading to the accomplishments noted below.

Did It Meet Its Objectives?

The Marshall Plan agencies, the ECA and OEEC, established a number of quantitative standards as their objectives, reflecting some of the broader purposes noted earlier.

Balance of Trade and the Dollar Gap

In 1948, participating countries could pay for only half of their imports by exporting. An objective of the ERP was to get European countries to the point where they could pay for 83% of their imports in this manner. Although they paid for 70% by exporting in 1938, the larger ratio was sought under ERP because earnings from overseas investment had declined.

Even though trade rose substantially, especially among participants, the volume of imports from the rest of the world rose substantially as well, and prices for these imports rose faster than did prices of exports. As a result, Europe continued to be strained. One obstacle to expansion of exports was breaking into the U.S. and South American markets, where U.S. producers were entrenched. OEEC exports to North America rose from 14% of imports in 1947 to nearly 50% in 1952.

Related to the overall balance of trade was the deficit vis-a-vis the dollar area, especially the United States. In 1947, the total gold and dollar deficit was over $8 billion. By 1949, it had dropped to $4.5 billion, by 1952 to half that figure, and by the first half of 1953 had reached an approximate current balance with the dollar area.

Trade Liberalization

In 1949, the OEEC Council asked members to take steps to eliminate quantitative import restrictions. By the end of 1949, and by February 1951, 50% and 75% of quota restrictions on imports were eliminated, respectively. By 1955, 90% of restrictions were gone. In 1951, the OEEC set up rules of conduct in trade under the Code of Liberalization of Trade and Invisible Transactions. At the end of 1951, trade volume within Europe was almost double that of 1947.

Psychological Boost

Many believe that the role of the Marshall Plan in raising morale in Europe was as great a contribution to the prevention of communism and stimulation of growth as any financial assistance. As the then-Director of Policy Planning at the State Department George Kennan noted, "The psychological success at the outset was so amazing that we felt that the psychological effect was four-fifths accomplished before the first supplies arrived."

Economic Integration

The United States had a view of itself as a model for the development of Europe, with individual countries equated with American states. As such, U.S. leaders saw a healthy Europe as one in which trade restraints and other barriers to interaction, such as the inconvertibility of currencies, would be eliminated. The European Recovery Program required coordinated planning for recovery and the establishment of the OEEC for this purpose. In 1949, the ERP Authorization Act was amended to make it the explicit policy of the United States to encourage the unification of Europe. Efforts in support of European integration, integral to the original Marshall Plan, were strengthened at this time.

To encourage intra-European trade, the ECA in its first year went so far as to provide dollars to participating countries to finance their purchase of vitally needed goods available in other participating countries (even if these were available in the United States). In a step toward encouraging European independence from the dollar standard, it also established an intra-European payments plan whereby dollar grants were made to countries that exported more to Europe as a group than they imported, on condition that these creditor countries finance their export balance in their own currencies.

The European Payments Union (EPU), an outgrowth of the payments plan, was established in 1950 by member countries to act as a central clearance and credit system for settlement of all payments transactions among members and associated monetary areas (such as the sterling area). At ECA request, the 1951 congressional authorization withheld funds specifically to encourage the pursuit of this program since successful conclusion of the EPU depended on an American financial contribution. In the end, the United States provided $350 million to help set up the EPU and another $100 million to assist it through initial difficulties. Many believe that these and other steps initiated under the ERP led to the launching of the European Coal and Steel Community in 1952 and eventually to the European Union of today.

Stability and Containment of Communism

Perhaps the greatest inducement to the United States in setting up the Marshall Plan had been the belief that economic hardship in Europe would lead to political instability and inevitably to communist governments throughout the continent. In essence, the ERP allowed economic growth and prosperity to occur in Europe with fewer political and social costs. Plan assistance allowed recipients to carry a larger import surplus with less strain on the financial system than would be the case otherwise. It made possible larger investments without corresponding reductions in living standards and could be anti-inflationary by mopping up purchasing power through the sale of imported assistance goods without increasing the supply of money. The production aspects of the Plan also helped relieve hunger among the general population. Human food consumption per capita reached the prewar level by 1951. In West Germany, economically devastated and besieged by millions of refugees from the East, one house of every five built since 1948 had received Marshall Plan aid.

Perhaps as a result of these benefits, communism in Europe was prevented from coming to power via the ballot box. It is estimated that communist strength in Western Europe declined by almost one-third between 1946 and 1951. In the 1951 elections, the combined pro-Western vote was 84% of the electorate.

U.S. Domestic Procurement

Champions of the Marshall Plan hold that its authorizing legislation was free of most of the potential restrictions sought by private interests of the sort to later appear in foreign aid programs. Nevertheless, restrictions were enacted that did benefit the United States and U.S. business in particular.

Procurement of surplus goods was encouraged under the Economic Recovery Program legislation, while procurement of goods in short supply in the United States was discouraged. It was required that surplus agriculture commodities be supplied by the United States; procurement of these was to be encouraged by the ECA Administrator. The ERP required that 25% of total wheat had to be in the form of flour, and half of all goods had to be carried on American ships.

In the end, an estimated 70% of European purchases using ECA dollars were spent in the United States.53 Types of commodities purchased from the United States included foodstuffs (grain, dairy products), cotton, fuel, industrial and raw materials (iron and steel, aluminum, copper, lumber), and industrial and agricultural machinery. Sugar and nonferrous metals made up the bulk of purchases from outside the United States.

Enhanced Role in Europe for the United States

U.S. prestige and power in Europe were already strong following World War II. In several respects, however, the U.S. role in Europe was greatly enhanced by virtue of the Marshall Plan program. U.S. private sector economic relations grew substantially during this period as a consequence of the program's encouragement of increased exports from Europe and ERP grants and loans for the purchase of U.S. goods. The book value of U.S. investment in Europe also rose significantly. Furthermore, while the Marshall Plan grew out of a recognition of the economic interdependence of the two continents, its implementation greatly increased awareness of that fact. The OEEC, which, in 1961, became the OECD (Organization for Economic Co-operation and Development) with the United States as a full member, endured and provided a forum for discussion of economic problems of mutual concern. Finally, the act of U.S. support for Europe and the creation of a diplomatic relationship which centered on economic issues in the OEEC facilitated the evolution of a relationship centered on military and security issues. In the view of ECA Administrator Hoffman, the Marshall Plan made the Atlantic Alliance (NATO) possible.

Proving Ground for U.S. Development Programs

Many of the operational methods and programs devised and tested under the Marshall Plan became regular practices of later development efforts. For example, the ECA was established as an independent agency with a mission in each participating country to ensure close interaction with governments and the private sector, a model later adopted by the U.S. Agency for International Development (USAID). Unlike previous aid efforts, the Plan promoted policy reform and used commodity import programs and counterpart funds to ease adoption of those reforms and undertake development programs, a practice of USAID programs in later decades. The Marshall Plan also launched the first participant training programs bringing Europeans to the United States for training and leveraged private sector investment in recipient countries through the use of U.S. government guaranties. Hundreds of American economists and other specialists who implemented the Marshall Plan gained invaluable experience that many later applied to their work in developing countries for the ECA's successor foreign aid agencies.

Critiques Of The Marshall Plan

Not everyone agrees that the Marshall Plan was a success. One such appraisal was that Marshall Plan assistance was unnecessary. It is, for example, difficult to demonstrate that ERP aid was directly responsible for the increase in production and other quantitative achievements noted above. Critics have argued that assistance was never more than 5% of the GNP of recipient nations and therefore could have little effect. European economies, in this view, were already on the way to recovery before the Marshall Plan was implemented. Some analysts, pointing out the experimental nature of the Plan, agree that the method of aid allocation and the program of economic reforms promoted under it were not derived with scientific precision. Some claim that the dollar gap was not a problem and that lack of economic growth was the result of bad economic policy, resolved when economic controls established during the Nazi era were eventually lifted.

Even at the time of the Marshall Plan, there were those who found the program lacking. If Marshall Plan aid was going to combat communism, they felt, it would have to provide benefits to the working class in Europe. Many believed that the increased production sought by the Plan would have little effect on those most inclined to support communism. In congressional hearings, some Members repeatedly sought assurances that the aid was benefiting the working class. Would loans to French factory owners, they asked, lead to higher salaries for employees? Journalist Theodore H. White was another who questioned this "trickle" (now called the "trickle-down") approach to recovery. "The trickle theory had, thus far," White wrote in 1953, "resulted in a brilliant recovery of European production. But it had yielded no love for America and little diminution of Communist loyalty where it was entrenched in the misery of the continental workers."

In addition, many did not want the United States to appear to be assisting colonial rule. Considerable concern was expressed that the aid provided to Europe would allow these countries to maintain their colonies in Africa and Asia. The switch in emphasis from economic development to military development that began in the third year of the Plan was also the subject of criticism, especially in view of the limited time frame originally allowed for the aid program. A staff member of the Senate Appropriations Committee's Special Sub-committee on Foreign Economic Cooperation believed that the original intent of the Marshall Plan could not be accomplished under these conditions.

The tactics employed to achieve Marshall Plan objectives were often questioned as well. "Much of our effort in France has been contradictory," reported the committee staffer. "On the one hand, we have been working toward the abolition of trade barriers between European countries and on the other we have been fostering, or rebuilding, uneconomic industries which cannot survive unhampered international competition." Another concern was the proportion of funding that went to the public rather than private sector. One contemporary writer noted that public investments from the Italian counterpart fund obtained twice the amount of assistance as did the private sector in that country. Another analyst has argued that the ECA promoted government intervention in the economy. In the 1950 authorization hearings, U.S. businessmen urged that assistance be provided directly to foreign business rather than through European governments. Only in this way, they said, could free enterprise be promoted in Europe.

From its inception, some Members of Congress voiced fears that the ERP would have a negative effect on U.S. business. Some noted that the effort to close the trade gap by encouraging Europeans to export and limit their imports would diminish U.S. exports to the region. Amendments, most defeated, were offered to ERP legislation to ensure that certain segments of the private sector would benefit from Marshall Plan aid. That strengthening Europe economically meant increased competition for U.S. business also was not lost on legislators. The ECA, for example, helped Europeans rebuild their merchant marine fleets and, by the end of 1949, had authorized over $167 million in European steel mill projects, most using the more advanced continuous rolling mill process that had previously been little used in Europe. As the congressional "watchdog" committee staff noted, "The ECA program involves economic sacrifice either in direct expenditure of Federal funds or in readjustments of agriculture and industry to allow for foreign competition." In the end, the United States seemed to be willing to make both sacrifices

Lessons of the Marshall Plan

The Marshall Plan was viewed by Congress, as well as others, as a "new and far-reaching experiment in foreign relations." Although in many ways unique to the requirements of its time, analysts have attempted over the years to draw from it various lessons that might possibly be applied to present or future foreign aid initiatives. These lessons represent what observers believe were some of the primary strengths of the Plan:

- Strong leadership and well-developed argument overcame opposition. Despite growing national isolationism, polls showing little support for the Marshall Plan, a Congress dominated by budget cutters, and an election looming whose outlook was unfavorable to the President, the Administration decided it was the right thing to do and led a campaign—with national commissions set up and Cabinet members travelling the country—to sell the Plan to the American people.

- Congress was included at the beginning to formulate the program. Because he faced a Congress controlled by the opposition party, Truman made the European Recovery Program a cooperative bipartisan creation, which helped garner support and prevented it from becoming bogged down with private-interest earmarks. Congress maintained its active role by conducting detailed hearings and studies on ERP implementation.

- Country ownership made reforms sustainable. The beneficiaries were required to put together the proposal. Because the Plan targeted changes in the nature of the European economic system, the United States was sensitive to European national sovereignty. European cooperation was critical to establishing an active commitment from participants on a wide range of delicate issues.

- The collective approach facilitated success. Recovery efforts were framed as a joint endeavor, with the Europeans joining together in the CEEC to propose the program and the OEEC to implement key features, including collaborating to make grant allocation decisions and cooperating to lower trade barriers.

- The Marshall Plan had specific goals. Resources were dedicated to meeting the goals of increased production, trade, and stability.

- The Marshall Plan fit the objective. In the main, the Plan was not a short-term humanitarian relief program. It was a multiyear plan designed specifically to bring about the economic recovery of Europe and avoid the repeated need for relief programs that had characterized U.S. assistance to Europe since the War.

- The countries to be assisted, for the most part, had the capacity to recover. They, in fact, were recovering, not developing from scratch. The human and natural resources necessary for economic growth were largely available; the chief thing missing was capital.

- Trade supplemented aid. Aid alone was insufficient to assist Europe economically. A report in October 1949 by the ECA and Department of Commerce found that the United States should purchase as much as $2 billion annually in additional goods if Europe was to balance its trade by the close of the recovery program. Efforts to increase intra-European trade, such as funding the European Payments Union, were meant to bolster bilateral efforts.

- Parochial congressional tendencies to put restrictions on the program on behalf of U.S. business were kept under control for the good of the program. American businessmen, for example, were not happy that the ECA insisted Europeans purchase what was available first in Europe using soft currency before turning to the United States.

- Technical assistance, including exchanges, while inexpensive relative to capital block grants, may have a significant impact on economic growth. Under the Marshall Plan, technical assistance helped draw attention to the management and labor factors hindering productivity. It demonstrated American know-how and helped develop in Europe a positive feeling regarding America.

- The long-term foreign policy value of foreign assistance cannot be adequately measured in terms of short-term consequences. The Marshall Plan continues to have an impact: in NATO, the OECD, the European Community, the German Marshall Fund, in European bilateral aid donor programs, and in the stability and prosperity of modern Europe.66

The Marshall Plan as Precedent

Although many disparate elements of Marshall Plan assistance speak to the present, the circumstances faced now by most other parts of the world are so different and more complex than those encountered by Western Europe in the period 1948-1952 that the solution posed for one is not entirely applicable to the other. As noted earlier, calls for new Marshall Plans have continued ever since the first, but the first was unique, and today's proposals share little detail with their predecessor apart from the suggestion that a problem should be solved with the same concentrated energies, if not funds, applied decades ago.

Even if there exist countries whose needs are similar in nature to what the Marshall Plan provided, the position of the United States has changed since the late 1940s as well. The roughly $13.3 billion provided by the United States to 16 nations over a period of less than four years equals an estimated $143 billion in 2017 currency. That sum surpasses the amount of development and humanitarian assistance the United States provided from all sources to 212 countries and numerous international development organizations and banks in the four-year period 2013-2016 ($138 billion in 2017 dollars).67 In 1948, when the United States appropriated $4 billion for the first year of the Marshall Plan, outlays for the entire federal budget equaled slightly less than $30 billion.68 For the United States to be willing to expend 13% of its budget on anyone program (versus 0.8% in FY2016 for foreign assistance), Congress and the President would have to agree that the activity was a major national priority.

Nevertheless, in pondering the difficulties of new Marshall Plans, it is perhaps worth considering the views of the ECA Administrator, Paul Hoffman, who noted 20 years after Secretary Marshall's historic speech that even though the

Plan was "one of the most truly generous impulses that has ever motivated any nation anywhere at any time," the United States "derived enormous benefits from the bread it figuratively cast upon the international waters." In Hoffman's view:

Today, the United States, its former partners in the Marshall Plan and in fact all other advanced industrialized countries … are being offered an even bigger bargain: the chance to form an effective partnership for world-wide economic and social progress with the earth's hundred and more low-income nations. The potential profits in terms of expanded prosperity and a more secure peace could dwarf those won through the European Recovery Program. Yet the danger that this bargain will be rejected out of apathy, indifference, and discouragement over the relatively slow progress toward self-sufficiency made by the developing countries thus far is perhaps even greater than was the case with the Marshall Plan. For the whole broadscale effort of development assistance to the world's poorer nations—an effort that is generally, but I think quite misleadingly, called "foreign aid"—has never received the full support it merits and is now showing signs of further slippage in both popular and governmental backing. Under these circumstances, the study of the Marshall Plan's brief but brilliantly successful history is much more than an academic exercise

The Marshall Plan And Its Relevance For The Present Times

The Marshall Plan as a political tool for reform

Bradford De Long and Barry Eichengreen have a slightly different interpretation from Milward's, as they stated that the Marshall Plan did play an important role in Western Europe's recovery, but more for its political influence and not as much in its financial aid role. They state that these economies would little by little start to expand and eliminate trade barriers between its members, prioritizing free markets, less regulation, and balanced budgets, among other macro-economic measures.

In the United States' point of view of the time, the relatively open market that served as the basis for its economic growth was to be replicated in Western Europe after World War II. However, following the economic crash of 1929, European economies were not that open for economic change certainly not in the direction of free markets. The Marshall Plan sought for a return of these goals to European economic policy: in 1948, for example, a parcel of the Marshall Plan funding had been given to France with a demand for the French government to balance its budget and deregulate its economy.

The Marshall Plan did play an important role in Western Europe's recovery, but more for its political influence and not as much in its financial aid role. Indeed, according to Long and Eichengreen, about 83% of Marshall aid was used on imports of various products, industrial commodities, and agricultural products. This would also greatly benefit the largest producer of manufactured goods for Western

Europe at the time: the United States. Only about 17% was used for machinery, transports or others. The Marshall Plan would thus provide more money for necessary and largely freer imports and greater intra-European trade and the injection of necessary capital movement.

The Marshall Plan: the foundation for a common European economy?

While France was focused on a primarily European community as its economic foundation, (aside from its colonial holdings) without the Marshall Plan, the French road to economic recovery might have been very different. The Marshall Plan was, therefore, not only an important economic aid but it was also a political device for reform in Western Europe. It presented a facilitated solution for the countries' treasuries as a structural reform plan, rather than simple aid.

The Marshall Plan was also strongly tied with the Bretton Woods system as another important global monetary and financial transformation. The Marshall Plan was, therefore, a facilitator for economic growth but not an initiator: it represented only 3% of the national incomes of the states that received it. Social programs were at the time struggling for more revenues at the same time as inflationary policies and budget deficits were still a risk.

Aid is important but reform is much more significant.

Therefore, although the United States' direct economic role in the European recovery is still debatable, as Milward and other authors have shown, the Marshall Plan should be understood in a context where the United States were ensuring the political and military safety and stability in Western Europe, without which many of these advancements would perhaps not have been possible.

Consequently, the execution of American foreign policy (whether politically or economically) can indeed be considered as having a predominantly positive effect on the evolution of later European integration.

Lessons from the Marshall Plan for the COVID-19 pandemic

The financial aid provided by the Marshall Plan was more important due to its economically reformative stance, rather than due to its purely material financial scope. The reformative stance of the Marshall Plan facilitated expanding free markets and increasing productivity for European, particularly West-German imports and exports. This can be seen to have fed into the forces that also led to the creation of the European Economic Community (and later the European Union).

Despite the differences between post-war Europe and the present Corona crisis, historical occurrences can be revisited, and old lessons learned anew: The Corona crisis is also a global economic crisis. The Marshall Plan can serve as an example of how a crisis can be fought not only relying on financial or monetary aid but also with an effective push for policy-reform. Both the lessons of the Marshall Plan and the Euro crisis must serve as important reminders on how to tackle the Corona crisis today.

The fact that the present American presidency is focused on greater protectionism led to European crisis relief efforts this time being handled by primarily the ECB and the European Commission. The ECB has coupled a vast monetary mass plan with low interest rates and controlled inflation, while the Commission has proposed an extra intergovernmental budget (2021-2027).

It consists of approximately €1.8 trillion, in both hand-outs and loans, designed to facilitate the financial recovery of states and companies, all the while grappling with the hard task of assuring medical and health stability of the population (together with states).

The 2008 financial crisis led to great divisions within the EU, high unemployment, and an economic recession. However, low inflation levels in the Eurozone were maintained (despite a much greater monetary mass) and economic recovery was attained for some years. Both the lessons of the Marshall Plan and the Euro crisis must serve as important reminders on how to tackle the Corona crisis today. Aid is important but reform is much more significant.

CONCLUSION

The ongoing digital revolution and the rise of large tech firms present the possibility of a radical departure from the traditional model of monetary exchange. The structure and technology underlying digital networks may lead to an unbundling of the separate roles of money, creating fiercer competition among specialized currencies. The association of digital currencies with large platform ecosystems, on the other hand, may lead to a remuddling of money in which payment services are packaged with an array of data services, encouraging differentiation but discouraging interoperability between platforms. Convertibility among monetary instruments and interoperability between platforms will be crucial in lowering barriers to trade and promoting competition. Digital currencies may also cause an upheaval of the international monetary system: countries that are socially or digitally integrated with their neighbors may face digital dollarization, and the prevalence of systemically important platforms could lead to the emergence of digital currency areas that transcend national borders. The rise of digital currencies will have implications for the treatment of private money, data ownership regulation, and central bank independence. For monetary policy to influence credit provision and risk sharing, public money must at least be used as a unit of account. In a digital economy where most activity is conducted through networks with their own monetary instruments, a regime in which all money is convertible to CBDC would uphold the unit of account status of public money.

As the digitalisation of banking business evolves, it would be desirable to construct appropriate metrics in common across the entire financial system, and which are applied transparently to the market. This should be done in such a way as to be able to check on whether the investments made are appropriate and whether they produce the expected results, where this is done on comparable terms among institutions and countries. This exercise should be carried out by both the banking institutions, to chart their progress, and the authorities, to monitor financial systems.

OTHER BOOKS BY THE AUTHOR

Cryptocurrency Millionaire Make Money
With Cryptocurrency

Secret Of Wealth Creation: Principle Lessons On The
Secrets Of Building A Long Lasting Wealth

Guide To Private Placement Project Fundingtrade
Programs: Understanding High-Level Project Funding
Trade Programs

Make Money Doing Nothing

The Blueprint To Intelligent Investors

The Blueprint To Intelligent Investors Volume 2

Financial Intelligence: Fundamentals Of Private Placement
Programs (PPP)

Private Placement Programs - The Holy Grail

Special Drawing Rights (SDR) And The Federal Reserve

Special Drawing Rights (SDR) And The Federal Reserve
Volume 2.

Cryptocurrency: The Next Level For Banking Reform

CPSIA information can be obtained
at www.ICGtesting.com
Printed in the USA
BVHW072325230822
645288BV00014B/725

9 781915 642028